Contents

To the Student

This book contains a number of exercises after each chapter. About half of them have answers at the back of the book. You will not be helping yourself at all if you merely copy out the answers which have been provided. You will merely be deceiving yourself – and nobody else.

Introduction

Accounting as an Information System

So far your studies have been concerned primarily with the recording function of accounting, often called book-keeping, and the drafting of the final accounts of different types of organizations, such as partnerships or limited companies. The term generally used for your studies up to this point is that of Financial Accounting. Much of it is concerned with legal requirements, such as complying with the provisions of the Companies Acts when drafting final accounts, or keeping an accounting record of a customer's legal indebtedness, ie. a debtor's account. With companies the final accounts represent the account given to the shareholders by the directors of their running of the company during a particular year, in other words it is a statement of the directors' "stewardship". These accounts are also given to other interested parties such as the bankers to the firm, creditors, Inspectors of Taxes etc.

Whilst Financial Accounting is necessary from a legal point of view, it cannot be said to be ideal from the point of view of controlling the activities of a firm. Your studies would therefore be incomplete if you had seen only the "stewardship" function of accounting. The use of accounting for controlling the activities of a firm is probably more important, therefore this book is concerned mainly with accounting for "Management Control" purposes. The word "management" does not necessarily mean that the firm is a limited company, although most of the large organisations in the private sector of industry would in fact be limited companies. It means instead the people who are managing the affairs of the firm, whether they are directors, partners, sole traders or "managers" classified as those employees who are in charge of other employees.

Before starting to examine Accounting for Management Control let us look first at the deficiencies of Financial Accounting when we want to control the activities of an organization. Its first deficiency is that it deals with operations that have already occurred: it deals with the past, not the future. It is possible to control something whilst it is happening, and control can be arranged for something that is going to happen, but when it has already happened without being controlled then the activity has ended and we are too late to do anything about control. In this way if a company incurs a loss and we do not realize it until long after the event then the loss cannot be prevented. What we really want to do is to control affairs so that a loss is not incurred if at all possible, and we should be able to call on accounting techniques to help in the control of activities. However, it certainly does not mean that we are not interested in the past. We can learn lessons from the past which can be very useful in understanding what is going on now, and what is likely to be happening in the future.

The second deficiency of Financial Accounting is that it is concerned with the whole of the firm. Thus the Trading Account of a firm may show a gross profit of £60,000, and whilst it is better to know that than to have no idea at all of what the gross profit is, it does not tell management much about past transactions. Suppose that in fact the firm manufactures three products — watches, pens and cigarette lighters. Some possibilities of how much profit (or loss) was attributable to each of the products might be as in Exhibit i.

Exhibit i

Various possibilities of profits and loss for each product

	1	2	3	4
Watches	20,000	5,000	30,000	(30,000)*
Pens	20,000	70,000	28,000	65,000
Lighters	20,000	(15,000)*	2,000	25,000
Total Gross Profit	£60,000	£60,000	£60,000	£60,000

*Losses are shown in brackets

These are only some of the possible figures of profit and loss for each product which could result in an overall gross profit of £60,000. Just the figure of total gross profit would give you very few clues as to what lessons can be learned from studying the past to help you control the firm in the future. If possibility number 2 was in fact the correct solution then it would stimulate further discussion and investigation as to why these results had occurred. It could result in the closing down of the section of the firm which makes cigarette lighters if, after investigation, it was found to be in the interests of the firm to cease manufacturing them. Many more lessons can therefore be learned from events if the firm's activities can be examined for each part of its activities instead of just the whole of its activities.

This means that Financial Accounting is of little use by itself for Management Control purposes. It does not mean that it is of no use at all for control purposes, as for instance the Financial accounting system may reveal that the debtors at a point in time are £50,000. Management need to know this if they are to control their finances properly, but although this is true of some accounting figures in Financial Accounting many of the other accounting figures may not be much use in controlling the business. For example if a building was bought in 1930 for £20,000 it may well be worth £200,000 today, whilst if we rented a similar building now it might cost us £30,000 a year. We would surely not use the original cost of £20,000 as the deciding factor as to what we will do now with the building. The original cost is now completely irrelevant for the control of the business now or in the future.

Objectives of the Firm

Before we can discuss Management Control we have to ask ourselves what it is for, we cannot really have control unless it is for a purpose. It would be generally agreed that Management Control is needed in guiding the firm so that it achieved its objectives. Before any plans can be drawn up in financial terms the objectives of the firm should be defined quite clearly by the director or owners of a firm. It must not be thought that to make as much profit as possible is the objective of every firm. It would still beg the question of whether it was maximum profit in the long term or the short term that was most important.

In fact it is very rare for the objectives of a firm to be spelled out clearly and unambiguously. Just because in theory it would be a good idea if all firms were to write down their objectives, so that misunderstandings could be cleared up more easily does not mean that it is done. In every walk of life there is a great deal of muddled thinking, and boards of directors and owners of firms are no exception to the general rule. There is a great deal of "muddling through" without any really clear ideas of in which direction the firm is heading. If the objectives are uncertain then management control must also be uncertain, and the muddled thinking will penetrate downwards from the board of directors to the shop floor.

Objectives could be expressed in terms of profit and in addition other factors could be brought in. Instances could be the size of the share of the market the firm wished to achieve, the quality of the goods manufactured, the sense of obligation to its employees or the duty of the firm to the community at large. As to whether or not a firm has good management control this can only be found by looking at how effective the management control system was in guiding the firm towards its objectives. Thus a firm making artificial limbs might conceivably set itself a much lower profit target than it could make, because the directors put product quality before profit. The management control system in that case is concerned more with quality than it would be with profit. But the directors may well have stipulated a profit figure they must achieve, even though it is lower than they could manage if they let quality slide, and therefore the management control system would have as its task the maintaining of the highest quality product possible whilst still achieving the profit target.

People and Management Control

It is also important to point out that the most important resource of any firm are the people who work on it. A danger exists that a great deal of care and attention may be given to designing a management control system and operating it, but this is absolutely of no use to management if it does not result in action by the human beings in the firm. Systems and figures do not themselves do anything, instead it is the people in the firm who take (or do not take) the necessary action.

You must bear in mind that figures thrown up by systems are only part of the evidence available when a decision has to be made as to the necessary action. A particular department may be incurring losses now, but the sales manager may give as his considered opinion that sales will increase soon and that the department will become profitable. If people accepted accounting figures as the only criteria on which action should be based then there would be some very bad actions by management. Many of the now very successful products have started off by incurring losses in the early stages, and have been eventually successful because the firm has persevered with the product because they had the faith that it would eventually make the grade.

If it was possible to have exactly the same system of management control in three different firms, it might be found in firm A that the control system was useless because no one acted on the data produced. In firm B the control system might result in damage being done to the firm because management used the data as though it was the only criteria in gauging the actions it should take. In firm C it might be an extremely good system because the management saw the data as a useful guide in the planning and control of the firm, and had also made certain that the rest of the organization took the same view.

How human beings react to a management control system is therefore right at the heart of the problem of ensuring that an effective management control system is in use.

Management Information

Part of this book is about information which is intended to be used by the management of an organisation. For a small and simple organisation the information needs of management may be limited and can be obtained by direct observation — using eyes to look and the voice to ask questions. For example a person managing a greengrocery stall on a market can often operate effectively without formal records to help him. What he buys is determined by the goods available in the local wholesale market and his personal knowledge of what his customers are prepared to buy at a given price. His records will probably centre around the recording of cash — the details of his sales and expenditures in order to prepare financial accounts. However apart from the essential requirement of maintaining proper cash levels these records do not help him in the day to day management of his business operations.

If in contrast we look at the manager responsible for buying greengrocery for a large supermarket chain certain differences emerge. The basic decision about what to buy at a given price remains the same. However in the large organisation there is a much wider choice of where and how to buy than in the small organisation. The large buyer may for example be able to enter into contracts directly with growers and to enter forward contracts for the supply of produce (for example a farmer agrees to sell all his potatoes at the end of the summer to the firm at a fixed price).

In the large organisation the buyer will not be in direct contact with the many different sales outlets and therefore needs written information to keep him in touch with demand. He does not have to listen to complaining customers! Similarly because the sources of supply are likely to be much wider for the big firm he needs more formal information to keep him in touch with market prices.

One of the other features about the large organisation which distinguishes it from the small, is that responsibility for running the business is shared between many different people. In order to ensure that the operations of the firm are carried out efficiently and effectively there needs to be some criteria to measure the performance of the managers. In a small firm the inadequate proprietor will either make a very poor living or become a bankrupt.

Thus his success or failure is clearly his own responsibility. In a large firm the same things can happen overall, but the situation may be obscured by a swings and roundabouts effect of some good sections making up for some bad. A management information system should help identify these problems in an organisation.

The Management Process

The way that management operates in an organisation may be conveniently described by a division into three areas:-

(1) Forecasting & Planning
(2) Controlling Operations
(3) Evaluating Performance

1. Forecasting and Planning is the process by which Senior Management decide on major overall issues concerning what the business is going to do, and how it is going to do it. It involves an assessment of information about the future which is called forecasting. When the forecast has been prepared then the company can plan how to achieve the objectives set by management based on the forecast. Planning is the process of co-ordinating the resources available to attain an objective.

2. Controlling Operations involves management in a number of processes and requires several different kinds of information. It involves converting top management plans into an operating pattern which matches the parts into which a company is divided. This changes the overall plan into detailed operating plans which relate to the management structure of the company. This process is called budgeting.

When actual events occur then the information recording the events needs to be measured in such a way that it can be compared with the plan. This important process of management gives a feedback on the success of the plan to those who set it in the first instance.

Controlling operations effectively also requires information designed to help managers take the decisions which their jobs require. For example information about the profit produced by one product as compared to another will enable a decision about how many of each product to make.

3. Evaluating Performance involves the analysis and assessment of actual results. This is partly a process of comparison with plans but not

exclusively. The information on which plans were based may have been wrong. Thus the analysis of performance whilst involving comparison of actual with planned results needs considerable judgement as to what the plan should have been had all the facts been known in advance.

The three elements we have described are by no means completely independent. One way of looking at them is as a cycle in which information is circulating continually from one area to another as in Exhibit ii.

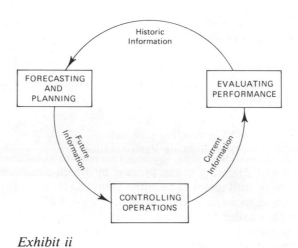

Exhibit ii

In this diagram information is shown to flow around from one part into the other. Thus for example forecasts in one period may be improved by taking account of the analysis of what happened last period.

The diagram we have just prepared only looks at internal information. In practice information is being fed into the process from outside. Top management will have to take into account all the information it can about the outside environment such as competition, economic cutbacks etc. The Control of Operations also receive information about actual events.

It is also useful to add to the diagram a time dimension as in Exhibit iii Forecasting and Planning must relate to the future. Controlling Operations relates to concurrent events — the here and now. Evaluating Performance can only be retrospective or historically based

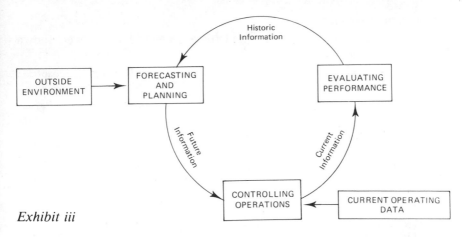

Exhibit iii

Types of Management Information

So far in this chapter no attempt has been made to describe the nature of the information which management requires. Information may come in many shapes and forms. In this book we are only concerned with information which is capable of being expressed in numerical terms, which in other words may be 'quantified'. Information of a more general nature about peoples' 'feelings' or 'views' may be very useful to management but cannot be quantified, and therefore is usually part of the informal rather than the formal information systems.

Within the body of quantified information it is normal to identify that part which can be measured in money terms. This is the part of the information system which is called Accounting Information. Accounting information is a very important element in the whole system since the organisation is basically an economic unit which must survive in conditions of economic scarcity and competition. In other words an organisation which does not meet its economic objectives will eventually fail or be taken over, hence the central importance of accounting information.

However other quantified information may be very important for management. For example if you are a farmer you will measure the yield of milk from your cows in the first instance as gallons. A production manager will be very concerned to monitor the tonnages produced on his machines.

Quantitative Methods in the Information System

A modern management information system collects all the data together (into what is called a data bank) and issues that part which is important to each manager. Thus the distinction between accounting and other types of management information has tended to become less meaningful in modern data processing systems. The techniques of quantitative analysis (or statistics) apply to all the data in this system whether it be accounting data or not.

8

Assignment Exercises

Assignment exercises followed by the letter x do NOT have answers shown at the back of the book.

(i)   Complete the following sentences by listing the missing words on a piece of paper:

      (a)   Most of the larger organisations in the private sector of industry are _____ _____.

      (b)   Financial Accounting is of _____ use by itself for management control purposes.

      (c)   Before we can discuss management control we must establish the _____ of the business.

      (d)   An effective management control system can only be judged by looking at how _____ the system was in guiding the firm towards its _____.

(ii)x   Complete the following sentences by listing the missing words on a piece of paper:

      (a)   Management Control states _____ shall be done, sees that it _____ done, checks _____ it has been done.

      (b)   A management control system is of no use if it does not _____ _____ _____ by the human beings in the firm.

      (c)   An accountant in management should cater for the _____ of _____.

      (d)   Accounting information is not the only _____ on which action should be based.

(iii)   In respect of the following statements write down whether you think they are TRUE or FALSE.

      (a)   An accountant can find all the solutions to the problems of the business in his textbooks, if he has a big enough library.

      (b)   The management control system of the business is concerned only with objectives which can be expressed only in terms of profits.

      (c)   Financial Accounting is normally of little use by itself for management control purposes.

      (d)   The majority of firms do not spell out their objectives clearly and objectively.

(iv)x   In respect of the following statements write down whether you think they are TRUE or FALSE.

      (a)   A firm might deliberately set itself a lower profit target than it could achieve.

      (b)   A management control system can function effectively even if the people in the firm do not react to control in the right way.

      (c)   Much information needed for management control will be in non-accounting terms.

      (d)   Quality may be more important than profits in some firms.

(v)x   A department store has four departments — (A) Clothing, (B) Furniture, (C) General, (D) Restaurant. A Trading Account has been drawn up which shows that the following gross profits or losses have been made:

(A)	Clothing Department	£10,000 gross profit
(B)	Furniture Department	£15,000 gross profit
(C)	General Department	£16,000 gross profit
(D)	Restaurant	£4,000 gross loss

What would you advise the management to do?

Chapter One

Elements of Costing

Cost Accounting is needed so that there can be an effective management accounting system. Without a study of costs such a system could not exist. Before entering into any detailed description of costs it is better if we ask ourselves first of all what use we are going to make of information about costs in the business. This can best be done by referring to something which is not accounting, and then relating it to accounting. Suppose that your employer asked you to measure the distance between Manchester and London, but walked away from you without giving any further information. As you thought about his request the following thoughts might go through your head:

1. *HOW* does he want the distance measuring? Some possibilities are:

(a) From the southern outskirts of Manchester to the northern outskirts of London.

(b) From the accepted geographical centre of London, to the accepted geographical centre of Manchester.

(c) To the centres of the two cities calculated as mathematically precise points.

(d) By road, this could be just major roads, just minor roads, or could be either major or minor roads the main requirement being the quickest route by road or the shortest route by road.

(e) By canal.

(f) By air; allowance may or may not be made for the distance covered by the aircraft which would include climbing to an altitude of 5,000 feet or perhaps 40,000 feet, or might ignore the distance travelling in achieving an altitude.

2. The *COST* of obtaining the information. Measuring distances (or measuring costs) is not costless itself. Using very sophisticated instruments to get accurate measurement can be very expensive indeed. On the other hand it might just be a matter of measuring the distance on a map with a rule and converting it into miles — this would cost hardly anything at all.

3. What is the *PURPOSE* for which the measurement will be used? This has been deliberately left as the last point, but in fact it should have been the first question that came into your mind. Illustrations of the use could have been as follows:

(a) He is going to drive from Manchester to London by car and wants a rough idea of the mileage so that he can gauge what time to set off if he is to arrive before it goes dark in London.

(b) He might conceivably want to walk it.

(c) Perhaps he wants to send goods by canal.

(d) He might be an amateur pilot who want to fly from Manchester Airport to London Airport.

(e) He might be submitting a tender for the building of a motorway by the shortest possible route, cutting tunnels through ranges of hills.

The lesson to be learned from this is that measurement depends entirely on the use that is to be made of the data. Far too often firms make measurements of financial and other data without looking first at the use that is going to be made of it. In fact it could be said that "information" is useful data that is provided for someone. Data given to someone which is not relevant to the purpose required is just not information. Data which is provided for a particular purpose, and which is completely wrong for the purpose, is worse than having no data at all. At least when there is no data the manager knows that he is making a guess, when useless data is collected it first of all has cost money to collect, in itself a waste of money; secondly it often gets taken to be useful data and misleads a manager into taking steps which are completely wrong and would not have happened if he had relied instead on his own hunches. Third it clogs up the communication system within a firm, so that other data is not acted on properly because of the general confusion that has been caused.

How is all this reflected in a study of costs?

1. What is the data on costs wanted for? It might be needed for the financial accounts, for management control or for decision making. Different data on costs are wanted for different purposes.

2. How are the costs to be measured? Only when the purpose for which the costs are to be used has been decided can the measurement process be decided. Financial accounting for instance needs a certain precision in calculating costs which is often not needed in management accounting, where sometimes the nearest thousand pounds will be good enough for the purpose.

3. The cost of obtaining costing data should not exceed the benefits to be gained from having it. This does not refer to some cost data which is needed to comply with various provisions of the law. Some cases of the benefits exceeding the costs could well be data which costs £1 to obtain but will be used as a basis for pricing many of the products of the firm — if the cost had been "guessed" instead of being found an error could have meant large losses for the firm if the prices had been set too low because of this. On the other hand to spend £10,000 to find data on sales which the sales manager will toss into the waste-paper basket because it is not the type of data he wants, is money wasted. Similarly, a great deal of the time spent in precise calculations can be wasted, e.g. if the managing director to know the figure of stock-in-trade for the financial accounts he will want to know that it is £2,532,198, but if he wants to know the figure for the purpose of having a

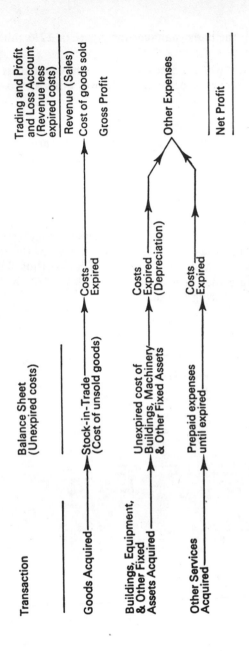

Exhibit 1.1

Here the costs are concerned with the past and are found for the purpose of calculating the gross and net profits, or to put it in a rather more academic way the purpose was that of the measurement of income.

general chat with the bank manager the figure of £2½ million will be quite accurate enough.

When it is known what the costs are for, how much is to be spent on studying the costs, then subsequently the way costs are to be measured can proceed further.

Past costs in Trading Companies

Past costs — often aptly called historic costs — are part of the ordinary Financial Accounting done in firms. Here the "original cost" concept is used. A diagram — Exhibit 1.1 shows costs flowing through Financial Accounts.

Past Costs in Manufacturing Companies

The costs flowing through the firm are analysed in a different fashion than Trading Companies because of the extra dimension, the fact that the firm manufacturers goods and then trades in them — thus the manufacturing elements constitute the extra dimension. Exhibit 1.2 shows costs flowing through a Manufacturing Company.

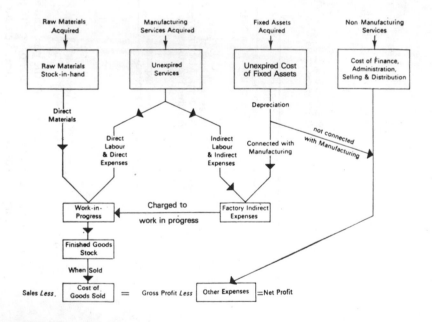

Exhibit 1.2

Direct Materials are those materials which become part of the finished good, subject to the proviso that the expense involved in tracing the cost is worthwhile. Some items, usually of insignificant amounts, are treated as indirect materials even though they are part of the finished product because the cost cannot be ascertained easily.

Direct Labour are those labour cost which are applied to convert the direct materials into the finished good, also subject to the proviso that the expense involved in tracing this cost is worthwhile.

Direct Expenses are those expenses which can be traced direct to the product being manufactured. These are fairly rare, but an instance would be a royalty where the production of each item resulted in say £1 being due to the owner of a patent.

Prime Cost: The total of Direct Materials + Direct Labour + Direct Expenses is called Prime Cost.

Naturally there will be disagreement between accountants as to whether certain costs are worth tracing as being of a Direct type, as it will often be a matter of judgement which defies any easy proof whether or not the expense of tracing the cost exceeds the benefit from so doing. You should get used to the idea in accounting that disagreement will often occur, which will only be settled by a compromise or appeal to someone in higher authority to settle the argument. This obviously relates to many things in accounting beside the decision as to whether an item is of a direct type or not.

Factory Indirect Expenses or Manufacturing Overhead are all those other expenses concerned with the manufacturing process which have not been treated as of the direct type. Because there is no easily traceable direct connection with the goods being manufactured these costs must be apportioned between the goods being manufactured in a logical fashion. The word "logical" must be stressed, remember that the accounting functions should be suited to the purpose in hand rather than the organization of the firm suited to meet the accounting system. As the saying goes "The tail should not wag the dog", meaning that the tail and accounting can be given the same meaning here.

Production Cost: The total of Prime Cost + Factory Indirect Expenses is called Production Cost.

Administration, Selling and Distribution and Finance Expenses are common to both trading and manufacturing firms.

Total Cost: If we add together Production Cost and Administration, Selling and Distribution, and Finance Expenses, the resultant figure is known as Total Cost. To summarise:

	Direct Materials
	Direct Materials
ADD	Direct Labour
ADD	Direct Expenses
Gives:	PRIME COST
ADD	Factory Indirect Expenses
Gives:	PRODUCTION COST
ADD	Administration Expenses
ADD	Selling and Distribution Expenses
ADD	Finance Expenses
Gives:	TOTAL COST

Exhibit 1.3 is a list of typical types of expenses found in a manufacturing firm. These can be analysed as to whether they are Direct Materials, Direct

Labour, Direct Expenses, Factory Indirect Expenses, Administration Expenses, Selling and Distribution Expenses, or Finance Expenses. See how well you can do yourself by covering up the right-hand column with a piece of paper, then sliding your paper down to reveal one answer at a time after you have mentally analysed it yourself.

Exhibit 1.3

Cost	*Cost Analysis*
1. Raw Materials for goods—identifiable with product made.	Direct Materials
2. Rent of Factory Buildings.	Factory Indirect Expenses
3. Salesmen's Salaries.	Selling and Distribution
4. Wages of Machine Operators in Factory.	Direct Labour
5. Wages of Accounting Machine Operators in Office.	Administration Expenses
6. Depreciation of Lathes in Factory.	Factory Indirect Expenses
7. Depreciation of Typewriters in Office.	Administration Expenses
8. Depreciation of Fixtures in Sales Showrooms.	Selling and Distribution Expenses
9. Foremen's Wages in Factory.	Factory Indirect Expenses
10. Royalty paid for each item manufactured.	Direct Expenses
11. Works Manager's salary: he reckons that he spends ¾ of his time in the factory and ¼ in general administration of the firm.	¾ Factory Indirect Expenses ¼ Administration Expenses
12. Raw Materials incorporated in goods sold, but too difficult to trace to the goods being made.	Indirect Expenses
13. Depreciation of Motor Vehicles used for delivery of finished goods to customers.	Selling and Distribution Expenses
14. Interest on Bank Overdraft.	Finance Expenses
15. Wages of crane drivers in factory.	Factory Indirect Expenses
16. Discounts Allowed.	Finance Expenses
17. Company Secretary's salary.	Administration Expenses
18. Advertising.	Selling and Distribution Expenses
19. Wages of Staff of Canteen used by Factory Staff only.	Factory Indirect Expenses
20. Cost of hiring special machinery for use in manufacturing one special item.	Direct Expenses

Assignment Exercises

Assignment Exercises followed by the letter x do NOT have answers at the back of the book.

1.1x If someone asked you to obtain a new type of cost data for them, what would you want to know before you commenced to work?

1.2 From the following information work out:

    (a) Prime Cost

    (b) Production Cost

	£
(c) Total Cost	
Salaries of employees in the Administrative Block	80,000
Wages of indirect labour force in the factory	110,000
Expenses of running firm's canteen attended by all workers,	
¾ work in the factory, ¼ in other parts of the firm	8,000
Interest on loans and overdraft	2,000
Wages: drivers of lorries used for distribution	2,500
Salaries: Salesmen	7,000
Commission on sales: paid to salesmen	1,200
Raw Materials used in production	210,000
Depreciation: Machinery in Factory	6,000
Accounting Machinery	500
Delivery Vehicles	1,500
Showroom Equipment	100
Labour costs directly connected with manufacture	120,000
Other Factory Indirect Expenses	66,000

1.3x From the following information work out:

    (a) Prime Cost

    (b) Production Cost

		£
(c) Total Cost		
Wages and Salaries of Employees:		
In Factory (60 per cent is directly concerned with units being		
manufactured)		150,000
In Sales Force		15,000
In Administration		26,000
Carriage Costs: On Raw Materials brought into the firm		1,800
On finished goods delivered to customers		1,100
Rent and Rates: Of Factory Block	4,900	
Of Sales Department and Showrooms	1,000	
Of Administrative Block	1,100	
		7,000
Travelling Expenses: Salesmen	3,400	
Administrative staff	300	
Factory Workers not connected directly		
with production	200	
		3,900
Raw Materials: Stock at start of period		11,400
Bought in the period		209,000
Stock at close of the period		15,600
Royalties: payable per unit of production		400
Depreciation: Salesmens' cars	500	
Vehicles used for deliveries to customers	300	
Cars of administrative staff	400	
Machinery in Factory	1,800	
Office Machinery	200	
		3,200
Interest Costs on Borrowed Money		800
Other Factory Indirect Expenses		6,000
Other Administrative Expenses		4,000
Other Selling Expenses		1,000

1.4 Analyse the following costs between:
   (i) Direct Materials
   (ii) Direct Labour
   (iii) Factory Indirect Expenses
   (iv) Administration Expenses
   (v) Selling and Distribution Expenses
   (vi) Finance Expenses
      (a) Wages of men maintaining machines in factory
      (b) Wages of man maintaining accounting machinery
      (c) Expenses of canteen run exclusively for factory workers
      (d) Expenses of canteen run exclusively for administrative workers
      (e) Grease used for factory machinery
      (f) Cost of raw materials
      (g) Carriage inwards on fuel used in factory boiler-house
      (h) Carriage inwards on raw material
      (i) Wages of managing director's chauffeur
      (j) Wages of cleaners in factory
      (k) Discounts Allowed
      (l) Rent of salesrooms
      (m) Wages of lathe operators in factory
      (n) Wages of security guards; The area of the factory buildings is four times as great as the other buildings
      (o) Debenture interest
      (p) Rent of annexe used by accounting staff
      (q) Managing director's remuneration
      (r) Salesmen's salaries
      (s) Running costs of salesmen's cars
      (t) Repairs to factory buildings
      (u) Audit fees
      (v) Power for machines in factory
      (w) Rates: ¾ for factory buildings and ¼ for other buildings
      (x) Rent of internal telephone system in factory
      (y) Bank Charges
      (z) Costs of advertizing products on television.

1.5x Analyse the following costs between
   (i) Direct Materials
   (ii) Direct Labour
   (iii) Factory Indirect Expenses
   (iv) Administration Expenses
   (v) Selling and Distribution Expenses
   (vi) Finance Expenses
      (a) Interest on bank overdraft
      (b) Factory Storekeepers Wages
      (c) Hire of Rolls-Royce for managing director's use
      (d) Repairs to factory roof
      (e) Hotel bills incurred by salesmen
      (f) Motor tax for vans used for delivering goods to customers
      (g) Chief Accountant's salary
      (h) Lubricants for factory machinery
      (i) Cost of paper-tape for firm's computer
      (j) Helicopter hire charges re special demonstration of company's products

(k) Debt collection costs
(l) Costs of painting advertising signs on London buses
(m) Cost of airplane tickets for salesmen
(n) Wages of painters engaged in production
(o) Wages of time-keepers in factory
(p) Postal charges for letters
(q) Wages of office boy in general office
(r) Postal charges — parcels sent to customers
(s) Repairs to vans used for taking goods to customers
(t) Cost of raw materials included in product
(u) Wages for charwomen engaged in administration block
(v) Carriage inwards on raw materials
(w) Repairs to neon sign in Piccadilly Circus
(x) Advertising agency fees
(y) Wages of crane drivers in factory
(z) Power costs of accounting machinery.

1.6   From the following information work out:

(a) Prime Cost
(b) Production Cost
(c) Total Cost

Wages and Salaries of Employees:		£
In Factory (70 per cent is directly concerned with units being manufactured)		220,000
Salaries: Salesman		8,000
Commission on Sales paid to Salesman		1,400
Salaries of administrative staff		72,000
Travelling Expenses:		
Salesmen	2,900	
Factory Workers not directly concerned with production	100	
Administrative Staff	200	3,200
Haulage costs on raw material bought		4,000
Carriage costs on goods sold		7,800
Depreciation: Factory Machinery	38,000	
Accounting & office machinery	2,000	
Motor Vehicles:		
Salemens cars	3,800	
Administrative staff	1,600	
Sales display equipment	300	45,700
Royalties payable per unit of production		1,600
Canteen costs used by all the workers, ⅔ work in the factory, ⅓ in other parts of the firm		6,000
Raw materials: Stock at start of period		120,000
Stock at close of period		160,000
Bought in the period		400,000
Interest on Loans and Overdrafts		3,800
Other Factory Indirect Expenses		58,000
Other Administrative Expenses		42,000
Other Selling Expenses		65,000

1.7 Analyse the following costs between:
- (i) Direct Materials
- (ii) Direct Labour
- (iii) Factory Indirect Expenses
- (iv) Administrative Expenses
- (v) Selling and Distribution Expenses
- (vi) Finance Expenses

    (a) Costs of electricity for office duplicating equipment
    (b) Hotel costs of salesmen
    (c) Haulage costs bringing materials to factory
    (d) Wages of drilling machine operators in factory
    (e) Raw material costs
    (f) Hiring hoardings for sale posters
    (g) Cost Accountant's salary
    (h) Legal costs re debt collection
    (i) Repairs to drilling machinery
    (j) Shipping cost of sending goods overseas
    (k) Chairman's remuneration
    (l) Rent of stand at an exhibition
    (m) Repairs to factory cranes
    (n) Salary of Secretary to managing director
    (o) Repairs to showrooms
    (p) Bank overdraft interest
    (q) Wages of lathe operators
    (r) Discounts Allowed
    (s) Printing sales brochures
    (t) Wages of service department apprentices in the factory
    (u) Costs of accounting stationery
    (v) Salary of nurse in factory accident room
    (w) Wages of women assembling goods
    (x) Fire Insurance of factory
    (y) Fees of management consultants reorganising office routines
    (z) Diesel oil for running factory machinery.

Chapter Two

Manufacturing Accounts

In a manufacturing account the production cost of goods completed during an accounting period is calculated. This means that all the items of Production Cost are charged to the manufacturing account. Administration and selling and distribution expenses are charged to the profit and loss account.

You should note that it is the production cost of goods *completed* in the period, irrespective as to when the work started on them. Because of this fact goods partly completed, known as work in progress, have to be taken into account.

Two exhibits are now given. In the first of these, 2.1, a case is shown of a firm without any work in progress, either at the beginning or the end of the accounting period.

Exhibit 2.1

The following are details of production cost for the year ended 31 December 19-4.

1 January 19-4, stock of raw materials	800
31 December 19-4, stock of raw materials	1,200
Purchase of raw materials	9,000
Manufacturing (direct) wages	15,000
Royalties	400
Indirect wages	8,000
Rent of factory (excluding administration and selling and distribution departments)	1,080
Factory rates	340
General indirect expenses	430
Depreciation of works machinery	550

Manufacturing Account for the year ended 31 December 19-4

	£		£
Stock of Raw Materials		Production cost	
1.1.19-4	800	of Goods	
Add Purchases	9,000	Completed c/d	34,400
	9,800		
Less Stock of Raw Materials			
31.12.19-4	1,200		
Cost of Raw Materials			
Consumed	8,600		
Manufacturing Wages	15,000		
Royalties	400		
Prime Cost	24,000		
Factory Overhead Expenses			
Rent	1,080		
Rates	340		
Indirect Wages	8,000		
Depreciation	550		
General Expenses	430	10,400	
		34,400	34,400

When the production cost of goods completed is known, it is carried down to the trading account, in the place where normally the purchases are shown. Sometimes a firm will additionally also buy goods for resale, and in this case the trading account will have both figures included.

Work in Progress

If there is work in progress i.e. goods only part completed at the beginning and end of an accounting period, then an adjustment will be needed. To calculate the production cost of goods completed during the period, the value of the work in progress at the beginning must be brought in as it is work which normally will be finished within the period. Likewise work in progress at the end of the period must be carried forward to the next period, as it will be completed during that next period. The adjustments are made by adding the value of work in progress at the beginning to the total production cost for the period, and the closing work in progress is deducted. This is shown in Exhibit 2.2.

	£
Exhibit 2.2	
1 January 19-3 Stock of raw materials	900
31 December 19-3 Stock of raw materials	1,250
1 January 19-3 Work in progress	460
31 December 19-3 Work in progress	540
For the year ended 31 December 19-3:	
Wages: Direct	5,440
Indirect	3,060
Raw Materials Purchased	12,800
Power and Fuel	520
Direct Expenses	260
Carriage inwards on raw materials	170
Factory rent and rates	840
Depreciation of factory machinery	360
Insurance of factory buildings	120
General factory expenses	390

Manufacturing Account for the year ended 31 December 19-3

		£			£
Stock of raw materials			Production cost of goods		
1.1.19-3		900	Completed c/d		23,530
Add Purchases		12,800			
Add Carriage Inwards		170			
		13,870			
Less Stock Raw Materials					
31.12.19-7		1,250			
Cost of Raw Materials					
Consumed		12,620			
Direct Wages		5,440			
Direct Expenses		260			
Prime Cost		18,320			
Factory Overhead Expenses					
Power and Fuel	520				
Indirect Wages	3,060				
Rent and Rates	840				
Depreciation of					
Machinery	360				
Insurance	120				
General Factory					
Expenses	390	5,290			
		23,610			
Add Work in Progress					
1.1.19-3		460			
		24,070			
Less Work in Progress					
31.12.19-3		540			
		23,530			23,530

The trading account deals with finished goods. If in Exhibit 2.2 there had been £4,800 stock of finished goods at 1 January 19-3 and £5,600 at 31 December 19-3, and also assuming that the sales of finished goods amounts to £37,000, the trading account would appear as follows:

Trading Account for the year ended 31 December 19-3

	£		£
Stock of Finished Goods		Sales	37,000
1.1.19-3	4,800		
Add Production Cost of			
Goods Completed b/d	23,530		
	28,330		
Less Stock of Finished Goods			
31.12.19-3	5,600		
	22,730		
Gross Profit c/d	14,270		
	37,000		37,000

The Profit and Loss Account is then drawn up in the normal way, and the expenses charged there will be Administration Expenses, Selling and Distribution Expenses and Finance Expenses. The items referring to stocks and work in progress will appear as follows in the Balance Sheet as at 31 December 19-3.

Current Assets
Stocks:

Raw Materials	1,250
Finished Goods	5,600
Work in Progress	540

Assignment Exercises

Assignment Exercises followed by the letter x do NOT have answers shown at the back of the book.

2.1   Prepare Manufacturing, Trading and Profit and Loss Accounts from the following balances of Logan for the year ended 31 December 19-7.

	£
Stocks at 1 January 19-7:	
Raw Materials	18,450
Work in Progress	23,600
Finished Goods	17,470
Purchases: Raw Materials	64,300
Carriage on Raw Materials	1,605
Direct Labour	65,810
Office Salaries	16,920
Rent and Rates	2,700
Office Lighting and Heating	5,760
Depreciation: Works Machinery	8,300
Office Equipment	1,950
Sales	200,600
Factory Fuel & Power	5,920

Rent and Rates are to be apportioned: Factory ⅔rds : Office ⅓. Stocks at 31 December 19-7 were: Raw Materials £20,210, Work in Progress £17,390, Finished Goods £21,485.

2.2x From the following details of Larkins & Son you are to draw up a Manufacturing, Trading and Profit and Loss Account for the year ended 30 September 19-4.

	30.9.19-3	30.9.19-4
	£	£
Stocks of Raw Materials, at cost	8,460	10,970
Work in Progress	3,070	2,460
Finished Goods Stock	12,380	14,570
For the year:		£
Raw Materials Purchased		38,720
Manufacturing Wages		20,970
Factory Expenses		12,650
Depreciation:		
Plant & Machinery		7,560
Delivery Vans		3,040
Office Equipment		807
Factory Power		6,120
Advertising		5,080
Office and Administration Expenses		5,910
Salesmens' Salaries and Expenses		6,420
Delivery Van Expenses		5,890
Sales		134,610
Carriage Inwards		2,720

2.3 D. August is a manufacturer. His trial balance at 31 December 19-6 is as follows:

	£	£
Delivery Van Expenses	2,500	
Light & Heat: Factory	2,859	
Office	1,110	
Manufacturing Wages	45,470	
Advertising	1,866	
General Expenses: Office	1,950	
Factory	5,640	
Salesmen: Commission	7,860	
Purchase of Raw Materials	39,054	
Rates: Factory	4,800	
Office	2,200	
Machinery (cost £50,000)	32,500	
Office Equipment (cost £15,000)	11,000	
Office Salaries	6,285	
Debtors	28,370	
Creditors		19,450
Bank	13,337	
Sales		136,500
Premises at Cost	40,000	
Stocks at 31 December 19-5:		
Raw Materials	8,565	
Finished Goods	29,480	
Drawings	8,560	
Capital		137,456
	293,406	293,406

Prepare the Manufacturing, Trading and Profit and Loss Accounts for the year ended 31 December 19-6 and a Balance Sheet as at that date. Give effect to the following adjustments:

1. Stocks at 31 December 19-6, Raw Materials £9,050, Finished Goods £31,200. There is no Work in Progress.
2. Depreciate Machinery £2,000, Office Equipment £1,500.
3. Manufacturing Wages due but unpaid at 31 December 19-6 £305, Advertising prepaid £108.

2.4x B. Little has a manufacturing business. His trial balance as on 31 December 19-7 was as follows:

	£	£
Carriage Outwards	2,760	
Rent and Rates: Office	990	
Factory	4,850	
Office Machinery (cost £6,000)	4,200	
Bank		14,360
Debtors	28,972	
Sales		184,715
Machinery (cost £50,000)	28,000	
Salaries to Salesmen	8,570	
Raw Material Purchases	57,245	
Sundry Expenses: Factory	1,362	
Office	898	
Creditors		15,477
Stocks at 31 December 19-6:		
Raw Materials	15,872	
Finished Goods	51,897	
Office Salaries	8,416	
Advertising	4,278	
Manufacturing Wages	64,371	
Light & Heat: Office	1,475	
Factory	4,896	
Drawings	9,900	
Capital		84,400
	298,952	298,952

You are to draw up a Manufacturing, Trading and Profit and Loss Account for the year ended 31 December 19-7, and a Balance Sheet as on that date. Give effect to the following adjustments:

(a) Depreciate Machinery £5,000, Office Machinery £800.
(b) The following were due but unpaid at 31 December 19-7, Advertising £188, Light & Heat:- Office £125, Factory £488.
(c) The factory rent had been prepaid £250 at 31 December 19-7.
(d) Stocks at 31 December 19-7, Raw Materials £13,820, Finished Goods £56,842.

Chapter Three

Product Costs and Period Costs

Product costs are those costs which are allocated to the units of goods manufactured. In fact product costs make up Production Cost. Such costs are charged up to the cost of goods manufactured in the Trading Account, and would normally be part of the valuation of unsold goods if the goods to which they refer had not been sold by the end of the period. Product costs are therefore matched up against revenue as and when the goods are sold and not before.

Period costs are those of a non-manufacturing nature and represent the selling and distribution, administration and the financial expenses. They are treated as expenses of the period in which they were incurred irrespective of the volume of goods sold.

Past Costs: Trading and Manufacturing Compared

There is a very important difference between costs in a Trading concern with that in a Manufacturing concern. In a Trading concern such items as wages, depreciation and indirect expenses are treated as period costs, i.e. they are charged to the Profit and Loss Account. In a manufacturing concern the wages, depreciation and indirect expenses are treated as part of the Production Cost, and the unsold goods at the end of the period are normally valued at Production Cost. These items, therefore, affect the closing valuation of stock-in-hand in the manufacturing firms but not in the trading concern, and different figures for stock-in-trade mean that the reported profits are different. Exhibit 3-1 gives and example of the first year of (a) a trading concern and (b) a manufacturing concern where total costs are the same but profits calculated are different because of the inclusion of a proportion of Indirect Expenses when Stock-in-Trade was valued at the end of each period in the manufacturing firm.

Exhibit 3.1

Retailing Firm—Expenses:

	£	£	£	£
Purchases—1,000 units		90,000		
Wages and Salaries		13,000		
General Expenses		17,000		
Finance Expenses		2,000		
(Same total as Manufacturing Firm)		122,000		
Sales: 800 units			£120,000	

Manufacturing Firm—Expenses:

	£	£	£	£
Cost of Raw Materials Used to make 1,000 units		50,000		
Wages: Direct Labour	20,000			
Factory Indirect Labour	12,000			
Salaries and Wages: Administration and Selling	8,000	40,000		
Other Factory Indirect Expenses	20,000			
Other Selling and Administration Expenses	10,000	30,000		
Finance Expenses		2,000		
(Same total as Retail Firm)		122,000		
Sales: 800 units				£120,000

Closing Stocks of Goods

Retailing Firm: Valued at cost

200 units in hand which cost $\dfrac{200}{1,000} \times £90,000 = £18,000$

Manufacturing Firm: Valued at Production Cost

200 units in hand which cost $\dfrac{200}{1,000} \times$ (Raw Materials 50,000 + Wages 32,000 + Factory Indirect Expenses 20,000)

$= \dfrac{200}{1,000} \times £102,000 = £20,400$

Retailing Firm's Trading and Profit and Loss Account

	£		£
Purchases	90,000	Sales	120,000
Less Closing Stock	18,000		
Cost of Goods Sold	72,000		
Gross Profit c/d	48,000		
	120,000		120,000
Wages and Salaries	13,000	Gross Profit b/d	48,000
General Expenses	17,000		
Finance Expenses	2,000		
Net Profit	16,000		
	48,000		48,000

Manufacturing Firm's Manufacturing and Trading and Profit and Loss Account

		£		£
Cost of Materials Used		50,000	Production Cost of Goods	
Direct Labour		20,000	Completed c/d	102,000
Prime Cost		70,000		
Factory Indirect Expenses				
Indirect Labour	12,000			
Other Indirect Expenses	20,000			
		32,000		
		102,000		102,000

Production Cost of Goods	£		£
Completed b/d	102,000	Sales	120,000
Less Closing Stock			
(see calculation)	20,400		
Cost of Goods Sold	81,600		
Gross Profit c/d	38,400		
	120,000		120,000
Salaries and Wages	8,000	Gross Profit b/d	38,400
Other Administration and			
Selling Expenses	10,000		
Finance Expenses	2,000		
Net Profit	18,400		
	38,400		38,400

The difference between the net profits of the two firms of £2,400 can be seen to be equal to the difference between the closing stocks, i.e. £20,400 and £18,000. The difference in profit calculations can be seen to be due to the different treatment of costs as product costs and period costs in the two firms.

You have now looked at the various elements of cost as far as the whole of the firm is concerned. Such a classification of costs is necessary so that the overall production cost can be ascertained in the case of a manufacturing company with its effect on the valuation of the closing stock of finished goods and of work-in-progress. What most businesses want to know is how much each item has cost to make. This means that the total costs for the whole firm are not sufficient, and so these costs must be analysed further.

Any costing system must bring about the better control of the firm in guiding it towards its objectives, and the benefits to be derived from the costing system must be greater than the expense of operating the costing system. We must, therefore, look at the possible advantages to be gained in carrying on further analyses of cost:

(a) Because expenditure is traced down to each item produced, or each batch of items, it becomes possible to ascertain the contribution of each item towards the profitability of the business. The desirability of stopping unprofitable activities can then be assessed.

(b) Once the profitability of each item is known the reasons for increases or decreases in profits can be seen more clearly.

(c) It becomes easier to forecast future results if we know more about the operations of all the various parts of the business. When forecasted results are not achieved it becomes possible to highlight the reasons for the failure to achieve the forecasted results.

(d) Estimates and tenders can be prepared in future with far greater confidence — previously such calculations as were done must have been largely guesswork. Fewer errors should be made because of the greater knowledge gained via the costing system.

(e) Improvements in various activities of the firm may come about because of the more relevant information that can be supplied. Thus a machine which had always been though to be quite cheap to use may turn out to be very expensive to use. This may bring about an investigation which would not otherwise have happened, and it may consequently be found that a simple attachment to the machine costing £10 brings about a saving of £100 a year.

(f) As will shortly be described, a very important advantage is the control of expenditure, and it can be achieved because an individual can be made responsible for the expenditure under his control.

The possible advantages which can be gained from having a costing system can be seen to be quite considerable. It is, however, now a convenient point to remind you that accounting techniques themselves do not solve problems. Instead it is people within the firm who, when armed with the information that accounting techniques can provide, are far more able to make sensible decisions about what should be done to aid the progress of the firm towards its objectives. Imagine trying to decide which item to stop producing out of twelve items made by a firm if you have little information as to the contribution of each item towards the profitability of the firm. Very often the solution will be that a new layout in the factory is needed; special training given to certain employees; changes made in the system of remunerating employees and so on. The information provided by accounting is, therefore, only one part of the whole story for any problem. It is important to remember that often it will be the least important information available to the decision-taker.

The Control of Costs

One of the most important features of cost accounting is its use for control purposes, meaning in this context the control of expenditure. But control of expenditure is possible only if you can trace the costs down to employees who are responsible for such costs. A convenient area for collecting costs is called a "cost centre". In a manufacturing firm all direct materials, direct labour and direct expenses are traced to cost centres, in this case they would be known as "product centres". A product centre may be such as a single machine used for jobbing work, i.e. quite a lot of separate jobs performed specially to conform with the customer's specifications. It could, however, be a group of similar machines or a production department.

In comparison factory indirect expenses by definition, i.e. because they are "indirect" expenses, cannot be traced (or it is not worthwhile tracing them) to product centres. These are traced to cost centres which give service rather than being concerned with work directly on the products, and such cost centres are, therefore, known as "service centres". Examples of service centres would be the factory canteen or the maintenance department. The costs from these service centres will then need allocating to the product centres in a logical fashion.

In practice there are a number of possible ways of allocating costs to cost centres. What must not be lost sight of is the endeavour to trace costs to a person responsible for the expenditure so that the costs can be controlled.

Costing: Manufacturing firms compared with retailing or wholesale firms

It is quite wrong to think that costing is concerned only with manufacturing firms. Both text-books and examinations papers often give the impression that only in manufacturing is costing needed or found. This is quite incorrect, as costing is just as relevant to retailing and wholesaling firms as it is to those in manufacturing. It is simply that manufacturing, which usually has more complex sorts of activities because of the manufacturing element, has attracted greater attention than other types of firms. There are, in addition, many other forms of organisations such as farming, shipping, banking and even charitable organisations where costing can aid management control. It would indeed be difficult to find any organisation which could not use some form of costing system profitably.

Assignment Exercises

Assignment Exercises followed by the letter x do NOT have answers shown at the back of the book.

3.1 From the following information draw up a Trading and Profit and Loss Account for C. Dean's retail business, and a Manufacturing and Profit and Loss Account for D. Warren's manufacturing business. These businesses were both started on 1 January, 19-3, accordingly neither of them had opening Stock-in-Trade, and the accounts are for the year ended 31 December, 19-3.

C. Dean	£
Purchases: 5,000 units	100,000
Wages and Salaries	50,000
Rent and Rates	9,000
Other Expenses	40,000
Finance Expenses	1,000
	£200,000
Sales: 4,200 units at £50 each =	£210,000

D. Warren		£
Cost of Raw Materials from which 5,000 units are manufactured during the year		100,000
Wages: Factory Direct	28,000	
Wages: Factory Indirect	8,000	
Salaries: Administration	10,000	
Salaries: Salesmen	4,000	
		50,000
Other Factory Indirect Expenses	38,000	
Other Selling and Administrative Expenses	11,000	49,000
Finance Expenses		1,000
		£200,000
(N.B. There is no work-in-progress.)		
Sales: 4,200 units at £50 each =		£210,000

(Keep your answer, you may need it for question 3.3.)

3.2x Draw up a Trading and Profit and Loss Account for J. Knight, a retail firm, and a Manufacturing, Trading and Profit and Loss Account for J. Hanson, a manufacturing firm for the year ended 31 December, 19-7. Both firms have just completed their first year of activity.

	£
J. Knight	
Purchases: 2,000 units	40,000
Selling and Distribution Expenses	30,000
Administration Expenses	7,000
Finance Expenses	3,000
	£80,000
Sales: 1,500 units at £52 each =	£78,000

	£
J. Hanson	
Cost of Raw Materials from which 2,000 units have been made	50,000
Direct Labour	10,000
Factory Indirect Expenses	12,000
Administration Expenses	5,000
Selling Expenses	1,200
Finance Expenses	1,800
	£80,000

(N.B. There is no work-in-progress).

Sales: 1,500 units at £52 each =	£78,000

(Keep your answer, you may need it for question 3.4).

3.3 This question is a continuation of 3.1. You are to bring forward the closing stocks goods at 31 December, 19-3 which become the opening stocks for the year ended 31 December, 19-4.

C. Dean's retail business and D. Warren's manufacturing businesses have now each completed their second year of operations. You are required to draw up a Trading and Profit and Loss Account for C. Dean and a Manufacturing, Trading and Profit and Loss Account for D. Warren, each for the year ended 31 December, 19-4.

	£
C. Dean	
Purchases during the year 6,000 units	120,000
Wages and Salaries	53,000
Rent and Rates	9,000
Other Expenses	42,000
Finance Expenses	2,000
	£226,000
Sales: 5,600 units at £50 each =	£280,000

D. Warren

Cost of Raw Materials from which 6,000 units have been manufactured during the year		120,000
Wages: Factory Direct	30,000	
Wages: Factory Indirect	9,000	
Salaries: Administrative Staff	10,000	
Salaries: Salesmen	4,000	53,000
Other Factory Indirect Expenses	39,000	
Other Selling Expenses	8,000	
Other Administrative Expenses	4,000	51,000
Finance Expenses		2,000
		£226,000
Sales: 5,600 units at £50 each =		£280,000

(N.B. There is no work-in-progress.)

3.4x This question is a continuation of 3.2x. You are to bring forward the closing stocks at 31 December, 19-7 which become the opening stocks for the year ended 31 December, 19-8.

J. Knight's retail business and J. Hanson's manufacturing business have now each completed their second year of operations. You are required to draw up a Trading and Profit and Loss Account for J. Knight, and a Manufacturing, Trading and Profit and Loss Account for J. Hanson, both for the year ended 31 December, 19-8.

J. Knight	£
Purchases during the year: 2,500 units	50,000
Selling and Distribution Expenses	36,000
Administration Expenses	9,000
Finance Expenses	2,000
	£97,000
Sales: 2,200 units at £52 each =	£114,400

J. Hanson	
Cost of Raw Materials from which 2,500 units have been made during the year	62,500
Direct Labour	12,500
Factory Indirect Expenses	14,000
Administration Expenses	5,000
Selling Expenses	2,000
Finance Expenses	1,000
	£97,000
Sales: 2,200 units at £52 each =	£114,400

3.5x What advantages can be gained by operating a costing system?

Chapter Four

Accounting for Materials

It may seem a simple matter that when materials are used in production they should be charged to the cost centre at "cost price". Before we look at other problems connected with materials, the ways in which these "cost prices" can be determined will be considered first. It should be mentioned that there are more methods than are described in this chapter, including the way in which they are calculated under standard costing — this is looked at in chapter Twelve, but the present chapter limits its survey to the three other main methods in use.

First of all a word of warning. Students often confuse the actual physical issue of the goods or materials to production etc. with the attempt to put a price on the issue of the goods. Suppose that we had always bought a particular type of item for £1 each ever since the firm began. When these are used in production the cost centre will be charged up with £1 for each item used. On the other hand this country, and the world generally, has experienced inflation for quite a few years now. This has meant that for most items the price per item has been increasing steadily over the past few decades. On the other hand some items have been falling in price. An instance of this are ballpoint pens which were about £3 each for the cheapest type when they were first produced around the year 1943. They now cost a few pence for the cheapest type. With other items the price fluctuates up and down. After all in a free society the price is the interaction of supply and demand. Physically you may have to follow a chronological pattern of issuing goods to production on the basis of the first goods to be received are the first to be issued to production. This would well be the case with perishable foodstuffs as for instance meat being put into meat pies. On the other hand it may not matter at all as to the order in which the goods received by the firm are issued to production, it may be an item such as a plastic clip which would not deteriorate at all with age. What we are going to consider is the calculation of the price of the item which is to be charged to production of the item issued. For this purpose we will ignore in the first instance which goods were actually issued to production, instead we will concentrate on which goods were "deemed" to be issued to production. Often a firm will know only how many items were issued, they may not know at all when the various items were received by the firm as, for instance, in the case of the plastic clips it does not matter to the firm at all in which order the goods are issued. If it does not benefit a firm to know the chronological order in which goods are received then it will surely not bother to go to the expense of finding out the information.

Let us now look at the mechanics of finding the price at which goods are charged out to production, or in a retail firm are priced to find the cost of goods sold. We will use the same basic information and find the cost of goods issued by the three main methods in use. The information is that the goods issued and received are as follows:

Received	
19-1	*Number and cost per item*
January	10 at £15 each = £150
March	10 at £17 each = £170
August	20 at £20 each = £400
Issued	*Number issued*
19-1	
April	8
December	24

1. *First In, First Out Method (abbreviated as F.I.F.O.)*

With this method the first goods received are deemed to be issued first, goods from earlier receipts are treated as being issued before any of the goods from later receipts.

In this case the cost of the goods issued is stated to be £120 + £440 = £560.

	Received	Issue Price	Stock after each transaction
January	10 at £15 each		10 at £15 each = £150
March	10 at £17 each		10 at £15 each = £150 10 at £17 each = £170 = £320
April		8 at £15 each = £120	2 at £15 each = £30 10 at £17 each = £170 = £200
August	20 at £20 each		2 at £15 each = £30 10 at £17 each = £170 20 at £20 each = £400 = £600
December		2 at £15 each = £30 10 at £17 each = £170 12 at £20 each = £240 = £440.	8 at £20 each = £160

2. Last In, First Out Method (abbreviated as L.I.F.O.)

This method treats each issue of goods as being made from the last lot of goods received previous to the date of issue. If that lot of goods is not enough then the balance of the issue is treated as being made from the next previous lot still unissued, and so on.

	Received	Issue Price	Stock after each transaction
January	10 at £15 each		10 at £15 each = £150
March	10 at £17 each		10 at £15 each = £150 10 at £17 each = £170 = £320
April		8 at £17 each = £136	10 at £15 each = £150 2 at £17 each = £34 = £184
August	20 at £20 each		10 at £15 each = £150 2 at £17 each = £34 20 at £20 each = £400 = £584
December		20 at £20 each = £400 2 at £17 each = £34 2 at £15 each = £30 = £464	8 at £15 each = £120

In this case the cost of the goods issued is stated to be £136 + £464 = £600.

3. Average Cost Method

Each time there is a receipt of goods the average cost of the goods held in stock is recalculated. Any issues then made are at that price until another receipt of goods when the price is recalculated for further issues, and so on.

	Received	Issued	Average Cost per unit of stock held £	Number of units in stock	Total value of stock £
January	10 at £15 each		15	10	150
March	10 at £17 each		16	20	320
April		8 at £16 each = £128	16	12	192
August	20 at £20 each		18.5	32	592
December		24 at £18.5 each = £444	18.5	8	148

In this case the cost of the goods issued is stated to be £128 + £444 = £572.

Periodic inventory valuation methods

So far we have looked at materials or goods being issued and the records being kept on a perpetual basis, meaning by this that each issue or sale was compared with the receipts strictly on a chronological basis and the price of issue calculated accordingly. The record was, therefore, being maintained perpetually throughout the year. For accounting purposes, however, especially in financial accounting, the calculation of the cost of the goods issued or sold may not be determined until the end of the accounting year. When this is done the exact date of issue of sale during the year is ignored — it is just looked at from the point of view of the total issued or sold. Using the average cost method the issue price is the average cost for the whole year rather than the different averages at different points in time. The LIFO method assumes that the last goods to come in during the year are the first to be issued, instead of the last to be received before the issue was made. The FIFO method will, however, give the same answer no matter whether the perpetual or the periodic method is used.

As an illustration of the way the two methods can give different answers is shown in Exhibit 4.1.

Exhibit 4.1
The following details are relevant to the receipt and issue of goods. There was no opening stock of goods.

Exhibit 4.1

	Receipts		Issues	
19-1	January	9 at £20 each	May	5 items
	July	6 at £30 each	November	4 items

Perpetual inventory — average cost

	Received	Issued	Average Cost per unit of stock held	Number of units in stock	Total value of stock
					£
January	9 at £20		20	9	180
May		5 at £20	20	4	80
July	6 at £30		26	10	260
November		4 at £26	26	6	156

Periodic Inventory — Average Cost

Received	9 at £20 =	180
	6 at £30 =	180
	15	£360

Fifteen items cost a total of £360, therefore the average cost at which issues will be priced is £360 = £24 each. As 9 items have been issued the total

$$\frac{£360}{15}$$

price that they will be charged out as cost of goods sold or materials used is 9 × £24 = £216. Compare this with the issue price of 5 × £20 plus 4 × £26 = £204 using the perpetual inventory method. The closing stocks are 6 × £24 = £144 under the periodic inventory method and £156 under the perpetual inventory method.

Similarly the LIFO method of pricing issues will give different answers, in fact 5 × £20 plus 4 × £30 = £220 with the perpetual method and 6 × £30 plus 3 × £20 = £240 with the periodic method. The FIFO method will give the same answer under both methods, that of 9 × £20 = £180 for the cost of the issues.

Assignment Exercises

Assignment Exercises followed by the letter x do NOT have answers shown at the back of the book.

4.1 From the following figures calculate the closing stock-in-trade that would be shown using (i) F.I.F.O., (ii) L.I.F.O., (iii) A.V.C.O. methods on a perpetual inventory basis.

Bought		Sold	
January	10 at £30 each	April	8 for £46 each
March	10 at £34 each	December	12 for £56 each
September	20 at £40 each		

4.2 For question 4.1 draw up the Trading Account for the year showing the gross profits that would have been reported using (i) F.I.F.O., (ii) L.I.F.O., (iii) A.V.C.O. methods on a perpetual inventory basis.

4.3x From the data in question 4.1 what would the answers have been if the periodic inventory method had been used for the valuation of stock-in-trade?

4.4x From the figures in question 4.3 draw up the Trading Accounts using (i) F.I.F.O., (ii) L.I.F.O., (iii) A.V.C.O. methods on a periodic inventory basis.

4.5 What does the relationship have to be between the physical issue of goods and the pricing out of goods?

4.6x Receipts and issues of a good are as follows:

Receipts		Sales	
January	20 at £30 each	June	6 for £45 each
May	10 at £33 each	August	22 for £46 each
July	16 at £38.5 each	December	10 for £48 each
October	12 at £39 each		

There was no opening stock-in-hand.

(a) Using the perpetual inventory method you are required to calculate the closing stock-in-trade using (i) F.I.F.O., (ii) L.I.F.O., (iii) A.V.C.O.

(b) Draw up the Trading Account showing the different reported gross profits from the figures given in (a).

(c) Using the periodic inventory method you are required to calculate the closing stock-in-trade using (i) F.I.F.O., (ii) L.I.F.O., (iii) A.V.C.O.

(d) Draw up the Trading Accounts showing the different reported gross profits calculated from the figures given in (c).

4.7 (a) From the following figures calculate the closing stock-in-trade that would be shown using (i) F.I.F.O., (ii) L.I.F.O., (iii) A.V.C.O. methods on a perpetual inventory basis.

Bought		*Sold*	
January	24 at £10 each	June	30 at £16 each
April	16 at £12.50 each	November	34 at £18 each
October	30 at £13 each		

(b) Draw up Trading Accounts using each of the three methods.

Chapter Five

Comparison of FIFO, LIFO and Average Cost Methods

The fact that accounts can be constructed to give widely differing answers and yet be within the law is a constant source of amazement to the general public. They feel, instinctively, that balance sheets should be "correct", and that for a firm only one answer is possible in the form of a Trading and Profit and Loss Account and Balance Sheet. We have already seen that issues of goods to production or as cost of goods sold can be on differing bases. There are many other factors which can be shown quite differently, a prime example of this are depreciation provisions as there are quite a number of ways of calculating depreciation, and in any event even where firms use the same method, e.g. the straight line method for similar assets, one firm may fix an asset life of five years and another ten years, one firm may estimate a residual value of £1,000 and the other firm may estimate it at £100.

The point that has to be brought home to the reader is that Final Accounts are concerned very much with matters of opinion. As matters are at present it would be impossible to get perfect uniformity between firms, as the opinions of one board of directors can never be exactly the same as the opinions of a board of directors of a similar firm, there are bound to be differences no matter how small. The late 1960's saw many disputes, especially where a firm had been taken over, because the accounts prior to the takeover were drafted on completely different bases than would have been used by the directors of the firm that had made the take-over bid. The figures involved have often been quite large, in one case the opinions of the figure that should have been included as stock varied by as much as four million pounds. The professional accountancy bodies have moved towards greater standardisation in stock valuation.

To illustrate this further we will now look at the accounts of three firms in Exhibit 5.1 for the first three years of operation. Each firm has exactly the same transactions, but they each use different methods of pricing out issues of goods with a corresponding effect on their stock valuations at the end of each year.

Exhibit 5.1

Each firm starts with Capital of £200 in the bank. All sales are cash sales and all purchases and expenses are paid for immediately. Each of the firms are in the same sort of retail trade. Receipts of goods are shown in chronological order, the periodic method of inventory control being used instead of the perpetual method.

	Receipts	Sales	General Expenses
Year 1	20 at £10 each	30 at £14 each	£50
	20 at £12 each		
Year 2	10 at £13 each	32 at £16 each	£60
	20 at £14 each		
Year 3	12 at £18 each	36 at £24 each	£80
	30 at £21 each		

We can now look at the calculation of the prices at which goods have been issued (sold in this case), then the Final Accounts are shown for each firm. The first firm uses Average Cost (AVCO), the second firm First In First Out (FIFO), and the third firm Last In First Out (LIFO).

Average Cost Method (A.V.C.O.)

	Receipts	£	Average Cost	Issues	Stock end of year
Year 1:	20 × £10 each =	200			
	20 × £12 each =	240			
	40	440	£440 ÷ 40 = £11	30 × £11 = £330	10 × £11 = £110

Year 2:

Stock b/f:	10 × £11 each =	110			
	10 × £13 each =	130			
	20 × £14 each =	280			
	40	520	£520 ÷ 40 = £13	32 × £13 = £416	8 × £13 = £104

Year 3:

Stock b/f:	8 × £13 each =	104			
	12 × £18 each =	216			
	30 × £21 each =	630			
	50	950	£950 ÷ 50 = £19	36 × £19 = £684	14 × £19 = £266

First In First Out Method (F.I.F.O.)

	Receipts	£	Issues	£	Stock end of year
Year 1:	20 × £10 each =	200	20 × £10 each =	200	
	20 × £12 each =	240	10 × £12 each =	120	10 × £12 each = 120
	40	440	30	320	

Year 2:

Stock b/f:	10 × £12 each =	120	10 × £12 each =	120	
	10 × £13 each =	130	10 × £13 each =	130	
	20 × £14 each =	280	12 × £14 each =	168	8 × £14 each = £112
	40	530	32	418	

Year 3:

Stock b/f:	8 × £14 each =	112	8 × £14 each =	112	
	12 × £18 each =	216	12 × £18 each =	216	
	30 × £21 each =	630	16 × £21 each =	336	14 × £21 each = £294
	50	958	36	664	

Last In First Out Method (L.I.F.O.)

	Receipts	£		Issues	£				£
Year 1:	$20 \times £10$ each =	200		$20 \times £12$ each =	240				
	$20 \times £12$ each =	240		$10 \times £10$ each =	100		$10 \times £10$ each =	£100	
	40	440		30	340				

Year 2:

		£			£				£
Stock b/f:	$10 \times £10$ each =	100		$20 \times £14$ each =	280				
	$10 \times £13$ each =	130		$10 \times £13$ each =	130				
	$20 \times £14$ each =	280		$2 \times £10$ each =	20		$8 \times £10$ each =	£80	
	40	510		32	430				

Year 3:

		£			£				£
Stock b/f:	$8 \times £10$ each =	80		$30 \times £21$ each =	630				
	$12 \times £18$ each =	216		$6 \times £18$ each =	108		$6 \times £18$ each =	£108	
	$30 \times £21$ each =	630					$8 \times £10$ each =	£80	
	50	926		36	738		=	£188	

Now we can look at the Trading and Profit and Loss Accounts and Balance Sheets for each of the three years. For simplicity we can assume that all goods were bought for cash and all sales were cash sales.

Trading and Profit and Loss Accounts — Year 1

	AVCO £	FIFO £	LIFO £		AVCO £	FIFO £	LIFO £
Purchases	440	440	440	Sales	420	420	420
Less Closing Stock	110	120	100				
Cost of Goods Sold	330	320	340				
Gross Profit c/d	90	100	80				
	420	420	420		420	420	420
Expenses	50	50	50	Gross Profit b/d	90	100	80
Net Profit	40	50	30				
	90	100	80		90	100	80

Balance Sheets—Year 1

	AVCO £	FIFO £	LIFO £		AVCO £	FIFO £	LIFO £
Capital	200	200	200	Stock	110	120	100
Add Net Profit	40	50	30	Bank	130	130	130
	240	250	230		240	250	230

	AVCO	FIFO	LIFO
Net Profit expressed as Return on Capital Employed*	$\dfrac{40}{240} \times \dfrac{100}{1} = 16.7\%$	$\dfrac{50}{250} \times \dfrac{100}{1} = 20\%$	$\dfrac{30}{230} \times \dfrac{100}{1} = 13\%$

*See Chapter 23 for a reference to this.

Trading and Profit and Loss Accounts—Year 2

	AVCO	FIFO	LIFO		AVCO	FIFO	LIFO
	£	£	£		£	£	£
Opening Stock	110	120	100	Sales	512	512	512
Add Purchases	410	410	410				
	520	530	510				
Less Closing Stock	104	112	80				
Cost of Goods Sold	416	418	430				
Gross Profit c/d	96	94	82				
	512	512	512		512	512	512
Expenses	60	60	60	Gross Profit b/d	96	94	82
Net Profit	36	34	22				
	96	94	82		96	94	82

Balance Sheets—Year 2

	AVCO	FIFO	LIFO		AVCO	FIFO	LIFO
Capital	240	250	230	Stock	104	112	80
Net Profit	36	34	22	Bank	172	172	172
	276	284	252		276	284	252

	AVCO	FIFO	LIFO
Net Profit expressed as Return on Capital Employed	$\dfrac{36}{276} \times \dfrac{100}{1} = 13\%$	$\dfrac{34}{284} \times \dfrac{100}{1} = 12\%$	$\dfrac{22}{252} \times \dfrac{100}{1} = 8.7\%$

Trading and Profit and Loss Accounts—Year 3

	AVCO	FIFO	LIFO		AVCO	FIFO	LIFO
	£	£	£		£	£	£
Opening Stock	104	112	80	Sales	864	864	864
Add Purchases	846	846	846				
	950	958	926				
Less Closing Stock	266	294	188				
Cost of Goods Sold	684	664	738				
Gross Profit c/d	180	200	126				
	864	864	864		864	864	864
Expenses	80	80	80	Gross Profit b/d	180	200	126
Net Profit	100	120	46				
	180	200	126		180	200	126

Balance Sheets—Year 3

	AVCO	FIFO	LIFO		AVCO	FIFO	LIFO
Capital	276	284	252	Stock	266	294	188
Net Profit	100	120	46	Bank	110	110	110
	376	404	298		376	404	298

42

	AVCO	*FIFO*	*LIFO*
Net Profit expressed as Return on Capital Employed	$\frac{100}{376} \times \frac{100}{1} = 26.6\%$	$\frac{120}{404} \times \frac{100}{1} = 29.7\%$	$\frac{46}{298} \times \frac{100}{1} = 15.4\%$

It will probably be easier to see the differences in reported profits using different cost methods of pricing out goods if a diagram is used. This can be shown as Exhibit 5.2.

Exhibit 5.2

Reported profits if different pricing methods used

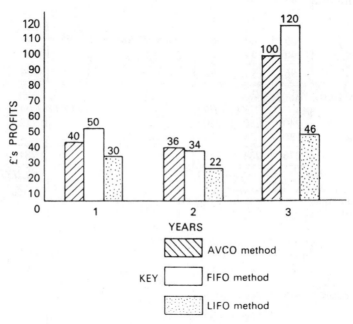

Accounting Practice and Stock Valuation

You may well think that Exhibit 5.1 was an artificial example in that in practice the same method would have been used by the three firms. This is far from the truth — surveys have shown that similar types of firms use different methods. Practice is very much conditioned by the high rates of taxation suffered by firms, this will be examined more closely in later chapters. Apart from the fact that accounting practice is so much affected by the desire to make the tax burden easier the other main reason is probably that of ease of calculation. Custom plays a part in some industries and very often it is found that a firm prices out goods, and therefore values stock, in a particular manner for no better reason than the accountant had used a particular method at his last firm and now puts it in use in his new firm.

Rising prices and pricing methods

In a period of rising prices, as is indeed the case in Exhibit 5.1 the LIFO method will tend to delay profit recognition as compared with the FIFO method. The AVCO method will usually lead to results in between the LIFO and FIFO methods. On the other hand, in a period of falling prices FIFO would tend to record lesser profits more quickly.

What should govern choice of method?

The Institute of Chartered Accountants in England and Wales give, as one of their recommendations, that the overriding consideration is the need to give a "true and fair view" of the state of the affairs of the organization as on the Balance Sheet date, and of the trend of the organisation's trading results. There is as yet, however no precise definition of "true and fair view", and it therefore rests on the judgement of the people concerned. Just as a large group of people could never agree as to which is the best football team in Great Britain, so also will it be impossible unless some very firm guidelines are laid down as to which would be the best method, i.e. LIFO, FIFO or AVCO, to keep to the "true and fair view". Especially since the movement towards Current Costs in Financial Accounts many firms have moved away from historic costs towards current cost values for inventory records. The following illustration shows the approach of Current Cost Accounting to periodic inventory valuation.

Replacement Cost Method

Under this method (called CCA for Current Cost Accounting) the balance of inventory is revalued to its current replacement value at the year end. The issues of material are also revalued at the average replacement value for the year. The revisions to the inventory values are transferred to an Inventory Revaluation Reserve Account. The revisions from revaluation are gains from holding inventories rather than from manufacturing and are not included in the Net Operating Profit.

Using the data from Exhibit 5.1 the following information is obtained in addition to that used in the historic cost accounts.

	Average Replacement Cost £	Year End Replacement Cost £
Year 1	11	12
2	13.50	14
3	20.00	22

The data will then be evaluated as follows:

	Receipts	£	Issue at Average Replacement Cost 1	£	Stock at Year End Replacement Cost 2	£	1 + 2 £	Adjustment to Revaluation Account £
Year 1	20 × £10 =	200						
	20 × £12 =	240						
	40	440	30 × £11 =	330	10 × £12 =	120	450	+ 10
Year 2								
Stock b/f	10 × £12 =	120						
	10 × £13 =	130						
	20 × £14 =	280						
	40	530	32 × £13.50 =	432	8 × £14 =	112	544	+ 14
Year 3								
Stock b/f	8 × £14 =	112						
	12 × £18 =	216						
	30 × £21 =	630						
		958	36 × £20 =	720	14 × £22 =	308	1,028	+ 70

Trading and Profit and Loss Accounts

	Year 1	Year 2	Year 3		Year 1	Year 2	Year 3
Opening Stock	–	120	112	Sales	420	512	864
Add Purchases	440	410	846				
Revaluation	10	14	70				
	450	544	1,028				
Less Closing Stock at Current Value	120	112	308				
Cost of Goods Sold at Current Values	330	432	720				
Gross Operating Profit c/d	90	80	144				
	420	512	864		420	512	864
Expenses	50	60	80	Gross Profit b/d	90	80	144
Net Operating Profit	40	20	64				
	90	80	144		90	80	144

Balance Sheets

	Year 1	Year 2	Year 3		Year 1	Year 2	Year 3
Capital	200	250	284				
Revaluation of Stock Reserve	10	14	70	Stock	120	112	308
Net Operating Profit	40	20	64	Bank	130	172	110
	250	284	418		250	284	418

Note that by comparison the net profits for: –

AVCO	40	36	100
FIFO	50	34	120
LIFO	30	22	46

In the first two years the FIFO profits of £50 and £34 are equivalent to the Net Operating Profit plus the Revaluation Reserve £40 + £10 = £50 and £20 + £14 = £34. In the third year a difference arises because the closing stock is valued at a replacement price of £22 per unit which is higher than any units actually bought in the year. Under FIFO the closing stock of 14 units is valued at £21 compared to £22 under CCA, which accounts for a different of £1 per unit – in total £14. This is the difference between the two results i.e. CCA £64 + 70 = £134 – FIFO £120. The CCA approach gives more information than the historic cost method as it distinguishes between 'holding gains' and 'operating profits'.

For costing on a perpetual basis where prices are changing frequently it would usually be more convenient to use Standard Costing methods which are shown in Chapter 13.

Assignment Exercises

Assignment Exercises followed by the letter x do NOT have answers shown at the back of the book.

5.1 D. Simon has been in business for 3 years, deals in only one product, and has used the F.I.F.O. method of valuing stock-in-trade on a perpetual inventory basis. The figures of receipts and sales are as follows:

		Receipts		Sales
Year 1	January	30 at £12 each	July	24 for £15.5 each
	May	30 at £14 each	November	16 for £18 each
Year 2	February	10 at £16 each	June	30 for £22 each
	April	10 at £18 each	December	20 for £23 each
	November	20 at £18 each		
Year 3	January	10 at £19 each	April	20 for £23 each
	March	20 at £20 each	July	10 for £24 each
	August	10 at £19 each	December	24 for £26 each
	November	20 at £21 each		

You are required to calculate the valuation of the closing stock-in-trade for each of the three years. Keep your answer, it will be used as a basis for later questions.

5.2 What would the stock-in-trade valuations have been at the end of each of the three years in 5.1 if the L.I.F.O. method had been used?

5.3 What would the stock-in-trade valuations have been at the end of each of the three years in 5.1 if the A.V.C.O. method had been used?

5.4 From the figures in 5.1 draw up the Trading Accounts for each of the three years assuming that the stock records were kept on a perpetual basis if (i) the F.I.F.O. method had been used, (ii) the L.I.F.O. method was used, (iii) the A.V.C.O. method was used. (Keep your answer — it will be used as the basis of a later question.)

5.5 If in 5.1 the periodic method had been in use rather than the perpetual method then what would the answer have been?

5.6 If in 5.2 the periodic method had been in use rather than the perpetual inventory method then what would the answer have been?

5.7 If in 5.3 the periodic method had been used rather than the perpetual inventory method then what would the answer have been?

5.8 If in 5.4 the periodic method had been used rather than the perpetual method then what would the answer have been? Keep your answer, it will be used as the basis of a later question.

5.9x Using the answer in 5.4(i), i.e. the F.I.F.O. method set of Trading Accounts, draft the Profit and Loss Accounts and Balance Sheets for the three years if the cash receipts and payments (includes the bank receipts and payments) were as follows (see note re depreciation at end of question):

Year 1

Capital Introduced	1,200	Fixed Assets bought	200
Cash Sales (all sales all for		Payments to Creditors for	
cash	660	goods (goods are bought	
		on credit)	500
		Expenses	100
		Drawings	80
		Balance carried forward	980
	£1,860		£1,860

Year 2

Balance brought forward	980	Payment to Creditors	750
Cash Sales	1,120	Expenses	110
		Drawings	190
		Balance carried forward	1,050
	£2,100		£2,100

Year 3

Balance brought forward	1,050	Payments to Creditors	900
Cash Sales	1,324	Expenses	130
		Drawings	240
		Balance carried forward	1,104
	£2,374		£2,374

You may assume that there was nothing owing for expenses at the end of each year. The Fixed Assets are to be depreciated £20 per annum.

5.10x Using the same figures of cash as in 5.9 draft Profit and Loss Accounts and Balance Sheets for the three years to the answer in 5.4(ii), i.e. the L.I.F.O. method set of Trading Accounts.

5.11x Using the same figures of cash as in 5.9 draft Profit and Loss Accounts and Balance sheets for the three years to the answer in 5.4(iii), i.e. the A.V.C.O. method set of Trading Accounts.

5.12x Using your answer to 5.8(i) i.e. Trading Accounts using F.I.F.O. on a periodic inventory basis, and using the same figures of cash as in 5.9, draw up Profit and Loss Accounts and Balance Sheets for the three years.

5.13x Using your answer to 5.8(ii), i.e. Trading Accounts using L.I.F.O. on a periodic inventory basis, and using the same figures of cash as in 5.9, draw up Profit and Loss Accounts and Balance Sheets for the three years.

5.14x Using your answer to 5.8(iii), i.e. Trading Accounts using A.V.C.O. on a periodic inventory basis, and using the same figures of cash as in 5.9, draw up Profit and Loss Accounts and Balance Sheets for the three years.

5.15x P. Paul has been in business for three years, deals in only one product, and has used the F.I.F.O. method of valuing stock-in-trade on a perpetual inventory basis. The figures of receipts and sales are as follows:

		Receipts		*Sales*
Year 1	January	28 at £10 each	March	11 for £16 each
	April	12 at £10 each	August	15 for £16 each
	November	14 at £11 each	December	10 for £16.5 each
Year 2	February	9 at £12 each	April	17 for £17 each
	June	10 at £13 each	July	8 for £17 each
	August	8 at £12 each	December	30 for £19 each
	November	20 at £13 each		
Year 3	January	15 at £15 each	February	15 for £19 each
	April	10 at £16 each	November	32 for £22 each
	June	10 at £17 each		
	October	20 at £19 each		

You are required to calculate the valuation of the closing stock-in-trade for each of the three years. Keep your answer, it will be used as a basis for later questions.

5.16x What would the stock-in-trade valuations have been in 5.15 if the L.I.F.O. method had been used?

5.17x What would the stock-in-trade valuations have been in 5.15 if the A.V.C.O. method had been used?

5.18x From the figures in 5.15 draw up the Trading Accounts for each of the three years assuming that the stock records were kept on a perpetual basis if (i) the F.I.F.O. method had been used, (ii) the L.I.F.O. method was used, (iii) the A.V.C.O. method was used.

5.19x If in 5.16 the periodic inventory method had been in use instead of the perpetual inventory method, what would the answer have been?

5.20x If in 5.17 the periodic inventory method had been in use instead of the perpetual inventory method, what would the answer have been? (nearest £)

5.21x If in 5.18 the periodic inventory method had been in use instead of the perpetual inventory method, what would the answer have been?

5.22 Using the data from 5.1 and the following additional information on replacement costs, construct Trading Accounts for the three years using Replacement Cost Method.

	Average Replacement Cost £	Year End Replacement Cost £
Year 1	13	15
2	18	18.50
3	19.50	21.00

5.23 Using the data from 5.22 and the following additional information on replacement costs, construct Trading Accounts for the three years using Replacement Cost Method.

	Average Replacement Cost £	Year End Replacement Cost £
Year 1	23	26.50
2	28	30.00
3	31	31.00

5.24x Using the data from 5.15x and the following additional information on replacement costs construct Trading Accounts for the three years using Replacement Cost Method.

	Average Replacement Cost £	Year End Replacement Cost £
Year 1	10.50	11.50
2	13.00	14.00
3	17.00	20.00

Chapter Six

Absorption and Marginal Costing

The most commonly accepted cost accounting theory used for purposes of the determination of profit is where all the Factory Indirect Expenses are allocated to the products manufactured. This is shown in Exhibit 3.2 where the Factory Indirect Expenses are seen as adding to the value of work-in-progress and thence to finished goods stock. The Production Cost of any article is thus comprised of Direct Materials, Direct Labour, any Direct Expenses and a share of Factory Indirect Expense.

After the financial year is over it is possible to look back and calculate what the Factory Indirect Expenses actually were, such as in Exhibit 3.1 where the Factory Indirect Expenses were seen to be £32,000. That firm had a calculation of the closing stock valuation which was:

$$\frac{\text{Unsold items}}{\text{Items produced}} \times \text{Production Cost of Goods Completed}$$

or in figures $\dfrac{200 \text{ units}}{1,000 \text{ units}} \times \text{Production Cost } £102,000 = £20,400$

Cost data is used for other purposes than valuing stock, and the question is, therefore, whether or not this method is suitable for all purposes in costing. This method of allocating all the Factory Indirect Expenses to products is known as absorption costing or full costing.

We can now look at a decision we might have to come to about a future action. Exhibit 6.1 shows a firm which has to make a decision about whether or not to take on an extra order.

Exhibit 6.1

Donald Ltd's factory has been making 1,000 units annually of a particular product for the past few years. Last year costs were:

	£
Direct Labour	2,000
Direct Materials	3,000
Factory Indirect Expenses	4,000
Production Cost	9,000
Administration and Other Expenses	1,000
	10,000

The units, 1,000 had been sold for £12 each = £12,000.

The production cost per unit can be seen to be $\dfrac{£9,000}{1,000} = £9$.

The current year is following exactly the same pattern of production and costs. Suddenly, part-way through the year, a foreign buyer says he will take 200 units if the price for him can be cut from £12 each to £8 each. A meeting is held and the managing director says, "What a pity. This could have been our first export order, something we have been waiting to happen for several years. The selling price overseas has no bearing on our selling price at home. But it costs us £9 a unit in production costs alone. We just cannot afford to lose money so as to export. Our shareholders would not tolerate the profits of the company falling to less than £2,000."

"I think that you are wrong," says John the accountant. "Let's look at this year's results (a) if we do not accept the order and (b) if the order is accepted." He then drafts the following:

	(a) Order not taken £		(b) Order taken £	
Sales 1,000 × £12		12,000		
1,000 × £12 + 200 × £8				13,600
Less Expenses:				
Direct Labour	2,000		2,400	
Direct Materials	3,000		3,600	
Factory Indirect Expenses	4,000		4,200	
Other Expenses	1,000	10,000	1,000	11,200
Net Profit		2,000		2,400

"More profit. This means that we take the order," says the sales director enthusiastically.

"Surely you've got your figures wrong, John," says the managing director. "Check your arithmetic."

"There's nothing wrong with my arithmetic," says John, "but perhaps it will be a little more enlightening if I draft (b) Order taken, more fully."

(b) Order taken

Sales		13,600
Less Costs which vary with production: Direct Labour. The men are on piece work of a type that means 20 per cent more production brings 20 per cent more wages (i.e. £2,000 for 1,000 units, £2,400 for 1,200 units).	2,400	
Direct Materials. 20 per cent greater production gives 20 per cent more materials (£3000 + £600).	3,600	
Factory Indirect Expenses: Some would not change at all, e.g. Factory Rent, Factory Rates. Some would alter, e.g. cost of electric power because machines are used more. Of the Factory Indirect Expenses one-quarter is variable. For this part £1,000 costs for 1,000 units means £1,200 costs for 1,200 units.	1,200	7,200
Sales less Variable Costs		6,400
Costs; i.e. costs which will not alter at all if 200 more units are produced.		
Factory Indirect Expenses; fixed part	3,000	
Administration and Other Expenses	1,000	4,000
Net Profit		2,400

"We can do all this without borrowing any money," says the managing director, "so I'll phone now to tell them we will start production immediately. By the way, John, come to my office this afternoon and tell me more about variable and fixed costs."

The Lesson to be Learned

We must not get lost in the technicalities of accounting. It is easy to think that calculations which look complicated must give the right answer. Logic must be brought to bear on such problems. This last case shows that different costs will often be needed when making decisions about the future than the costs which were used for calculating profit earned in the past. £9 per unit had been taken for stock valuation, but this case proves that a firm could still manufacture units and sell at less than £9 each and still increase profits. The reason for this state of affairs is the very essence of the differences between fixed and variable costs which we will now consider.

Fixed and Variable Costs

The division of costs into those that are fixed and those that are variable is not an easy matter. Even factory rent is not always a fixed cost, for if production had to be increased to a certain figure the firm might have to rent further premises. Such a change would not usually happen in the short-term, it would take a while to rent and set-up a new factory or extra premises before production could start. When fixed costs are mentioned it is normally assumed that this means costs which are fixed in the short-term.

In the firm Donald Ltd., Exhibit 6.1 assumed that variable costs were 100 per cent variable, by this meaning that if production rose 20 per cent then the cost would rise 20 per cent, if the production rose 47 per cent then the cost would also rise 47 per cent. This is not necessarily true. The cost of power may rise 20 per cent if production rose 20 per cent, but the cost of repairing and maintaining the machines may rise by only 10 per cent if production rose 20 per cent. In this case the machine maintenance would be a semi-variable cost, this being the term for a cost which varies with production but not at a proportionate rate.

Cost Behaviour

Intelligent cost planning and control is dependent on the knowledge of how costs behave under certain conditions. What is important is how costs behave in a particular firm, there is no substitute for experience in this respect.

Raw materials are examples of variable costs which normally vary in strict proportion to the units manufactured. Labour costs, on the other hand, usually move in steps, thus the name "step-variable" costs. For instance, a job may be done by two men, and then a slight increase in activity means that the two men cannot manage it so that a third man is added. In fact it may represent only 2⅓ men's work, but the acquisition of workers comes in

52

indivisible chunks. There can still be a further increase in activity without any more workers, but then the time will come when a fourth man is needed. This is shown on the two graphs in Exhibit 6.2.

Exhibit 6.2

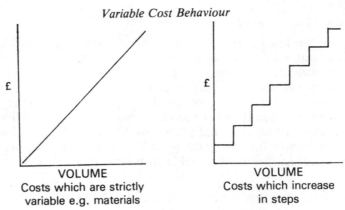

Variable Cost Behaviour

VOLUME
Costs which are strictly
variable e.g. materials

VOLUME
Costs which increase
in steps

Marginal Costing and Absorption Costing Contrasted

Where costing is used which takes account of the variable cost of products rather than the full production cost, then this is said to be Marginal Costing. We have seen that a marginal costing approach to the decision as to whether or not to accept the foreign order by Donald Ltd. gave us the answer which increased the firm's profitability, whereas to use absorption costing of £9 a unit in a blind fashion would have meant us rejecting the order and therefore passing up the chance to increase profits and break into the foreign market. Let us look now at what would happen if we used either marginal costing or absorption costing in the calculation of profits for a whole firm, i.e. income determination.

Exhibit 6.3

The final accounts of a firm, Burke Ltd., are now shown drafted as if (A) Marginal Costing had been used, (B) Absorption Costing had been used. The following information is available:

1. All fixed factory overheads amounted to £4,000 per annum.

2. Variable overheads amounted to £2 per unit.

3. Direct labour and direct materials total £3 per unit.

4. Sales remain constant at 1,000 units per annum at £12 per unit.

5. Production in year 1 is 1,200 units, year 2 is 1,500 units and year 3 is 900 units.

Year 1	(A) Marginal Costing £		(B) Absorption Costing £	
Sales		12,000		12,000
Less Variable Costs:				
Direct Labour and Material, 1,200 × £3	3,600		3,600	
Variable overheads, 1,200 × £2	2,400		2,400	
Total Variable Cost	6,000			
Less in (A) Valuation Closing Stock				
200 × £6,000	1,000*			
1,200				
	5,000			
Fixed Factory Overhead	4,000	9,000	4,000	
Total Production Costs			10,000	
Less in (B) Valuation Closing Stock				
200 × £10,000			1,666*	8,334
1,200				
Gross Profit		3,000		3,666

*see note later

Year 2				
Sales		12,000		12,000
Less Variable Costs:				
Direct Labour and Material 1,500 × £3	4,500		4,500	
Variable Overheads, 1,500 × £2	3,000		3,000	
Total Variable Cost	7,500			
Add in (A) Opening Stock b/fwd	1,000			
	8,500			
Less in (A) Closing Stock				
700 × £7,500 (see note later)	3,500			
1,500				
	5,000			
Fixed Factory Overhead	4,000	9,000	4,000	
Total Production Costs			11,500	
Add Opening Stock in (B) b/fwd			1,666	
			13,166	
Less Closing stock in (B) (see note later)				
700 × £11,500			5,366	7,800
1,500				
Gross Profit		3,000		4,200

Year 3		(A) *Marginal Costing*		(B) *Absorption Costing*	
			£		£
Sales			12,000		12,000
Less Variable Costs:					
Direct Labour and Material, 900 × £3		2,700		2,700	
Variable Overheads, 900 × £2		1,800		1,800	
Total Variable Cost		4,500			
Add in (A) Opening Stock b/fwd		3,500			
		8,000			
Less in (A) Closing Stock 600 × £4,500		3,000			
900					
		5,000			
Fixed Factory Overheads		4,000	9,000	4,000	
				8,500	
Add in (B) Opening Stock b/fwd				5,366	
				13,866	
Less in (B) Closing Stock 600 × £8,500				5,666	8,200
900					
Gross Profit			3,000		3,800

Notes: The Closing Stock each year for (A) is made up of:

$$\frac{\text{Unsold units}}{\text{No. of units produced in year}} \times \text{Total Variable Cost of that year}$$

Units produced year 1   1,200 − sold 1,000 = Stock 200 units

Units produced year 2   1,500 + 200 opening stock − sales 1,000 = Closing Stock 700 units

Units produced year 3   900 units + 700 opening stock − sales 1,000 = Closing Stock 600 units

So in year 1 unsold units are 200 units; units produced 1,200; total variable cost is £6,000, therefore stock valuation is

$$\frac{200}{1,200} \times £6,000 = £1,000$$

The Closing Stock each year for (B) is made up of:

$$\frac{\text{Unsold units}}{\text{No. of units produced in year}} \times \text{Total Production Cost of that year.}$$

So in year 1 Stock valuation becomes $\frac{200}{1,200} \times £10,000 = £1,666$.

Exhibit 6.4 shows in diagrammatic form the reported profits shown in Exhibit 6.2.

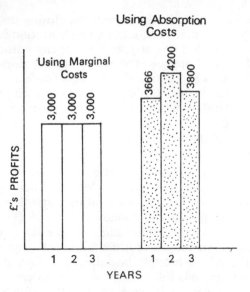

Using Absorption Costs

Using Marginal Costs

Exhibit 6.4

YEARS

Comparison of reported gross profits using marginal cost and absorption cost methods — constant sales and uneven production

Exhibit 6.3 has illustrated that Burke Ltd., a firm which has had the same amount of sales each year at the same prices, and the variable costs per unit have not changed at all, shows quite different profit figures using a Marginal Costing approach compared with Absorption Costing. As these were the gross profits that were calculated let us assume that the selling, distribution, administration and finance expenses were £1,000 for each of these years. The net profits would therefore be as follows:

	(A) Marginal Costing	(B) Absorption Costing
	£	£
Year 1	2,000	2,666
Year 2	2,000	3,200
Year 3	2,000	2,800

Because of the Absorption Costing approach year 2 shows the biggest profit. As sales etc. are the same, only production being different, this means that the year which has the greatest closing stock has shown the greatest profit. Because of greater production the amount of fixed factory overhead is less. For instance in year 1 with 1,200 units produced and £4,000 fixed factory overhead this means $\frac{£4,000}{1,200}$ = £3.3 per unit, year 2 $\frac{£4,000}{1,500}$ = £2.7 per unit, year 3 $\frac{£4,000}{900}$ = £4.4 per unit (only taken to one decimal place).

By calculating the value of closing stock bringing in fixed factory overhead means that less gets charged for fixed factory overhead when production is greatest, and thus there is a tendency for a greater profit to be shown.

Of course it gets more complicated because the closing stock of one year is the opening stock of the next year, and under absorption costing the values of units of stock will vary. Look at year 3: the opening stock of 700 units is shown as £5,366 = £7.7 approximately; the closing stock of 600 units is shown as £5,666 = £9.4 approximately. Yet these are exactly the same kind of things, and because we have made costs the same each year we have been ignoring inflation. To show a higher profit in a year when the closing stock is higher than usual is often dangerous. In fact the stock may be rising because we cannot sell the goods, we are really getting into trouble, yet the accounts sublimely show a higher profit!

Many experts have argued for or against the Marginal and the Absorption approach in income determination. The Marginal approach really states that fixed Factory Overhead is a function of time and should not be carried forward to the next period by including it in stock valuations. The Absorption approach states that such overhead is concerned with production and therefore the goods produced in that year, but not yet sold, should have such overhead brought into the calculation of its value carried forward to the next period. Put bluntly — do such costs "attach" to the product or to time? Accountants are divided on this issue, perhaps what has been written in this chapter may have brought you down in favour of one side or the other. It does seem that the marginal approach will become used much more frequently than in the past.

Assignment Exercises

Assignment Exercises followed by the letter x do NOT have answers shown at the back of the book.

6.1 Drake Ltd's cost and revenues for the current year are expected to be:

	£	£
Direct Labour		6,000
Direct Materials		7,000
Factory Indirect Expenses:		
Variable	4,500	
Fixed	500	5,000
Administration Expenses		1,200
Selling and Distribution Expenses		600
Finance Expenses		200
		£20,000

It was expected that 2,000 units would be manufactured and sold, the selling price being £11 each.

Suddenly during the year two enquiries were made at the same time which would result in extra production being necessary. They were:

(A) An existing customer said that he would take an extra 100 units, but the price would have to be reduced to £9 per unit on this extra 100 units. The only extra costs that would be involved would be in respect of variable costs.

(B) A new customer would take 150 units annually. This would mean extra variable costs and also an extra machine would have to be bought costing £1,500 which would last for 5 years before being scrapped. It would have no scrap value. Extra running costs of this machine would be £600 per annum. The units are needed for an underdeveloped country and owing to currency difficulties the highest price that could be paid for the units was £10 per unit.

On this information, and assuming that there are no alternatives open to Drake Ltd., should the company accept or reject these orders? Draft the memo that you would give to the managing director of Drake Ltd.

6.2x Hawkins Ltd. expects its costs per unit — assuming a production level of 100,000 per annum — to be:

	£
Direct Materials	2.8
Direct Labour	2.4
Factory Indirect Expenses: Variable	0.8
Fixed	0.4
Selling and Distribution Expenses	0.2
Administration Expenses	0.3
Finance	0.1
	£7.0

Selling price is £7.5 per unit.

The following propositions are put to the managing director. Each proposition is to be considered on its own without reference to the other propositions.

(a) If the selling price is reduced to £7.4 per unit sales could be raised to 120,000 units per annum instead of the current 100,000 units. Apart from Direct Materials, Direct Labour and Factory Variable Expenses there would be no change in costs.

(b) If the selling price is put up to £7.7 per unit sales would be 80,000 per annum instead of 100,000. Apart from variable costs there would also be a saving of £2,000 per annum in Finance Costs.

(c) To satisfy a special order, which would not be repeated, 5,000 extra units could be sold at £6.3 each. This would have no effect on fixed expenses.

(d) To satisfy a special order, which would not be repeated, 3,000 extra units could be sold for £5.9 each. This would have no effect on fixed expenses.

Draft a memo stating what you would advise the managing director to do giving your reasons and workings.

6.3x Assume that by coincidence two firms have exactly the same costs and revenue, but that Magellan Ltd. uses a marginal costing approach to the valuation of stock-in-trade in its final accounts, whilst Frobisher Ltd. has an absorption cost approach. Calculate the gross profits for each company for each of their first three years of operating from the following:

(a) All fixed factory overhead is £9,000 per annum.

(b) Direct Labour costs over each of the three years — £3 per unit.

(c) Direct Material costs over each of the three years — £5 per unit.

(d) Variable overheads which vary in direct ratio to production were £2 per unit.

(e) Sales are: Year 1 900 units: Year 2 1,200 units: Year 3 1,100 units. The selling price remained constant at £29 per unit.

(f) Production is at the rate of: Year 1 1,200 units: Year 2 1,300 units: Year 3 1,250 units.

6.4x Gould Ltd. have been in business for three years and have always used an absorption cost approach to the valuation of stock-in-trade for their final accounts. They are approached by a take-over bidder who prefers to use a marginal cost approach. The price for the shares is agreed at a formula:

Average Gross Profit for the three years calculated using the marginal cost approach times 5, add Gross Profit for year 3 using the absorption cost approach times 2 = Price to be given for all the shares of Gould Ltd.

The following information is available:
(a) Sales were: Year 1   10,000 units: Year 2   12,000 units: Year 3   11,000 units.
(b) Production is at the rate of: Year 1   13,000 units: Year 2   11,000 units: Year 3   12,000 units.
(c) Direct Labour costs per unit were constant at £6 per unit.
(d) Direct Material costs per unit over the three years were constant at £11 per unit.
(e) Variable Overheads which vary in direct proportion to production were £4 per unit.
(f) Fixed expenses are: factory overhead £80,000 per annum.
(g) Selling price remained constant at £30 per unit.

You are required to calculate the amount that would have to be paid for the shares of Gould Ltd. by the take-over bidder.

6.5 The costs and revenues for Garrick Limited for the present year are expected to be as follows:

	£
Direct Labour	16,000
Direct Materials	21,000
Factory Indirect Expenses*	9,000
Administration Expenses	3,000
Selling and Distribution Expenses	2,000
Finance Expenses	1,000
	52,000
Net profit	8,000
Sales: 4,000 units (at £15 each)	60,000

*Made up of one-third fixed and two-thirds variable expenses.

Towards the end of the year two additional projects come under consideration. Both of these would require extra production. They are:

(a) A new customer would take 200 units annually. The order would bring about extra variable costs in direct proportion to the extra production needed. In addition an extra machine would have to be bought for £3,000, it would last for four years before being scrapped, there being a scrap value of £200. The extra running costs of this machine would be £1,800 per annum. The highest price that could be paid by this customer, it is an overseas company, is £25 per unit.

(b) An existing customer says he will take 50 units additionally per annum, but the price would have to fall to £13 per unit on these 50 units.

Based on the information above, what advice would you give to your Managing Director? You are also to state how you would qualify your advice. Show all of your workings to substantiate your advice.

6.6 Your firm has been trading for three years. It has used a marginal costing approach to the valuation of stock-in-trade in its final accounts. Your directors are interested to know what the recorded profits would have been if the absorption cost approach had been used instead. Draw up the three year's accounts using both methods.

(a) Fixed factory overhead is £16,000 per annum.

(b) Direct Labour costs per unit over each of the three years £4 per unit.

(c) Direct Material costs over each of the three years £3 per unit.

(d) Variable overheads which vary in direct ratio to production were £5 per unit.

(e) Sales are: Year 1   9,000 units; Year 2   10,000 units; Year 3   15,000 units. All at £16 per unit.

(f) Production is at the rate of: Year 1   10,000 units; Year 2   12,000 units; Year 3   16,000 units.

Chapter Seven

Job and Process Costing

The earlier chapters on costing have been concerned mainly with the firm as a whole. You have seen the effects of Marginal and Absorption Costing if applied to the firm, and you have seen the flow of costs through manufacturing and retail businesses. Now we have to consider the use of these concepts in the application of costing in firms. So far there has been a certain amount of simplification just so that the concepts could be seen without too much detail obscuring your view. For instance it has been usually assumed in most of the Exhibits that the firms have been making only one kind of product, and that there has really been only one cost centre. Without stretching your imagination greatly you will realize that firms manufacture many different types of goods, and that there are many cost centres in most firms.

When looking at the costing systems in use it can be seen that they can usually be divided into two main types, (a) Job Costing, (b) Process costing. These two main types have either an absorption or marginal costing approach, they use FIFO or LIFO or AVCO methods of pricing issues etc. It is important to realize that Marginal Costing is not a costing system, it is instead an approach to costing which is used when Job or Processing Costing systems are used. The same applies to Absorption Costing.

The Choice of Job Costing or Process Costing

Process costing is relevant where production is regarded as a continuous flow, and would be applicable to industries where production is repetitive and continuous. One example would be an oil refinery where crude oil is processed continually, emerging as different grades of petrol, paraffin, motor oil, etc. Another instance would be a salt works where brine (salt water) is pumped into the works, and the product is slabs or packets of salt. Salt works and oil refineries will have a repetitive and continuous flow of production and would, therefore, use Process Costing.

Contrasted with this would be production which consisted of separate jobs for special orders which could be just one item or of a batch of items. For instance where bodies of Rolls-Royce cars are made to each customers' specifications, each car can be regarded as a separate job. Compared with this would be a printer's business where books are printed, so that the printing of say 5,000 copies of a book can also be regarded as a job. The "job" can thus be one item or a batch of similar items.

1. *Job Costing*

Each job will be given a separate job number, and direct materials and direct labour used on the job will be charged to the job. The accumulation of the costs will be done on a "job cost sheet". The materials will have been charged to the job on FIFO, or LIFO, or AVCO, etc., basis. The direct labour costs will be found by recording the number of direct labour hours of each type of direct worker, and multiplying by the labour cost per hour for each type.

The job is thus the cost centre, and direct labour and direct materials can be charged direct to the cost centre. The indirect expenses cannot be charged direct to the job, such costs are charged instead to a service cost centre and the cost of the service centre is then apportioned between the various jobs to give the cost of each job including indirect expenses. Now it is only after the accounting period is over that the exact costs of each service centre are known, but you will want to know how much each job costs as it is finished. You will not want to wait months to find out the cost of each job. This is solved by estimating the indirect expenses, and then fixing the method of apportioning these estimated expenses as will be seen in Exhibit 7.1.

Suppose there are three jobs being performed and these are in separate production departments, Departments A, B and C. There are also two service centres, Departments G and H. Some of the indirect labour expenses and other indirect expenses can be allocated direct to the production departments — for instance the wages of the foremen of each of Departments A, B and C, or items such as lubricating materials if each department used quite different lubricants. Other indirect labour can be traced to the two centres G and H as well as expenses. The problem then is that of apportioning the costs of G and H between Departments A, B and C. We can now look at Exhibit 7.1, and see what answer this firm came up with.

Exhibit 7.1

Indirect Labour Costs and Other Indirect Expenses have been allocated to Production Departments A, B and C and Service Departments G and H as follows:

| | Production Departments | | | Service Departments | |
	A	B	C	G	H
Indirect Labour	2,000	3,000	4,000	500	1,000
Other Expenses	1,000	2,000	3,000	1,500	2,000
	£3,000	£5,000	£7,000	£2,000	£3,000

The problem is to apportion the costs of G and H to the production departments. G was a department which maintained factory buildings whilst H maintained factory machinery. A study of the costs of G produced a very easy answer. There was no doubt that the costs were in direct relationship to the floor space occupied by each department. But it must not be overlooked that department H also needed the attention of G's workforce so that part of the costs of G would have to be apportioned to H. These costs would then increase the total of costs of department H which would then need apportioning to the production departments. Floor space in square feet was A 2,000, B 4,000, C 3,000, and H 1,000. The £2,000 costs were therefore apportioned:

$$\text{Each department:} \quad \frac{\text{Its floor space}}{\text{Total floor space}} \times £2,000$$

Therefore:

$$\text{A} \quad \frac{2,000}{10,000} \times £2,000 = £400 \quad : \quad \text{B} \quad \frac{4,000}{10,000} \times £2,000 = £800$$

$$\text{C} \quad \frac{3,000}{10,000} \times £2,000 = £600 \quad : \quad \text{H} \quad \frac{1,000}{10,000} \times £2,000 = £200$$

(Department H's costs have now increased by £200 and become £3,200).

Department H's costs presented a far more difficult problem. Consideration was given to apportionment based on numbers of machines, volumes of production, and types of machinery. It was, however, felt that there was a high relationship in this case (although this would certainly not always be true in other firms) between the values of machinery in use and the costs of maintaining them. The more costly equipment was very complicated and needed a lot of attention. Consequently it was decided to apportion H's costs between A, B and C on the basis of the value of machinery in each department. This was found to be A £3,000; B £6,000; C £7,000. The costs were therefore apportioned:

$$\frac{\text{Value of machinery in department}}{\text{Total value of machinery in all 3 departments}} \times £3,200$$

Therefore:

$$\text{A} \quad \frac{3,000}{16,000} \times £3,200 = £600 \quad : \quad \text{B} \quad \frac{6,000}{16,000} \times £3,200 = £1,200$$

$$\text{C} \quad \frac{7,000}{16,000} \times £3,200 = £1,400$$

The costs and their apportionment can, therefore, be shown:

	Production Departments			Service Departments	
	A	B	C	G	H
Indirect Labour	2,000	3,000	4,000	500	1,000
Other Expenses	1,000	2,000	3,000	1,500	2,000
	3,000	5,000	7,000	2,000	3,000
Department G's costs apportioned	400	800	600	(2,000)	200
					3,200
Department H's costs apportioned	600	1,200	1,400		(3,200)
	£4,000	£7,000	£9,000	—	—

Now we have the estimated overhead for each department for the ensuing accounting period. We now have another problem as to how the overhead is going to be taken into the calculation of the cost of each job in these departments. After investigation the conclusion is that in departments A and B there is a direct relationship between direct labour hours and overhead, but in department C the guiding fact is machine hours. If the total overhead of departments A and B are therefore divided by estimated number of direct labour hours this will give the overhead rate per direct labour hour, whilst in department C the total overhead will be divided by the estimated machine hours. The calculation of the overhead rates are therefore:

	Production Departments		
	A	B	C
Direct Labour hours	5,000	4,000	
Machine hours			6,000
Overhead rate per			
Direct Labour hour	$\dfrac{£4,000}{5,000}$	$\dfrac{£7,000}{4,000}$	
	$= £0.8$	$= £1.75$	
Overhead rate per			$\dfrac{£9,000}{6,000}$
Machine hour			$= £1.5$

We can now calculate the costs of four jobs performed in this factory:

Department A

Job A/70/144 Started 1.7.19-2.   Completed 13.7.19-2.
Cost of Direct Materials £130.
Number of Direct Labour hours 100.
Cost rate of direct labour per hour £0.9.

Department B

Job B/96/121 Started 4.7.19-2.   Completed 9.7.19-2.
Cost of Direct Materials £89.
Number of Direct Labour hours 40.
Cost rate of direct labour per hour £1.1.

Department C

Job C/67/198 Started 8.7.19-2. Completed 16.7.19-2.
Cost of Direct Materials £58.
Number of Direct Labour hours 50.
Cost rate of direct labour per hour £1.0.
Number of machine hours 40.

Departments A and C

Job AC/45/34 Started in A 3.7.19-2. Passed on to C 11.7.19-2. Completed in
C 16.7.19-2.
Cost of Materials £115.
Number of Direct Labour hours (in dept. A) 80.
Number of Direct Labour hours (in dept. C) 90.
Cost rate per direct labour hour dept. A £0.9.
dept. C £1.0.
Number of machine hours, dept. C 70.

Job Cost Sheet. Job No. A/70/144.

Started 1.7.19-2   Completed 13.7.19-2

	Hours	Rates £	£
Materials			130
Direct Labour	100	0.9	90
Factory Overhead	100	0.8	80
Total Job Cost			£300

Job Cost Sheet. Job No. B/96/121

Started 1.7.19-2.   Completed 9.7.19-2.

	Hours	Rates £	£
Materials			89
Direct Labour	40	1.1	44
Factory Overhead	40	1.75	70
Total Job Cost			£203

Job Cost Sheet. Job No. C/67/198

Started 8.7.19-2.   Completed 16.7.19-2.

	Hours	Rates £	£
Materials			58
Direct Labour	50	1.0	50
Factory Overhead	40	1.5	60
Total Job Cost			£168

Job Cost Sheet. Job No. AC/45/34

Started 3.7.19-2.   Completed 16.7.19-2.

	Hours	Rates £	£
Materials			115
Direct Labour (dept. A)	80	0.9	72
Direct Labour (dept. C)	90	1.0	90
Factory Overhead (dept. A)	80	0.8	64
Factory Overhead (dept. C)	70	1.5	105
Total Job Cost			£446

In the Exhibit and when the job costs were worked out it has not been stated whether or not this is using a marginal or absorption costing approach. Assume that in fact an absorption approach has been used in that overhead is deemed to include both fixed and variable overhead. If instead a marginal costing approach was to be used then the overhead brought into the calculations of job costs would exclude fixed overhead, so that the overhead rate would be a variable overhead rate.

Cost Centres — Job Costing and Responsibility

It must be pointed out that a cost centre for job costing is not necessarily the same as tracing the costs down to the individual who is responsible for controlling them. There are two questions here (a) Finding the cost of a job to check on its profitability and (b) Controlling the costs by making someone responsible for them so that he will have to answer for any variations from planned results. Many firms therefore keep separate records of costs to fulfil each of these functions.

2. *Process Costing*

Job costing treats production as a number of separate jobs being performed, whereas process costing sees production as a continuous flow. In process costing there is correspondingly no attempt to allocate costs to specific units being produced.

There is, however, usually more than one process in the manufacture of goods. We can take for an example a bakery producing cakes. There are three processes: (a) The mixing of the cake ingredients, (b) The baking of the cakes, (c) The packaging of the cakes. Each process is treated as a cost centre, and therefore costs for (a), (b) and (c) are collected separately. Overhead rates are then calculated for each cost centre in a similar fashion to that in job costing.

In the case of the bakery each accounting period would probably start and finish without any half-mixed or half-baked cakes, but some types of firms which use process costing have processes which take rather longer to complete than baking cakes. A typical case would be the brewing of beer. At the beginning and end of each period there would be partly processed units. It is a matter of arithmetic to convert production into "equivalent production". For instance, production during a particular period may be as in Exhibit 7.2.

Exhibit 7.2

Started in previous year ¾ completed then, and ¼ completed in current period, 400 units, $400 \times ¼$	100
Started and completed in current period	680
Started in current period and ⅛ completed by end of period, 160 units, $160 \times ⅛$	20
Equivalent Production	800 units

If the total costs of the cost centre amounted to £4,000 then the unit cost would be $\frac{£4,000}{800} = £5$.

In fact process costing can become very complicated because some of the part-produced items are complete in terms of say, materials, but incomplete in terms of labour, or else say ⅔ complete for materials and ¼ complete for labour. Although it becomes complicated the principles are no different from that described of calculating equivalent production.

We can now look at an example of process costing in Exhibit 7.3. So that we do not get involved in too many arithmetical complications, we will assume that there are no part completed goods in each process at the start and end of the period considered.

Exhibit 7.3

A bakery making cakes has three processes, process (A) The mixing of the cake ingredients, (B) The baking of the cakes, (C) The packaging of the cakes.

January activity was as follows:

Materials used:	£
Process (A)	4,000
Process (B)	—
Process (C)	1,000
Direct Labour:	
Process (A)	1,500
Process (B)	500
Process (C)	800
Factory Overhead:	
Variable:	
Process (A)	400
Process (B)	1,300
Process (C)	700
Fixed: (allocated to processes)	
Process (A)	600
Process (B)	500
Process (C)	400

During January 100,000 cakes were made.
The Process Cost accounts will appear as:

Process (A)

	£		£
Materials	4,000	Transferred to Process (B)	
Direct Labour	1,500	100,000 units at £0.065	6,500
Variable Overhead	400		
Fixed Overhead	600		
	£6,500		£6,500

Process (B)

Transferred from Process (A)		Transferred to Process (C)	
100,000 units at £0.065	6,500	100,000 units at £0.088	8,800
Direct Labour	500		
Variable Overhead	1,300		
Fixed Overhead	500		
	£8,800		£8,800

Process (C)

	£		£
Transferred from Process (B)		Transferred to Finished	
100,000 units at £0.088	8,800	Goods Stock 100,000 units at	
Materials	1,000	£0.117	11,700
Direct Labour	800		
Variable Overhead	700		
Fixed Overhead	400		
	£11,700		£11,700

Other Kinds of Firms

Process costing is found most often in industries such as oil, canning, paint manufacture, steel, textiles, and food processing.

The Problem of Joint Costs

Usually a manufacturing operation results in one simple product. Any excess is regarded as scrap, and the small cost that could be traced to it is ignored, e.g. the manufacture of a suit where the cost is traced to the suit, the small unusable bits of cloth being ignored.

This is not always the case, and where a group of separate products is produced simultaneously, each of the products having relatively substantial sales values, then the products are called "joint products". Thus crude oil taken into an oil refinery is processed and the output is in terms of different grades of petrol, paraffin, motor oil etc. This means that in costing terms the costs of the materials and processes etc. have to be split between the joint products.

Many problems exist in this area. Perhaps you will see why when the problem of allocating costs between joint products is concerned with the cutting-up of a cow for beef. From a cow there is rump-steak, the fillet steaks, the T-bone steaks, sirloin, silverside, brisket etc. If the cow cost the butcher £130, then how would you allocate the cost between all of these various joint products? This gives you some idea of the problem which exists, in many industries this becomes involved with complex technological problems.

68

Assignment Exercises

Assignment Exercises followed by the letter x do NOT have answers shown at the back of the book.

7.1 A factory has six departments. In departments A, B and C factory overhead is allocated using overhead rates per direct labour hour at A £1.3: B £1.4: C £2.3; Departments D, E and F use an overhead rate per machine hour of D £2.8: E £1.5: F £4.0.

The cost rate of direct labour per hour in the department is A £0.9: B £1.0: C £1.1: D. £1.2: E £0.9: F £1.0.

You are required to calculate the cost of the following jobs:

Job 1001: Dept. A.	Cost of Direct Materials	£118
	Number of direct labour hours	60
Job 1002: Dept. A.	Cost of Direct Materials	£206
	Number of direct labour hours	50
Job 1003: Dept. B.	Cost of Direct Materials	£310
	Number of direct labour hours	71
Job 1004: Dept. C.	Cost of Direct Materials	£205
	Number of direct labour hours	80
Job 1005: Dept. D.	Cost of Direct Materials	£98
	Number of direct labour hours	60
	Number of machine hours	50
Job 1006: Dept. E.	Cost of Direct Materials	£306
	Number of direct labour hours	110
	Number of machine hours	80
Job 1007: Dept. F.	Cost of Direct Materials	£401
	Number of direct labour hours	130
	Number of machine hours	130
Job 1008: Dept. E.	Cost of Direct Materials	£180
	Number of direct labour hours	70
	Number of machine hours	60
	Then passed on to Dept. A to complete where Additional Raw Materials used	£44
	Number of direct labour hours	40
Job 1009: Dept. C.	Cost of Direct Materials	£388
	Number of direct labour hours	50
	then passed to Dept. A where no additional materials used but spent direct labour hours	40
	then passed on to Dept. F. where it was completed	
	Additional materials cost	£68
	Number of direct labour hours	70
	Number of machine hours	59
	(Show your workings)	

7.2x A factory has five departments. In department J, K and L factory overhead is allocated using an overhead rate per machine hour of J £2.3: K £4.3: L £3.2. Departments M and N use an overhead rate per direct labour hour of M £2.7: N £1.9.

The cost rate of direct labour per hour in the departments is J £1.5: K. £1.3: L. £2.1: M. £1.8: N. £2.0.

You are required to calculate the cost of the following jobs:

Job 1551: Dept. J.	Cost of Direct Materials	£359
	Number of direct labour hours	115
	Number of machine hours	77
Job 1552: Dept. K.	Cost of Direct Materials	£1,498
	Number of direct labour hours	206
	Number of machine hours	117
Job 1553: Dept. L.	Cost of Direct Materials	£115
	Number of direct labour hours	66
	Number of machine hours	66
Job 1554: Dept. M.	Cost of Direct Materials	£110
	Number of direct labour hours	46
	Number of machine hours	24
Job 1555: Dept. N.	Cost of Direct Materials	£1,390
	Number of direct labour hours	279
	Number of machine hours	250
Job 1556: Dept. M.	Cost of Direct Materials	£889
	Number of direct labour hours	104
	Then passed on to Dept. L where Additional	
	Direct Materials cost	£65
	Direct Labour hours	55
	Machine hours	46
Job 1557: Dept. K.	Cost of Direct Materials	£506
	Number of direct labour hours	80
	Number of machine hours	76
	Then passed on to Dept. N where Additional	
	Direct Materials cost	£45
	Direct labour hours	40
	Then passed on to Dept. L where Additional	
	Direct Materials cost	£49
	Direct labour hours	50
	Machine hours	37

(Show your workings)

7.3 In a firm there are 4 types of jobs performed in separate production departments A, B, C and D. In addition there are 3 service departments, K, L and M. Costs have been allocated to the departments as follows:

	Production Departments				Service Departments		
	A	B	C	D	K	L	M
	£	£	£	£	£	£	£
Indirect Labour	4,000	6,000	8,000	2,000	1,500	3,000	4,100
Other Expenses	2,700	3,100	3,600	1,500	4,500	2,000	2,000

The expenses of the Service Departments are to be allocated between other departments as follows:

Dept. K to Depts. A 25 per cent: B 30 per cent: C 20 per cent: D 10 per cent: M 15 per cent.

Dept. L to Depts. A 60 per cent: C 30 per cent: D 10 per cent.

Dept. M to Depts. B 30 per cent: C 50 per cent: D 20 per cent.

In departments A and C the job costing is to use an overhead rate per direct labour hour, whilst in B and D a machine hour rate will be used. The number of direct hours and machine hours per department is expected to be:

	A	B	C	D
Direct labour hours	2,000	4,000	4,450	2,700
Machine hours	1,900	2,600	2,900	2,400

You are required to calculate:

(a) The overhead rates for departments A and C.

(b) The overhead rates for departments B and D.

(Keep your answer — it will be used as a basis for the next question.)

7.4x In the firm mentioned in 7.3 what would be the costs of the following jobs given that the direct labour costs per hour are Dept. A £2.1: B £1.7: C £2.4: D £2.3.

Job 351: Dept. A.	Direct Materials cost		£190
	Number of direct labour hours		56
	Number of machine hours		40
Job 352: Dept. B.	Direct Materials cost		£1,199
	Number of direct labour hours		178
	Number of machine hours		176
Job 353: Dept. C.	Direct Materials cost		£500
	Number of direct labour hours		130
	Number of machine hours		100
Job 354: Dept. D.	Direct Materials cost		£666
	Number of direct labour hours		90
	Number of machine hours		64
Job 355: Dept. C.	Direct Materials cost		£560
	Number of direct labour hours		160
	Number of machine hours		150
	Job passed on to Dept. B where Additional		
	Direct Materials cost		£68
	Number of direct labour hours		30
	Number of machine hours		20

7.5x In a firm there are five types of jobs performed in separate production departments P, Q, R, S and T. In addition there are two service departments F and G. Costs have been allocated to the departments as follows:

	Production Departments					Service Departments	
	P	Q	R	S	T	F	G
	£	£	£	£	£	£	£
Indirect Labour	5,000	7,000	3,000	6,000	8,000	10,000	9,000
Other Expenses	500	1,800	1,000	1,200	1,300	6,000	7,000

The expenses of the Service Departments are to be allocated between other departments as follows:

Dept. F to Depts. P 10 per cent: Q 20 per cent: S 30 per cent: T 15 per cent: G 25 per cent.

Dept. G to Depts. P 12.5 per cent: Q 20 per cent: R 25 per cent: S 30 per cent: T 12.5 per cent.

In departments R and T the job costing is to use an overhead rate per direct labour hour, whilst in the other production departments a machine hour rate will be used. The number of direct labour hours and machine hours per department are expected to be:

	P	Q	R	S	T
Direct labour hours	4,000	5,000	3,600	10,000	3,550
Machine hours	3,000	4,000	3,000	8,000	2,800

You are required to calculate:

(a) The overhead rates for departments R and T.

(b) The overhead rates for departments P, Q and S.

(Keep your answer — it will be used for question 7.6.)

7.6x In the firm mentioned in 7.5 what would be the costs of the following jobs, given that the direct labour rate per hour is Dept. P £1.9: Q £2.5: R. £2.0: S £2.7: T £2.4.

Job 701: Dept. R.	Direct Materials cost	£115
	Number of direct labour hours	35
	Number of machine hours	29
Job 702: Dept. T.	Direct Materials cost	£1,656
	Number of direct labour hours	180
	Number of machine hours	160
Job 703: Dept. P.	Direct Materials cost	£546
	Number of direct labour hours	100
	Number of machine hours	90
Job 704: Dept. S.	Direct Materials cost	£65
	Number of direct labour hours	250
	Number of machine hours	60
Job 705: Dept. Q.	Direct Materials cost	£4,778
	Number of direct labour hours	305
	Number of machine hours	280
Job 706: Dept. P.	Direct Materials cost	£555
	Number of direct labour hours	200
	Number of machine hours	180
	Then passed to Dept. T for completion where	
	Direct Materials cost	£11
	Number of direct labour hours	18
	Number of machine hours	2

7.7x   A factory uses process costing. There are three departments, each concerned with a separate process, called Departments A, B and C. Departments A and C where the labour content predominates, and therefore a labour overhead rate is used. Department B employs a great deal of expensive machinery and a machine hour rate for overhead is in use there.

The following details relate to estimates of overhead:

	Dept. A £	Dept. B £	Dept. C £
Indirect labour	17,000	2,000	24,000
Other Indirect expenses	3,000	8,000	6,000

The number of labour hours worked will be A 10,000, B 1,000, C 12,000. The number of machine hours in department B will be 500.

Find the cost of producing 100 units which had raw materials costing £3,000 taken into Department A, processed in 200 labour hours, then passed on to Department B where 100 labour hours are spent on them and 45 machine hours, and finished off in Department C where £168 additional materials are incorporated, and 270 labour hours are spent on them. The cost per hour of direct labour is Dept. A £2.2: Dept. B £1.8: Dept. C £2.4.

Chapter Eight

Budgeting and Budgetary Control

In chapter one of this book it was stated that management control was needed to try to ensure that the organisation achieved its objectives. Once the objectives have been agreed, plans should be drawn up so that the progress of the firm can be directed towards the ends specified in the objectives. Now it must not be thought that plans can be expressed only in accounting terms, for example quality of the product might be best shown in engineering terms, or social objectives shown in a plan concerned with employee welfare. But some of the objectives, such as the attainment of a desired profit, or of the attainment of a desired growth in assets can be expressed in accounting terms. When a plan is expressed quantitively it is known as a "budget" and the process of converting plans into budgets is known as "budgeting". In this book we are concerned primarily with budgets shown in monetary terms, i.e. financial budgets.

The budgeting process may be quite formal in a large organisation with committees set up to perform the task. On the other hand in a very small firm the owner may jot down his budget on a piece of scrap paper or even on the back of a used envelope. Some even manage without writing anything down at all, they have done the budgets in their heads and can easily remember them. This book is concerned with budgeting in a formal manner.

Budgets and People

Probably in no other part of accounting is there a greater need for understanding other people than in the processes of budgeting. Budgets are prepared to try to guide the firm towards its objectives. There is no doubt that some budgets that are drawn up are even more harmful to a firm than if none were drawn up at all.

Budgets are drawn up for control purposes, that is an attempt to control the direction that the firm is taking. Many people, however, look upon them, not as a guide, but as a straightjacket. We can look at a few undesirable actions that can result from people regarding budgets as a straightjacket rather than as a guide.

(a) The sales manager refuses to let a salesman go to Sweden in response to an urgent and unexpected request from a Swedish firm. The reason — the overseas sales expenses budget has already been spent. The result — the most profitable order that the firm would have received for many years is taken up instead by another firm.

(b) The works manager turns down requests for overtime work, because the budgeted overtime has already been exceeded. The result — the job is not completed on time, and the firm has to pay a large sum under a penalty clause in the contract for the job which stated that if the job was not finished by a certain date then a penalty of £20,000 would become payable.

(c) Towards the end of the accounting year a manager realises that he has not spent all of his budget for a particular item. He then launches on a spending spree, completely unnecessary items being bought, on the basis that "If I don't spend this amount this year they will cut down next year when I will really need the money." The result: a lot of unusable and unnecessary equipment.

(d) The education budget has been spent, therefore the education manager will not let anyone go on courses for the rest of the year. The result: the firm starts to fall behind in an industry which is highly technical, the staff concerned become fed up, and the better ones start to look for jobs in other firms which are more responsive to the need to allow personnel to keep in touch with changing technology.

Studies have shown that the more that managers are brought into the budgeting process, then the more successful budgetary control is likely to be. A manager on whom a budget is imposed, rather than a manager who had an active part in the drafting of his budget, is more likely to pay less attention to the budget and use it unwisely in the control process.

Having sounded the warning that needs to be borne in mind constantly when budgeting, we can now look at the positive end of budgeting — to see the advantages of a good budgetary control system.

Budgets and Profit Planning

The methodology of budgetary control is probably accountancy's major contribution to management. Before we get down to the mechanics of constructing budgets we should first of all look at the main outlines of drafting budgets.

When the budgets are being drawn up the two main objectives must be uppermost in the mind of top management, that is that the budgets are for:

(a) Planning. This means a properly co-ordinated and comprehensive plan for the whole business. Each part must interlock with the other parts.

(b) Control. Just because a plan is set down on paper does not mean that the plan will carry itself out. Control is exercised via the budgets, thus the name budgetary control. To do this means that the responsibility of managers and budgets must be so linked that the responsible manager is given a guide to help him to produce certain desired results, and the actual achieved results can be compared against the expected, i.e. actual compared with budget.

Preparation of Estimates

The first thing to establish is what the limiting factors are in a firm. It may well be the fact that sales cannot be pushed above a certain amount, otherwise it might be the fact that the firm could sell as much as it can produce, but the productive capacity of the firm sets a limit. Whatever the limiting factor is, there is no doubt that this aspect of the firm will need more attention than probably any other. There would not, for instance, be much point in budgeting for the sale of 1,000 units a year if production could not manufacture more than 700, or to manufacture 2,000 a year if only 1,300 of them could be sold.

There is no doubt that usually the most difficult estimate to make is that of sales revenue. This can be done by using one of two methods:

(i) Make a statistical forecast on the basis of the economic situation conditions applying reference to the goods sold by the company, and what is known about the actions of competitors.

(ii) The opposite is to make an internal forecast. This is usually done by asking each salesman, or group of salesmen, to estimate the sales in their own areas, and then total the estimates. Sometimes the salesmen are not asked at all.

Now we should remember that much of the subject matter that you have read about, or are currently reading in Economics, is very relevant here. A knowledge of elasticity of demand, whether the product is a complementary product, e.g. the price of egg-cups is linked to the demand for eggs, whether it is a substitute, e.g. that a rise in the price of butter may induce housewives to turn to other commodities instead, is very relevant in this area. Factors such as whether the firm has a monopoly, whether the firm has many small customers, a few large customers, or even one large customers, are of crucial importance. Estimating sales revenue is very much a matter of taking all the economic factors into account allied to other factors.

The sales budget is, however, more than just a sales forecast. Budgets should show the actions that management is taking to influence future events. If an increase in sales is desired the sales budget may show extra sales, which may well be an indication of the action that management is going to take by means of extra television advertising, making a better product, or to give retailers better profit margins and push up sales in that way.

The Production Budget

The production budget stems from the sales budget, but the first question that has to be settled is that of the level of the stock of finished goods which will be held by the firm.

If sales are even over the year, then production can also be in keeping with the sales figure, and the stock figure can remain constant. Suppose that the firm sells 50 units every month, then the firm can produce 50 units per month. In almost every firm, a stock level will have to be maintained, the amount of stock will be dependent on factors such as amount of storage space, the estimated amount needed to cater for breakdowns in production or for delays in receiving raw materials etc. Nonetheless, if the stock level was to be a minimum of 70 units it would still mean that production was at the rate of 50 units per month.

On the other hand sales may not be constant. Sales may average 50 units per month, but the figures may well be as follows:

January	20 units	February	30 units	March	60 units
April	80 units	May	70 units	June	40 units

This would mean that if production levels were kept at 50 units per month the stock levels would usually have to be more than 100 units, whilst if the stock levels were to be kept at 100 units minimum the production figures each month would equal the sales figures. We can now compare the two levels of production.

(a) Even Production Flow

The problem here is to find the stock level that the firm would need on 1st January if (i) sales are as shown, (ii) the stock must not fall below 100 units, (iii) production is to be 50 per units per month. It can be found by trial and error. For instance, if you decided to see that would happen if the firm started off with 100 units in stock at 1st January you would find that, after adding production and deducting sales each month, the stock level would fall to 90 units in May. As 100 units of stock is the minimum needed you would need to start off on 1st January with 110 units. The method is that if you start off your calculation with an estimated figure of stock, which must at least be the minimum figure required, then if you find that the lowest figure of stock shown during the period is 10 units less than the minimum stock required, go back and add 10 units to the stock to be held on 1st January. If the lowest figure is 30 units less than required add 30 units to the 1st January stock, and so on. We can now look at the figures in Exhibit 8.1.

Exhibit 8.1

UNITS	January	February	March	April	May	June
Opening Stock	110	140	160	150	120	100
Add Units Produced	50	50	50	50	50	50
	160	190	210	200	170	150
Less Sales	20	30	60	80	70	40
Closing Stock	140	160	150	120	100	110

Before we look at the implications of maintaining an even production flow we can look at another example. Try and work it out for yourself before looking at the answer in Exhibit 8.2. The Sales are expected to be January 70, February 40, March 50, April 120, May 140 and June 70. The stock level must not fall below 120 units and an even production flow of 80 units is required. What stock level would there have to be on 1st January?

Exhibits 8.2

UNITS	January	February	March	April	May	June
Opening Stock	140	150	190	220	180	120
Add Units Produced	80	80	80	80	80	80
	220	230	270	300	260	200
Less Sales	70	40	50	120	140	70
Closing Stock	150	190	220	180	120	130

It is more important in many firms to ensure a smooth production flow than to bother unduly about stock levels, assuming that the minimum stock level is always attained. If the work is skilled then that type of labour force may take several years to become trained, and skilled labour in many industries does not take kindly to being sacked and re-employed as the demand for the goods fluctuates. This is not always true with skilled labour, for instance in the building industry such craftsmen as bricklayers may go to a builder until he has completed a contract such as building a college, a hospital, or a housing estate, and then leave and go to another employer on the completion of the job.

On the other hand, a skilled engineer concerned with the manufacturer of say, diesel engines, would not expect to be fired and re-employed continuously. The bricklayer has a skill that is easily transferable to many other building employers in an area, whereas the diesel engineer may have only one firm within fifty miles of his home where he can perform his skills properly. A man employed as labourer might work on a building site in one part of a year and then transfer as a labourer to an engineering factory as a labourer in another part of the year. Whether a firm could carry on production with widely uneven production levels depends so much on the type of firm and the type of labour involved. A firm would only sack skilled labour which it needed again shortly if it could persuade the men or women to come back when required. If the people who had been sacked were likely to find other employment, and not return to the firm when required, then this would mean that the firm would probably keep them on its payroll and production would continue and stocks of finished goods would begin to pile up. Many firms do in fact realise their social obligations by only laying off workers when no other alternative is at all reasonable. In many organisations there are probably more workers from time to time than the firm actually needs — this is known as "organisational slack", so that there is a leeway between the increasing of production and having to take on extra workers.

(b) Uneven Production Levels

Some firms by their very nature will have uneven production levels, and this will be accepted by their labour force. An ice-cream firm would find sales at the highest levels in summer, tailing off in winter. It is not really possible to build up stock of ice-cream in the winter for summer sales! Even if it could be done technically, the costs of refrigerating large quantities of ice-cream for several months could hardly be economic. The large labour force used in the summer months will probably include quite a few students occupying their vacation periods profitably, and not able anyway to work at the job all the year round even if they wanted to. Such a kind of firm will normally have a far greater relationship between current stock levels and current sales than a firm which has even production levels.

The calculation of the quantity to be produced is then:

$$\text{Opening Stock} + \text{Units Produced} - \text{Sales} = \text{Closing Stock}$$

This means that if the opening stock will be 80 units, the sales are expected to be 100 units and the desired closing is 50 units it becomes:

	units
Opening Stock	80
Add Production	?
Less Sales	100
Closing Stock	50

Production will, therefore, be the missing figure, i.e. 70 units (80 + Production 70 = 150 for sale less actually sold 100 = closing stock 50).

Exhibit 8.3 shows the units to be produced if the following information is known — Stock required 1st January 40, at end of each month, January 60, February 110, March 170, April 100, May 60, June 20. Sales are expected to be January 100, February 150, March 110, April 190, May 70, June 50.

Exhibit 8.3

UNITS	January	February	March	April	May	June
Opening Stock	40	60	110	170	100	60
Production required(?)	120	200	170	120	30	10
	160	260	280	290	130	70
Less Sales	100	150	110	190	70	50
Closing Stock	60	110	170	100	60	20

Linked with the production budget will be a materials purchase budget. It may well be that an order will have to be placed in January, received in March and issued to production in April. The purchase of materials will have to be planned as scientifically as possible.

Assignment Exercises

Assignment Exercises followed by the letter x do NOT have answers shown at the back of the book.

8.1x For the year ended 31 December, 19-6 the sales of units are expected to be:

January	70	July	20
February	90	August	30
March	60	September	60
April	40	October	70
May	30	November	90
June	20	December	50

The opening stock at 1 January, 19-6 will be 120 units. The closing stock desired at 31 December, 19-6 is 150 units.

(a) What will production be per month if an even production flow is required and stock levels during the year could be allowed to fall to zero?

(b) Given the same information plus the constraint that stock levels must never fall below 110 units, and that extra production will be undertaken in January 19-6 to ensure this, what will the January production figure be?

8.2x A firm wants to maintain an even production flow for the first six months of 19-4 followed by an even production flow of 20 units per month greater for the last six months of 19-4.

Opening stock of units at 1 January, 19-4 are	50
Closing stock of units wanted at 31 December, 19-4	120
Sales of units during the year	650

How many units should be manufactured per month (a) January to June 19-4, (b) July to December 19-4?

8.3x What stock should be held by a firm on 1 July, 19-7 if the following data is available:

Units	19-7	July	Aug.	Sept.	Oct.	Nov.	Dec.
(i)	Sales expected to be	100	140	180	270	190	130
(ii)	Production expected to be	160	200	220	250	210	180

(iii) Desired stock level at 31 December, 19-7 is 320 units.

8.4 What would the production levels have to be for each month if the following data was available:

Units	19-5	Jan.	Feb.	March	April	May	June
(i)	Stock levels wanted at the end of each month	690	780	1,100	1,400	1,160	940
(ii)	Expected sales each month	800	920	1,090	1,320	1,480	1,020

(iii) The stock level at 1 January, 19-5 will be 740 units.

8.5 For the year ended 31 December, 19-9 the sales of units are expected to be:

January	110	July	70
February	180	August	30
March	170	September	170
April	150	October	110
May	120	November	150
June	100	December	190

The opening stock at 1 January 19-9 will be 140 units. The closing stock desired at 31 December, 19-9 is 150 units.

(a) What will production be per month if an even production flow is required and stock levels during the year could be allowed to fall to zero?

(b) Given the same information plus the constraint that stock levels must never fall below 80 units, and that extra production will be undertaken in January 19-9 to ensure this, what will be the January production figure?

8.6 What stock should be held by a firm on 1 January 19-7 if the following data is available:

Units	19-7	Jan.	Feb.	Mar.	April	May	June
(i)	Sales expected to be	160	190	300	180	110	290
(ii)	Production expected to be	200	220	240	260	280	300
(iii)	Desired stock level at 30 June, 19-7 is 430 units.						

Chapter Nine

Cash Budgets

It is no use budgeting for production and for sales if sometime during the budget period the firm runs out of cash funds. When talking about cash in budgets we are also usually including bank funds, and therefore in this book we will not be differentiating between cash and cheque payments or between cash and cheques received. Cash is, therefore, also budgeted for, so that any shortage of cash can be known in advance and action taken to obtain permission for a loan or a bank overdraft to be available then, rather than wait until the shortage or deficiency occurs. Bank managers, or anyone concerned with the lending of money, certainly resent most strongly one of their customers needing a bank overdraft without prior warning, when in fact the customer could have known if he had drawn up a cash budget in advance which revealed the need for cash funds on a particular date.

The finance needed may not just be by way of borrowing from a bank or finance house, it may well be a long-term need that can only be satisfied by an issue of shares or debentures. Such issues need planning well in advance, and a cash budget can reveal (a) that they will be needed (b) how much is needed and (c) when it will be needed.

We can now look at a very simple case. Without being concerned in this first exhibit with exactly what the receipts and payments are for, just to keep matters simple at this stage, we can see the dangers that are inherent in not budgeting for cash.

Exhibit 9.1

Mr. Muddlem had a meeting with his accountant on 1st July, 19x3. He was feeling very pleased with himself. He had managed to get some very good orders from customers, mainly because he was now allowing them extra time in which to pay their accounts. Sprite, the accountant, said, "Can you afford to do all that you are hoping to do?"

Muddlem laughed, "Why, I'll be making so much money I won't know how to spend it."

"But have you got the cash to finance everything?" asked Sprite.

"If I'm making a good profit then of course I'll have the cash," said Muddlem. "I know the bank manager says that any bank overdraft could not be more than £1,000, but I doubt if I need it."

"Don't let us rely on guesses," says Sprite. "Let's work it out."

After an hour's work the following facts emerge.

(a) Present cash balance (including bank balance) £800.

(b) Receipts from debtors will be: July £2,000, August £2,600, September £5,000, October £7,000, November £8,000, December £15,000.

(c) Payments will be: July £2,500, August £2,700, September £6,900, October £7,800, November £9,900, December £10,300.

This is then summarised:

	July £	August £	Sept. £	Oct. £	Nov. £	Dec. £
Balance at start of the month:	+800	+300	+200			
Deficit at the start of the month:				−1,700	−2,500	−4,400
Receipts	2,000	2,600	5,000	7,000	8,000	15,000
	2,800	2,900	5,200	5,300	5,500	10,600
Payments	2,500	2,700	6,900	7,800	9,900	10,300
Balance at end of the month:	+300	+200				+300
Deficit at the end of the month:			−1,700	−2,500	−4,400	

"I'm in an awkward position now," says Muddlem. "I just cannot borrow £4,400 nor can I cut down on my sales, and anyway I don't really want to as these new sales are very profitable indeed. If only I'd known this, I could have borrowed the money from my brother only last week but he's invested it elsewhere now."

"Come and see me tomorrow," says Sprite. "There may well be something we can do."

Fortunately for Muddlem his luck was in. He arrived to see his accounant the following morning waving a cheque. "My wife won £5,000 on a jackpot bingo last night," he said.

"Thank goodness for that, at least in future you'll learn to budget ahead for cash requirements. You can't be lucky all the time," says Sprite.

Timing of Cash Receipts and Payments

In drawing up a cash budget it must be borne in mind that all the payments for units produced would very rarely be at the same time as production itself. For instance the raw materials might be bought in March, incorporated in the goods being produced in April, and paid for in May. On the other hand the raw materials may have been in hand for some time, so that the goods are bought in January, paid for in February, and used in production the following August. Contrary to this, the direct labour part of the product is usually paid for almost at the same time as the unit being produced. Even here a unit may be produced in one week and the wages paid one week later, so that a unit might be produced on say 27th June and the wages for the direct labour involved paid for on 3rd July.

Similarly the date of sales and the date of receipt of cash will not usually be at the same time, except in many retail stores. The goods might be sold in May and the money received in August, or even paid for in advance so that the goods might be paid for in February but the goods not shipped to the buyer until May. This is especially true, at least for part of the goods when a cash deposit is left for specially made goods which will take sometime to manufacture. A simple example of this would be a made-to-measure suit on which a deposit would be paid at the time of order, the final payment being made when the completed suit is collected by the buyer.

Exhibit 9.2

A cash budget for the six months ended 30th June, 19x3 is to be drafted from the following information.

(a) Opening cash balance at 1st January, 19x3 £3,200.

(b) Sales; at £12 per unit: cash received three months after sale.

Units: 19-2			19-3								
Oct.	*Nov.*	*Dec.*	*Jan.*	*Feb.*	*Mar.*	*April*	*May*	*June*	*July*	*Aug.*	*Sept.*
80	90	70	100	60	120	150	140	130	110	100	160

(c) Production: in units.

19-2			19-3								
Oct.	*Nov.*	*Dec.*	*Jan.*	*Feb.*	*Mar.*	*April*	*May*	*June*	*July*	*Aug.*	*Sept.*
70	80	90	100	110	130	140	150	120	160	170	180

(d) Raw Materials used in production costs £4 per unit of production. They are paid for two months before being used in production.

(e) Direct Labour. £3 per unit paid for in the same month as the unit produced.

(f) Other variable expenses, £2 per unit, ¾ of the cost being paid for in the same month as production, the other ¼ paid in the month after production.

(g) Fixed Expenses of £100 per month are paid monthly.

(h) A Motor Van is to be bought and paid for in April for £800.

Schedules of payments and receipts are as follows:

PAYMENTS: (The month shown in brackets is the month in which the units are produced)

January	£	February	£
Raw Materials: 130 (March) × £4	520	140 (April) × £4	560
Direct Labour: 100 (January) × £3	300	110 (February) × £3	330
Variable: 100 (January) × ¾ × £2	150	110 (February) × ¾ × £2	165
90 (December) × ¼ × £2	45	100 (January) × ¼ × £2	50
Fixed:	100		100
	£1,115		£1,205

March	£	April	£
Raw Materials: 150 (May) × £4	600	120 (June) × £4	480
Direct Labour: 130 (March) × £3	390	140 (April) × £3	420
Variable: 130 (March) × ¾ × £2	195	140 (April) × ¾ × £2	210
110 (February) × ¼ × £2	55	130 (March) × ¼ × £2	65
Fixed:	100		100
Motor Van			800
	£1,340		£2,075

May	£	June	£
Raw Materials: 160 (July) × £4	640	170 (August) × £4	680
Direct Labour: 150 (May) × £3	450	120 (June) × £3	360
Variable: 150 (May) × ¾ × £2	225	120 (June) × ¾ × £2	180
140 (April) × ¼ × £2	70	150 (May) × ¼ × £2	75
Fixed:	100		100
	£1,485		£1,395

RECEIPTS: (The month shown in brackets is the month in which the sale was made)

				£
January	80 (October)	× £12		960
February	90 (November)	× £12		1,080
March	70 (December)	× £12		840
April	100 (January)	× £12		1,200
May	60 (February)	× £12		720
June	120 (March)	× £12		1,440

CASH BUDGET

	Jan.	Feb.	Mar.	April	May	June
	£	£	£	£	£	£
Balance from previous month	3,200	3,045	2,920	2,420	1,545	780
Add Receipts (per schedule)	960	1,080	840	1,200	720	1,440
	4,160	4,125	3,760	3,620	2,265	2,220
Less Payments (per schedule)	1,115	1,205	1,340	2,075	1,485	1,395
Balance carried to next month	3,045	2,920	2,420	1,545	780	825

Assignment Exercises

Assignment Exercises followed by the letter x do NOT have answers shown at the back of the book.

9.1x B. Ukridge comes to see you in April 19-3. He is full of enthusiasm for a new product that he is about to launch on to the market. Unfortunately his financial recklessness in the past has led him into being bankrupted twice, and he has only just got discharged by the court from his second bankruptcy.

"Look here laddie," he says, "with my new idea I'll be a wealthy man before Christmas."

"Calm down," you say, "and tell me all about it."

Ukridge's plans as far as cash is concerned for the next six months are:

(a) Present cash balance (including bank) £5.

(b) Timely legacy under a will — being received on 1 May, 19-3, £5,000. This will be paid into the business bank account by Ukridge.

(c) Receipts from debtors will be: May £400, June £4,000, July £8,000, August £12,000, September £9,000, October £5,000.

(d) Payments will be: May £100, June £5,000, July £11,000, August £20,000, September £12,000, October £7,000.

You are required: (i) To draw up a cash budget, showing the balances each month, for the six months to 31 October, 19-3.

(ii) The only person Ukridge could borrow money from would charge interest at the rate of 100 per cent per annum. This is not excessive considering Ukridge's past record. Advise Ukridge.

9.2x Draw up a cash budget for J. Clarke from the following information for the six months 1 July, 19-9 to 31 December, 19-9.

(a) Opening cash (includes bank) balance 1 July 19-9 £1,500.

(b) Sales at £20 per unit:

	April	May	June	July	Aug.	Sept.	Oct.	Nov.	Dec.
Units	110	120	140	160	180	190	130	80	70

Debtors will pay two months after they have bought the goods.

(c) Production in units:

	April	May	June	July	Aug.	Sept.	Oct.	Nov.	Dec.	Jan.
Units	150	170	180	200	130	110	100	90	70	60

(d) Raw materials cost £6 per unit and are paid for 3 months after the goods are used in production.

(e) Direct labour of £5 per unit is payable in the same month as production.

(f) Other variable expenses are £3 per unit. Two-thirds of this cost is paid for in the same month as production and one-third in the month following production.

(g) Fixed expenses of £150 per month are paid one month in arrears — these expenses have been at this rate for the past two years.

(h) A machine is to be bought and paid for in September for £6,000.

(i) Clarke will borrow £3,000 from a relative in December 19-9. This will be put into the business bank account immediately.

9.3x Draw up a cash budget for L. Jones, showing clearly the balance at the end of each month, from the following information for the six months ended 30 June, 19-2:

(a) Opening cash (includes bank) balance £800.

(b) Production in units:

19-1			19-2						
Oct.	Nov.	Dec.	Jan.	Feb.	March	April	May	June	July
300	400	460	540	700	640	560	500	420	380

(c) Raw materials used in production cost £3 per unit. Of this one-third is paid one month before production and two-thirds in the same month as production.

(d) Direct labour costs of £5 per unit are payable in the same month as production.

(e) Variable expenses are £4 per unit, payable three-quarters in the same month as production and one-quarter in the month following production.

(f) Sales at £15 per unit:

19-1			19-2					
Oct.	Nov.	Dec.	Jan.	Feb.	Mar.	April	May	June
240	360	480	580	620	720	680	520	360

Debtors to pay their accounts: one-fifth as a deposit in the months of the sale and the remainder two months later.

(g) Fixed expenses are £300 per month payable each month.

(h) Extensions to the premises costing £6,000 are to be paid for in February 19-2.

(i) An income tax refund of £3,700 will be received in June 19-2.

9.4 R. Jeeves seeks your advice. He has exactly £1,000 cash with which to start a business. He has also received permission from a bank manager to have an overdraft of up to £10,000 during his first six months of business starting 1 January 19-8.

His plans for his first six months trading are:

(a) Payments for goods and supplies: January £5,500, February £7,200, March £9,700, April £10,500, May £9,600, June £6,900.

(b) Receipts from debtors will be: January £3,900, February £5,900, March £6,000, April £7,100, May £8,400, June £9,500.

(c) Loan receivable on 1 March £700 to be repaid in full plus £100 interest on 1 June 19-8.

(d) Drawings £300 per calendar month.

You are required to draw up a cash budget, showing the balances each month for the six months to 30 June 19-8. Also make any suitable comments.

9.5 Draw up a cash budget for N. Morris showing the balance at the end of each month, from the following information for the six months ended 31 December 19-2:

(a) Opening Cash (including bank) balance £1,200

(b) Production in units:

19-2								19-3	
April	*May*	*June*	*July*	*Aug.*	*Sept.*	*Oct.*	*Nov.*	*Dec.*	*Jan.*	*Feb.*
240	270	300	320	350	370	380	340	310	260	250

(c) Raw Materials used in production cost £5 per unit. Of this 80 per cent is paid in the month of production and 20 per cent in the month after production.

(d) Direct Labour costs of £8 per unit are payable in the month of production.

(e) Variable expenses are £2 per unit, payable one-half in the same month as production and one-half in the month following production.

(f) Sales at £20 per unit:

19-2									19-3
Mar.	*April*	*May*	*June*	*July*	*Aug.*	*Sept.*	*Oct.*	*Nov.*	*Dec.*
260	200	320	290	400	300	350	400	390	400

Debtors to pay their accounts three months after that in which sales are made.

(g) Fixed expenses of £400 per month payable each month.

(h) Machinery costing £2,000 to be paid for in October 19-2.

(i) Will receive a legacy £2,500 in December 19-2.

(j) Drawings to be £300 per month.

Chapter Ten

Co-ordination of Budgets

The various budgets have to be linked together and a "Master Budget", which is really a budgeted set of Final Accounts drawn up. We have in fact looked at the Sales, Production and Cash Budgets. There are, however, many more budgets for parts of the organization, for instance there may be:

(i)   A selling expense budget,
(ii) An administration expense budget,
(iii) A manufacturing overhead budget,
(iv) A direct labour budget,
(v)   A purchases budget,

and so on. In this book we do not wish to get entangled in too many details, but in a real firm with a proper set of budgeting techniques there will be a great deal of detailed backing for the figures that are incorporated in the more important budgets.

Now it may be that when all the budgets have been co-ordinated, or slotted together, the Master Budget shows a smaller profit than the directors are prepared to accept. This will mean recasting budgets to see whether a greater profit can be earned, and if at all possible the budgets will be altered. Eventually there will be a Master Budget that the directors can agree to. This then gives the target for the results that the firm hopes to achieve in financial terms. Remember that there are other targets such as employee welfare, quality product etc. that cannot be so expressed.

The rest of this chapter is concerned with the drawing up of budgets for an imaginary firm, Walsh Ltd., culminating in the drawing up of a Master Budget.

To start with we can look at the last Balance Sheet of Walsh Ltd. as at 31st December, 19-4. This will give us our opening figures of stocks of raw materials, stock of finished goods, cash (including bank) balance, creditors, debtors etc.

Walsh Ltd.
Balance Sheet as at 31 December 19-4

Assets Employed:

Fixed Assets	Cost £	Depreciation to date £	Net £
Machinery	4,000	1,600	2,400
Motor Vehicles	2,000	800	1,200
	6,000	2,400	3,600

Current Assets		
Stocks: Finished Goods (75 units)	900	
Raw Materials	500	
Debtors (19x4 October £540 + November £360 + December £450)	1,350	
Cash and Bank Balances	650	3,400
		£7,000

Financed By:	
Share Capital, 4,000 shares of £1 each	4,000
Profit and Loss Account	2,600
	6,600

Current Liabilities		
Creditors for Raw Materials (November £120 + December £180)	300	
Creditors for Fixed Expenses (December)	100	400
		£7,000

The plans for the six months ended 30th June, 19-5 are as follows:

(i)   Production will be 60 units per month for the first four months, followed by 70 units per month for May and June.

(ii) Production costs will be (per unit):

	£
Direct Materials	5
Direct Labour	4
Variable Overhead	3
	£12

(iii) Fixed overhead is £100 per month, payable always one month in arrears.

(iv) Sales, at a price of £18 per unit, are expected to be:

	January	February	March	April	May	June
No. of units	40	50	60	90	90	70

(v)   Purchases of direct materials (raw materials) will be:

January £	February £	March £	April £	May £	June £
150	200	250	300	400	320

(vi) The creditors for raw materials bought are paid two months after purchase.

(vii) Debtors are expected to pay their accounts three months after they have bought the goods.

(viii) Direct Labour and variable overhead are paid in the same month as the units are produced.

(ix) A machine costing £2,000 will be bought and paid for in March.

(x) 3,000 shares of £1 each are to be issued at par in May.

(xi) Depreciation for the six months: Machinery £450, Motor Vehicles £200.

We must first of all draw up the various budgets and then incorporate them into the Master Budget. Some of the more detailed budgets which can be dispensed with in this illustration will be omitted.

Materials Budget

	Jan.	Feb.	March	April	May	June
Opening Stock £	500	350	250	200	200	250
Add Purchases £	150	200	250	300	400	320
	650	550	500	500	600	570
Less Used in Production:						
Jan.—April 60×£5	300	300	300	300		
May and June 70×£5					350	350
Closing Stock £	350	250	200	200	250	220

Production Budget (in units)

	Jan.	Feb.	March	April	May	June
Opening Stock (units)	75	95	105	105	75	55
Add Produced	60	60	60	60	70	70
	135	155	165	165	145	125
Less Sales	40	50	60	90	90	70
Closing Stock	95	105	105	75	55	55

Production Cost Budget (in £'s)

	Jan.	Feb.	March	April	May	June	Total
Materials Cost £	300	300	300	300	350	350	1,900
Labour Cost £	240	240	240	240	280	280	1,520
Variable Overhead £	180	180	180	180	210	210	1,140
	720	720	720	720	840	840	4,560

Creditors Budget

	Jan.	Feb.	March	April	May	June
Opening Balance £	300	330	350	450	550	700
Add Purchases £	150	200	250	300	400	320
	450	530	600	750	950	1,020
Less Payments £	120	180	150	200	250	300
Closing Balance £	330	350	450	550	700	720

Debtors Budget

	Jan.	Feb.	March	April	May	June
Opening Balances	1,350	1,530	2,070	2,700	3,600	4,320
Add Sales £	720	900	1,080	1,620	1,620	1,260
	2,070	2,430	3,150	4,320	5,220	5,580
Less Received £	540	360	450	720	900	1,080
Closing Balances £	1,530	2,070	2,700	3,600	4,320	4,500

Cash Budget

	Jan.	Feb.	March	April	May	June
Opening Balance £	+650	+550	+210			+1,050
Opening Overdraft £				−2,010	−2,010	
Received (see schedule) £	540	360	450	720	3,900	1,080
	1,190	910	660	1,290	1,890	2,130
Payments (see schedule) £	640	700	2,670	720	840	890
Closing Balance £	+550	+210			+1,050	+1,240
Closing Overdraft £			−2,010	−2,010		

Cash Payments Schedule

	Jan.	Feb.	March	April	May	June
Creditors for goods bought two months previously £	120	180	150	200	250	300
Fixed Overhead £	100	100	100	100	100	100
Direct Labour £	240	240	240	240	280	280
Variable Overhead £	180	180	180	180	210	210
Machinery £			2,000			
£	640	700	2,670	720	840	890

Cash Receipts Schedule

	Jan.	Feb.	March	April	May	June
Debtors for goods sold three months previously £	540	360	450	720	900	1,080
Shares Issued £					3,000	
					3,900	

Master Budget

Forecast Operating Statement for the Six months ended 30 June 19-5

	£		£
Sales			7,200
Less Cost of Goods Sold:			
Opening Stock of Finished Goods		900	
Add Cost of Goods Completed		4,560	
		5,460	
Less Closing Stock of Finished Goods		660	4,800
Gross Profit			2,400
Less:			
Fixed Overhead		600	
Depreciation: Machinery	450		
Motors	200	650	1,250
Net Profit			1,150

Forecast Balance Sheet as at 30 June 19-5
  Assets Employed:
    Fixed Assets

	Cost £	Depreciation to date £	Net £
Machinery	6,000	2,050	3,950
Motor Vehicles	2,000	1,000	1,000
	8,000	3,050	4,950

Current Assets		
Stocks: Finished Goods	660	
Raw Materials	220	
Debtors	4,500	
Cash and Bank Balances	1,240	6,620
		11,570

Financed By:	
Share Capital	7,000
Profit and Loss Account (2,600 + 1,150)	3,750
	10,750

Current Liabilities		
Creditors for Goods	720	
Creditors for Overhead	100	820
		11,570

Capital Budgeting

The plan for the acquisition of fixed assets such as machinery, buildings etc. is usually known as a Capital Budget. Management will evaluate the various possibilities open to it, and will compare the alternatives. This is a very important part of budgeting. So far in this book it has been assumed that any capital budgeting has already been done.

Assignment Exercises

Assignment Exercises followed by the letter x do NOT have answers shown at the back of the book.

10.1x D. Smith is to open a retail shop on 1 January, 19-4. He will put in £25,000 cash as Capital. His plans are as follows:

(i) On 1 January 19-4 to buy an pay for Premises £20,000, Shop Fixtures £3,000, Motor Van £1,000.

(ii) To employ two assistants, each to get a salary of £130 per month, to be paid at the end of each month. (P.A.Y.E. tax, National Insurance contributions etc. are to be ignored.)

(iii) To buy the following goods (shown in units):

	Jan.	Feb.	March	April	May	June
Units	200	220	280	350	400	330

(iv) To sell the following number of units:

	Jan.	Feb.	March	April	May	June
Units	120	180	240	300	390	420

(v)   Units will be sold for £10 each. One-third of the sales are for cash, the other two-thirds being on credit. These latter customers are expected to pay their accounts in the second month following that in which they received the goods.

(vi)   The units will cost £6 each for January to April inclusive, and £7 each thereafter. Creditors will be paid in the month following purchase. (Value stock-in-trade on F.I.F.O. basis.)

(vii)   The other expenses of the shop will be £150 per month payable in the month following that in which they were incurred.

(viii)   Part of the premises will be sub-let as an office at a rent of £600 per annum. This is paid in equal instalments in March, June, September and December.

(ix)   Smith's cash drawings will amount to £250 per month.

(x)   Depreciation is to be provided on Shop Fixtures at 10 per cent per annum and on the Motor Van at 20 per cent per annum.

You are required to:

(a)   Draw up a Cash Budget for the six months ended 30 June, 19-4, showing the balance of cash at the end of each month.

(b)   Draw up a forecast Trading and Profit and Loss Account for the six months ended 30 June 19-4 and a Balance Sheet as at that date.

10.2x B. Cooper is going to set up a new business on 1 January, 19-8. He estimates that his first six months in business will be as follows:

(i)   He will put £10,000 into a bank account for the firm on 1 January, 19-8.

(ii)   On 1 January, 19-8 he will buy Machinery £2,000, Motor Vehicles £1,600 and Premises £5,000, paying for them immediately out of the business bank account.

(iii)   All purchases will be effected on credit. He will buy £2,000 goods on 1 January and he will pay for these in February. Other purchases will be rest of January £3,200, February, March, April, May and June £4,000 each month. Other than the £2,000 worth bought in January all other purchases will be paid for two months after purchase.

(iv)   Sales (all on credit) will be £4,000 for January and £5,000 for each month after that. Debtors will pay for the goods in the third month after purchase by them.

(v)   Stock-in-trade on 30 June, 19-8 will be £2,000.

(vi)   Wages and Salaries will be £150 per month and will be paid on the last day of each month.

(vii)   General Expenses will be £50 per month, payable in the month following that in which they were incurred.

(viii)   He will receive a legacy of £5,500 on 21 April, 19-8. This will be paid into the business bank account immediately.

(ix)   Insurance covering the 12 months of 19-8 will be paid for by cheque on 30 June, 19-8, £140.

(x)   Rates will be paid as follows: for the three months to 31 March, 19-8 by cheque on 28 February, 19-8: for the 12 months ended 31 March, 19-9 by cheque on 31 July 19-8. Rates are £360 per annum.

(xi)   He will make drawings of £80 per month by cheque.

(xii) He has substantial investments in public companies. His bank manager will give him any overdraft that he may require.

(xiii) Depreciate Motors 20 per cent per annum, Machinery 10 per cent per annum.

You are required to:

(a) Draft a cash budget (includes bank) month by month showing clearly the amount of bank balance or overdraft at the end of each month.

(b) Draft the projected Trading and Profit and Loss Account for the first six month's trading, and a Balance Sheet as at 30 June, 19-8.

10.3x The balance sheet of Gregg Ltd. at 30 June, 19-6 was expected to be as follows:

Balance Sheet 30 June, 19-6

	Cost	Depreciation to date	Net
Fixed Assets			
Land and Buildings	40,000	—	40,000
Plant and Machinery	10,000	6,000	4,000
Motor Vehicles	6,000	2,800	3,200
Office Fixtures	500	220	280
	56,500	9,020	47,480
Current Assets			
Stock-in-Trade: Finished Goods		1,800	
Raw Materials		300	
Debtors (19-6 May £990 + June £900)		1,890	
Cash and Bank Balances		7,100	11,090
			£58,570
Financed By:			
Share Capital			50,000
Profit and Loss Account			7,820
			57,820
Current Liabilities			
Creditors for Raw Materials (April £240 + May £140 + June £160)		540	
Creditors for variable overhead		210	750
			£58,570

The plans for the six months to 31 December 19-6 can be summarised as:

(i) Production costs per unit will be:

	£
Direct Materials	2
Direct Labour	5
Variable overhead	3
	£10

(ii) Sales will be at a price of £18 per unit for the three months to 30 September and at £18.5 subsequently. The number of units sold would be:

	July	Aug.	Sept.	Oct.	Nov.	Dec.
Units	60	80	100	100	90	70

All sales will be on credit, and debtors will pay their accounts two months after they have bought the goods.

(iii)   Production will be even at 90 units per month.

(iv)   Purchases of direct materials — all on credit — will be:

July	Aug.	Sept.	Oct.	Nov.	Dec.
£	£	£	£	£	£
220	200	160	140	140	180

Creditors for direct materials will be paid three months after purchase.

(v)   Direct labour is paid in the same month as production occurs.

(vi)   Variable overhead is paid in the month following that in which the units are produced.

(vii)   Fixed overhead of £90 per month is paid each month and is never in arrears.

(viii)   A machine costing £500 will be bought and paid for in July. A motor vehicle costing £2,000 will be bought and paid for in September.

(ix)   A debenture of £5,000 will be issued and the cash received in November. Interest will not start to run until 19-7.

(x)   Provide for depreciation for the six months: Motor Vehicles £600, Office Fixtures £30, Machinery £700.

You are required to draw up as a minimum:

(a)   Cash Budget, showing figures each month.

(b)   Debtors Budget, showing figures each month.

(c)   Creditors Budget, showing figures each month.

(d)   Raw Materials Budget, showing figures each month.

(e)   Forecast Operating Statement for the six months.

(f)   Forecast Balance Sheet as at 31 December, 19-6.

In addition you may draw up any further budgets you may wish to show the workings behind the above budgets.

10.4x The balance sheet of Brahms Ltd. at 31 December, 19-4 was expected to be:

Balance Sheet 31 December, 19-4

Assets Employed:		Depreciation	
Fixed Assets	Cost	to date	Net
Plant and Machinery	20,000	7,000	13,000
Motor Vehicles	8,000	3,000	5,000
Office Equipment	1,000	400	600
	29,000	10,400	18,600
Current Assets			
Stock-in-Trade: Finished Goods		7,600	
Raw Materials		3,600	
Debtors (December)		4,500	
Cash and Bank Balances		700	16,400
			£35,000
Financed By:			
Share Capital			30,000
Profit and Loss Account			1,700
Current Liabilities			31,700
Creditors for fixed expenses		300	
Creditors for Raw Materials			
(November £1,400, December £1,600)		3,000	3,300
			£35,000

Plans for the six months ended 30 June, 19-5 are as follows:

(a) Sales will be a price of £50 per unit. The number of units sold are expected to be:

	Jan.	Feb.	March	April	May	June
Units	80	70	120	150	130	100

All sales will be on credit. Debtors will pay their accounts in the month after purchase.

(b) Production will be at the rate of 100 per month for January, February and March, and 120 per month thereafter.

(c) Production costs per unit will be:

	£
Direct Material	20
Direct Labour	12
Variable overhead	6
	£38

(d) Purchases of direct materials — all on credit — will be:

January	February	March	April	May	June
£2,000	£1,800	£2,200	£2,800	£2,600	£2,400

Creditors for direct materials are paid two months after the goods are bought.

(e) Direct labour and variable overhead are paid in same month as production. Fixed expenses of £300 per month are paid one month after expenses incurred.

(f) Fixed expenses of £300 per month are paid one month in arrears.

(g) A machine costing £4,000 will be bought and paid for in February.

(h) Provide for depreciation for the 6 months: Plant and Machinery £1,400, Motor Vehicles £800, Office Equipment £50.

You are required to draw up as a minimum:

(i) Cash budget, showing figures for each month.

(ii) Debtors budget, showing figures each month.

(iii) Creditors budget, showing figures each month.

(iv) Raw materials budget, showing figures each month.

(v) Forecast Operating statement for the six months ended 30 June, 19-5.

(vi) Forecast Balance Sheet as at 30 June, 19-5. In addition you may wish to show the workings behind the above budgets.

10.5 Newman and Harris are to form a private limited company in the name of Craft Limited. They tell you that their plans for their first six months of trading for the period 1 January 19-4 to 30 June 19-4 are:

(a) Harris will put £20,000 into the business bank account on 1 January 19-4. He will be issued with 20,000 ordinary shares of £1 each at par.

(b) Newman will put £40,000 into the business bank account on 1 January 19-4. He will then be issued with 32,000 ordinary shares of £1 each at par, and a 7 per cent debenture of £8,000.

(c) Sales, all on credit, will be; January £12,000; February £16,000; March £28,000; April £22,000; May £24,000; June £26,000. All debtors will pay their accounts three months after that in which they buy the goods.

(d) Purchases, all on credit, will be: January £48,000; February £16,000; March £18,000; April £20,000; May £14,000; June £10,000. Creditors will be paid in the month following that in which the goods are bought.

(e) Wages and salaries will be £800 per month, payable on the last day of each month.

(f) Newman and Harris are to be the only directors. They are to be paid directors' remuneration totalling £1,200 per month, payable on the last day of each month.

(g) The first debenture interest will be paid on 31 December 19-4.

(h) Premises costing £30,000 will be occupied on 1 January 19-4 and will be paid for in February 19-4.

(i) All other expenses of £600 per month for the first five months and £840 for June are to be paid in the month following that in which they are incurred.

(j) Equipment will be bought on 1 January 19-4 for £12,000, payment being made of £6,000 in March 19-4 and £6,000 in June 19-4.

(k) Stock-in-Trade at 30 June 19-4 will be £21,800.

(l) Depreciation is to be written off the equipment at the rate of 20 per cent per annum.

You are required to:

(i) Draft a cash budget, showing clearly the bank balance at the end of each month.

(ii) Draft the budgeted Trading and Profit and Loss Account for the six months ended 30 June 19-4 and a Balance Sheet as at that date.

Ignore Taxation.

10.6 The following is a summary of the Trading and Profit and Loss Accounts of Blakes Ltd. for the 6 months to 31 May 19-8, and a Balance Sheet as at that date.

Trading and Profit and Loss Account

Stock	13,600	Sales	72,000
Purchases	55,000	Stock	11,000
Gross Profit	14,400		
	83,000		83,000
Wages and Salaries	5,800	Gross Profit	14,400
Administration expenses	3,600		
Net Profit	5,000		
	14,400		14,400

Balance Sheet

Issued Share Capital	10,000	Fixed Assets	9,000
(Ordinary £1 shares)		Stock	11,000
Profit and Loss Account	15,070	Debtors	9,600
Trade Creditors	9,330	Bank	5,400
Administration Expenses			
outstanding	600		
	£35,000		£35,000

At a meeting of the directors the following forward projections for the 6 months to 30 November 19-8 were agreed to:

1. Rate of gross profit to be reduced from 20% to 16⅔% of sales. The period of credit is to be increased from 1 month to 2 months, and it is expected that every customer will pay for the goods 2 months after the date of sale. It is expected that sales will be increased immediately from £12,000 to £18,000 each calendar month.

2. It is assumed that Blakes Ltd. will pay for all purchases 1 month after purchase. The stock is to be increased to £20,000 by the end of November. Purchases each month are of an equal amount.

3. Wages and Salaries will be £1,100 per calendar month payable each month.

4. Administration expenses will be £720 per calendar month, and it is expected that on the last day of each month there will be one month's expenses owing.

5. The firm is to issue 5,000 Ordinary Shares of £1 each in September at a premium of 25p. payable in full on application. The issue is expected to be a success.

6. Further finance is expected to be by bank overdraft. All sums received are to be paid into the bank and all payments made by cheque. No discounts will be received or allowed.

You are required to prepare a summary of the company's bank account for each of the six months, the Trading and Profit and Loss Account for the same period and a summary of the Balance Sheet as at the last day. Depreciate fixed Assets at the rate of 10 per cent per annum.

Chapter Eleven

Further Thoughts on Budgets

The process of budgeting with the necessary participation throughout management, finally producing a profit plan, is now a regular feature in all but the smallest firms. Very often budgeting is the one time when the various parts of management can really get together and work as a team rather than just as separate parts of an organisation. When budgeting is conducted under favourable conditions, there is no doubt that a firm which budgets will tend to perform rather better than a similar firm that does not budget. Budgeting means that managers can no longer give general answers affecting the running of the firm, they have to put figures to their ideas, and they know that in the end their estimated figures are going to be compared with what the actual figures turn out to be.

It has often been said that the act of budgeting is possibly of more benefit than the budgets which are produced. However, the following benefits can be claimed for good budgeting:

(a) The strategic planning carried on by the board of directors or owners can be more easily linked to the decisions by managers as to how the resources of the business will be used to try to achieve the objectives of the business. The strategic planning has to be converted into action, and budgeting provides the ideal place where such planning can be changed into financial terms.

(b) Standards of performance can be agreed to for the various parts of the business. If sales and production targets are set as part of a co-ordinated plan, then the sales department cannot really complain that production is insufficient if they had agreed previously to a production level and this is being achieved, nor can production complain if its production exceeds the amount budgeted for and it remains unsold.

(c) The expression of plans in comparable financial terms. Some managers think mainly in terms of say units of production, or of tons of inputs or outputs, or of lorry mileage etc. The effect that each of them has upon financial results must be brought home to them. For instance a transport manager might be unconcerned about the number of miles that his haulage fleet of lorries covers until the cost of doing such a large mileage is brought home to him, often during budgeting, and it may then be and only then that he starts to search for possible economies. It is possible in many cases to use mathematics to find the best ways of loading vehicles, or of the routes taken by vehicles so that fewer miles are covered and yet the same delivery service is maintained. This is just one instance of many when the expression of the plans of a section of a business in financial terms sparks off a search for economies, when otherwise such a search may never be started at all.

(d) Managers can see how their work slots into the total activities of the firm. It can help to get rid of the feeling of "I'm only a number not a person", because he can identify his position within the firm and can see that his job really is essential to the proper functioning of the firm.

(e) The budgets for a firm cannot be set in isolation. This means that the situation of the business, the nature of its products and its work force etc., must be seen against the economic background of the country. For instance it is no use budgeting for extra labour when labour is in extremely short supply, without realising the implications, possibly that of paying higher than normal wage rates. Increasing the sales target during a "credit squeeze" needs a full investigation of the effect of the shortage of money upon the demand for the firms's goods and so on.

The charges made against budgeting are mainly that budgets bring about inflexibility, and that managers will not depart from budget even though the departure would bring about a more desirable result. Too many budgets are set at one level of sales or production when in fact flexible budgets (discussed later in this chapter) ought to be used. It is very often the case that budgeting is forced upon managers against their will, instead the firm should really set out first of all to do a "selling job" to convince managers that budgets are not the monsters so often thought. A trial run for part of a business is far superior than starting off by having a fully detailed budget set up right away for the whole of the business. Learning to use budgets is rather like learning to swim. Let a child get used to the water first and remove its fear of the water, then it will learn to swim fairly easily. For most children (but not all), if the first visit to the baths meant being pushed into the deep end immediately, then reaction against swimming would probably set in. Let a manager become used to the idea of budgeting, without the fear of being dealt with severely during a trial period, and most managers will then become used to the idea and participate properly.

Flexible Budgets

So far in this book budgets have been drawn up on the basis of one set of expectations, based on just one level of sales and production. Later, when the actual results are compared with the budgeted results expected in a fixed budget, they will have deviated for two reasons:

(1) Whilst the actual and budgeted volumes of production and sales may be the same there may be a difference in actual and budgeted costs.

(2) The volumes of actual and budgeted units of sales and production may vary, so that the costs will be different because of different volumes.

The variations, or variances as they are more commonly known, are usually under the control of different managers in the organisation. Variances coming under (1) will probably be under the control of the individual department. On the other hand variances under (2) are caused because of variations in plans brought about by top management because of changing sales, or at least the expectation of changing sales.

Budgets are used for control purposes, therefore a manager does not take kindly to being held responsible for a variance in his spending if the variance is caused by a type (2) occurrence if he is working on a fixed budget. The answer to this is to construct budgets at several levels of volume, and to show what costs etc. they should incur at different levels. For instance, if a budget had been fixed at a volume of 500 units and the actual volume was 550, then the manager would undoubtedly feel aggrieved if his costs for producing 550 units are compared with the costs he should have incurred for 500 units. Budgets which do allow for changing levels are called "Flexible Budgets".

To draft a full set of flexible budgets is outside the scope of this book, but an instance of one department's flexible budget for manufacturing overhead can be shown in Exhibit 11.1.

Exhibit 11.1

Data Ltd.
Budget of Manufacturing Overhead, Department S.
(This would in fact be in greater detail)

Units	400	450	500	550	600
	£	£	£	£	£
Variable overhead	510	550	600	680	770
Fixed overhead	400	400	400	400	400
Total overhead (A)	£910	£950	£1,000	£1,080	£1,170
Direct Labour hours (B)	200	225	250	275	300
Overhead rates (A) divided by (B)	£4.55	£4.22	£4.0	£3.92	£3.9

Notice that the Variable costs in this case do not vary in direct proportion to production. In this case once 500 units production have been exceeded they start to climb rapidly. The flexible budget makes far greater sense than a fixed budget. For instance if a fixed budget had been agreed at 400 units, with variable overhead £510, then if production rose to 600 units the manager would think the whole system unfair if he was expected to incur only £510 variable overhead (the figure for 400 units). On the contrary, if the comparison was on a flexible budget then costs at 600 units production would instead be compared with £770 (the figure at 600 units).

Assignment Exercises

Assignment Exercises followed by the letter x do NOT have answers shown at the back of the book.

11.1x What are the disadvantages of NOT budgeting?

11.2x What are the two reasons why, in a fixed budget, actual results may vary from budgeted results?

11.3x What are the advantages of flexible budgets over fixed budgets?

Chapter Twelve

Standard Costing: An Introduction

A cost accounting system can be said to be either an actual cost system or a standard cost system. The difference is not in the systems themselves but rather on the kind of costs that are used. In the costing systems already shown we have seen that they have consisted of the actual costs for direct materials and direct labour, and overhead has been charged by reference to a pre-determined overhead rate. Standard costing uses instead the costs that should have been incurred. So standard costing has costs that should have been incurred, whilst other systems use costs that have been incurred.

In an actual cost accounting system costs are traced through the records as product costs. On the other hand standard costing uses standards of performance and of prices derived from studying operations and of estimating future prices. Each unit being produced can have a standard material cost, a standard direct labour cost and a standard overhead cost. As with any form of management accounting this does not in fact have to be carried out fully, for instance some companies will use standard labour and standard overhead costs but may use actual material costs. In the rest of this chapter we will consider firms that use standard costing system for all items.

As with all management accounting the benefits flowing from using standard costing should exceed the costs of operating it, so that there should be advantages accruing from having a standard costing system, and these are:

1. Usually it is simpler and needs less work than an actual cost system. This is because once the standards have been set they are adhered to, and the standard costs will remain unchanged for fairly long periods. Other systems need constant recalculations of cost. For instance the average cost method of pricing issues of materials needs a recalculation of the price each time there are further receipts, whereas standard cost of materials will remain at a constant figure. This can bring about a reduction in the costs of clerical work.

2. The unit costs for each identical product will be the same, whereas this may not be the same with actual costing systems. For instance, in an actual cost system two men making identical units may be paid at different wage rates, the materials issued to one man may have come from a slightly later lot of raw materials received which cost more than the previous lot and therefore the issue price may be higher, and so on. In a standard costing system the same amount would be charged for each of these men, until such time as the standards were altered.

3. A standard cost system provides a better means of checking on the efficiency with which production is carried on, in that the differences between the standard costs and the actual costs, i.e. the variances throw up the changes in efficiency.

4. One important advantage may be that standard costing might make faster reporting available. This is certainly most important, as generally the later information is received the less useful it will be. Standard costing has a great deal of predetermined data when compared with an actual costing system, therefore entering up job order sheets, job sheets and many other tasks can be speeded up if the actual costs do not have to be waited for.

The costs that will have been flowing through the standard costing system is that of standard costs and as actual costs will normally be different, then the difference or variance if adverse (i.e. actual costs have exceeded standard costs) will be debited to the profit and loss account. If the variance is a favourable one (i.e. actual costs have been less than standard costs) then this would be credited to the profit and loss account. This must be done as all the costs used for the calculation of gross profit etc. have been standard costs, and if the variances were not put in the profit and loss account then the net profit would not be the net profit actually made.

Setting Standards

Standard cost accounting is a classic case of the use of the principle of "management by exception". Put roughly this means that when things are going according to plan leave them alone, and concentrate instead on the things that are deviating from planned results. With standard costing the actual results that conform to the standards require little attention. Instead management's interest is centred on the exceptions to standards.

Getting the "right" standards is, therefore, of prime importance. If the "wrong" standards are used, not only will a lot of time and money have been wasted, but it may bring worse results than if no standard had been set al all. Standards may be unsuitable because they were not set properly, or else that conditions have changed greatly since they were set.

Standards of one of two types can be used; ideal standards and maintainable standards. These are as follows:

1. Ideal standards. These are set at a maximum level of efficiency, and thus represent conditions that really can very rarely be attained. This approach can be seriously objected to, in that if standards are too high, employees who might otherwise be motivated by standards which are possible to achieve may become discouraged.

2. Attainable standards. It is simple for someone to say that individuals will be motivated to attain standards that they are capable of, that they will not exert very much effort to exceed standards, and that standards outside the capability of a person will not motivate him. From this follows the also easy conclusion that standards should be neither "too easy" nor "too difficult" but should be "just right". The difficult part of this is in saying what the "just right" figures are to ask as standards. There is no doubt that the work

of behavioural scientists in this area has brought about a far greater insight into such problems. In a very large firm such specialists may be members of the team setting the standards.

The standards for materials and for labour can be divided between those which are concerned with (i) prices and (ii) quantities. Standard overhead costs are divided between standard variable overhead costs, and standard fixed overhead costs. The standard fixed overhead costs will be used in absorption costing only, as marginal costing does not bring the fixed costs into its figures.

Assignment Exercises

Assignment Exercises followed by the letter x do NOT have answers shown at the back of the book.

12.1x What are the disadvantages of having an actual cost system compared with a standing costing system?

12.2x What is "management by exception"?

12.3x What harm can "wrong standards" bring about?

12.4x What objections are there to "ideal" standards?

12.5x What are the benefits of using "attainable standards?

Chapter Thirteen

Introduction to Variance Analysis I: Material Variances

The difference between standard cost and actual cost has already been stated to be a variance. Remember these are classified:

> Adverse: Actual cost greater than standard cost.
> Favourable: Actual cost less than standard cost.

The use of the words favourable and adverse should not be confused with their meaning in ordinary language usage, they are technical terms. Whether a variance is "good" or "bad" can only be determined after the cause(s) of the variance have been fully investigated and ascertained.

There is a great deal of difference between the *computation* of the variances and their *analysis*. The computation is simply the mathematical calculation of the variance. The analysis of the variance is a matter requiring a fair amount of judgement, it just cannot be performed in a mechanical fashion.

We can now look at some computations of variances. In fact there are many variances which can be computed, but we will concentrate on a few of the more important ones. In order that sense can be made of the computations and a reasonable job of analysis done, it will be assumed that the standards set were calculated on a rational basis.

N.B. In the computations of variances which follows this, there are diagrams to illustrate the variances which have been calculated. The lines drawn on the diagrams will be as follows:

Representing standard costs _____

Representing actual costs ....

Where actual costs and standards costs are the same __.__.__.__.__.__

1. Materials Variances — Computations

(a) Material Price Variances:

(i) Favourable variance:

Material J	
Standard price per foot	£4
Standard usage per unit	5 feet
Actual price per foot	£3
Actual usage per unit	5 feet

Usage is the same as standard, therefore the only variance is that of price calculated:

	£
Actual cost per unit 5 × £3	15
Standard cost per unit 5 × £4	20
Variance (favourable)	£5

The diagram illustrates this in that the variance is represented by the shaded area. This is £1 by a quantity of 5, therefore the variance is £5. The variance extends to the price line and not the quantity line, therefore it is a price variance.

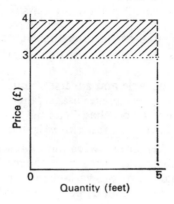

(ii) Adverse variance:

Material K	
Standard price per foot	£9
Standard usage per unit	8 feet
Actual price per foot	£11
Actual usage per unit	8 feet
Variance computed:	£
Actual cost per unit 8 × £11	88
Standard cost per unit 8 × £9	72
Variance (adverse)	£16

The shaded part of the diagram is the variance, this extends £2 times a quantity of 8, therefore the variance is £16. Notice that the shaded area is outside the lines marked ------------ representing standard costs. In the diagrams when the variance is outside the standard cost area as marked by the standard cost lines then it will be an adverse variance. When it is inside the standard cost area as marked by the standard cost lines then it will be a favourable variance.

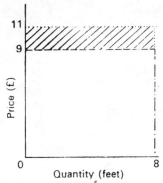

(b) Materials Usage variances

(i) Favourable variance:

Material L

Standard price per ton	£5
Standard usage per unit	100 tons
Actual price per ton	£5
Actual usage per unit	95 tons

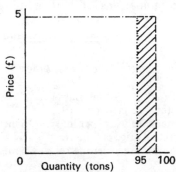

Cost is the same as standard, therefore the only variance is that of usage calculated:

	£
Act ...l cost per unit 95 × £5	475
Standard cost per unit 100 × £5	500
Variance (favourable)	25

(ii) Adverse variance:

Material M

Standard price per yard	£8
Standard usage per unit	11 yards
Actual price per yard	£8
Actual usage per unit	13 yards
Variance computed:	£
Actual cost per unit 13 × £8	104
Standard cost per unit 11 × £8	88
Variance (adverse)	16

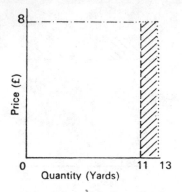

Here again the variances for Materials L and M are shown in diagrams by means of shaded areas. The variances extend to the quantity lines and are, therefore, usage variances. With material L the variance is shown inside the standard cost area, and is, therefore, a favourable variance, whereas material M shows an adverse variance as it is outside the standard cost area.

(c) Combinations of Material and Usage Variances

Most variances are combinations of both material and usage variances. Sometimes one variance will be favourable whilst the other is an adverse one, sometimes both will be adverse variances, and at other times both will be favourable variances.

(i) Favourable and Adverse variances combined:

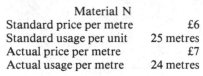

Material N
Standard price per metre   £6
Standard usage per unit   25 metres
Actual price per metre   £7
Actual usage per metre   24 metres

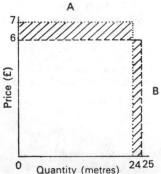

The net variance is calculated as:

	£
Actual cost per unit 24 × £7	168
Standard cost per unit 25 × £6	150
Variance (adverse)	£18

As the diagram shows this is in fact made up of two variances. The first variance, shown as the shaded portion A, is an adverse price variance (i.e. it is outside the standard cost lines, therefore actual cost has exceeded standard cost). The second variance, shown as the shaded portion B, is a favourable usage variance (i.e. it is inside the standard cost lines, therefore actual usage has been less than standard usage).

The adverse price variance can therefore be seen to be £1 by a quantity of 24 = £24. The favourable usage variance can be seen to be a length of 1 metre by a price of £6 = £6. The net (adverse) variance is therefore made up:

Adverse material price variance	24
Favourable material usage variance	6
Net (adverse) variance	£18

(ii) Both Adverse variances combined:

Material O	
Standard price per kilo.	£9
Standard usage per unit	13 kilos
Actual price per kilo.	£11
Actual usage per unit	15 kilos

The net variance is computed:

	£
Actual cost per unit $15 \times £11$	165
Standard cost per unit $13 \times £9$	117
Variance (adverse)	£48

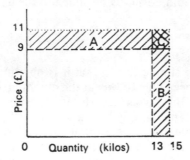

The diagram shows the shaded area A which is definitely a price variance of £2 × 13 = £26 adverse. Shaded area B is definitely a usage variance of 2 × £9 = £18 adverse. This makes up £44 of the variance, but there is the double shaded area, C, of 2 × £2 = £4. This is really an area which is common to both usage and price. Sometimes, although not very often, this would be treated as a separate variance, but as detail is necessarily limited in this book we will just add it to the price variance, making it £26 + £4 = £30, the usage variance being left at £18.

(iii) Both Favourable variances combined:

Material P

Standard price per ton	£20
Standard usage per unit	15 tons
Actual price per ton	£19
Actual usage per unit	13 tons

The net variance is computed:

	£
Actual cost per unit 13 × £19	247
Standard cost per unit 15 × £20	300
Variance (favourable)	£53

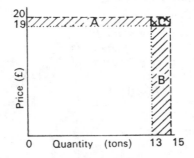

The diagram shows the shaded area A which is deinfitely a price variance of £1 × 13 = £13 favourable. Shaded area B is a usage variance of 2 × £19 = £38 favourable. The double shaded area C of £1 × 2 = £2, making up the total variance of 53 would normally be added to the usage variance to make it £38 + £2 = £40.

2. Materials Variances — Analysis

(a) Price Variances

The price variance is a simple one in that it is obvious that the purchasing department have not been able to buy at the anticipated price. How far this is completely outside the powers of the purchasing department depends entirely on the facts. It may simply be that the rate of inflation is far greater than it had been possible to foresee, or that special forms of extra taxes have been introduced by the Government. No one can surely blame the purchasing department for not knowing the secrets of the government's budget each year! On the other hand it may have been that poor purchasing control has meant that orders for materials have been placed too late for the firm to manage to get the right price in the market, or that materials which ought to have been bought in bulk have been in fact bought in small lots at uneconomic prices. If there are regular suppliers, a short-term gain by buying a cheaper lot from somewhere else could militate against the firm's benefit in the long run if the firm's regular suppliers took umbrage.

Buying the cheapest materials does not always bring about the achievement of the greatest profit. It may result in more wastages, a greater amount of labour time because the men take longer to do the job with inferior materials, and a unit made up of poor materials may well damage the image of the firm because its products do not last as long as they used to do.

All the same there must be someone to whom the responsibility for the price variance can be traced and he is then accountable for it.

(b) Usage Variances

There are many reasons for excessive use of material. Inferior materials can bring about a lot of waste, so can workers who are not as skilled as they ought to be. Perhaps the machinery is not suitable for the job, or there might even be deliberate wastage of material, e.g. wood wasted so that it can be taken home by workers as fuel etc. The theft of material obviously aggravates a usage variance. Here again responsibility must be traced.

Key Questions of Variances

Before we look at the computation or analysis of any further variances this is a convenient point to raise some fundamental questions about variances. They are:

1. Why do we wish to calculate this particular variance?

2. When it has been calculated what action are we going to take about it?

3. If we are not going to make an effective use of the variance, then why bother at all to calculate it?

Inventory Records under Standard Costing

It is worth noting at this point that when a firm adopts a Standard Costing system it avoids the difficulties described earlier in Chapters 4 and 5 involving FIFO, LIFO or Average Stock methods. In a Standard Costing system all materials received and issued are valued at the Standard Cost in the inventory account. There is no recording problem associated with changing prices during the period since they are separately recorded as variances.

Provided that standards are reviewed sufficiently often this system should ensure that the values of inventories are maintained close to their current value.

Disposition of Variances

The question arises as to how the variances are to be brought into the final accounts of the business. There are, in fact, several methods of dealing with them.

They can be treated entirely as costs (if adverse variances) which are period costs and are, therefore, not included in the valuation of closing stocks of finished goods or work in progress. Alternatively they may be brought in as product costs and therefore used in the valuation of closing stocks. Another variation is to treat those variances which are controllable as period costs, but the uncontrollable variances be treated as product costs. All of these methods are acceptable for the final accounts which are used for external reporting.

Example of Standard Costing in Inventory Records

Using the data from Exhibit 5.1 and assuming the following standard costs which were revised at the beginning of each year: –
Year 1   £11 per unit: Year 2   £14 per unit: Year 3   £20 per unit.

	Opening Stock	Price Variance	Receipts	Issues	End of Year Stock
Year 1	Nil	Nil	40 × £11 = £440	30 × £11 = £330	10 × £11 = £110
2	10 × £14 = £140	Opening Stock F 30			
		Receipts F 10	30 × £14 = £420	32 × £14 = £448	8 × £14 = £112
3	8 × £20 = £160	Opening Stock F 48			
		Receipts A 6	42 × £20 = £840	36 × £20 = £720	14 × £20 = £280

Note the Price Variances include the adjustment of the opening stock to the new standard at the start of the period, and the difference between standard and actual price of goods received in the period.

Trading and Profit and Loss Accounts

Year	1		2		3	
	£	£	£	£	£	£
Sales		420		512		864
Opening Stock at standard cost	–		140		160	
Purchases	440		420		840	
	440		560		1,000	
Less Closing Stock	110		112		280	
Cost of Goods Sold		330		448		720
Standard Gross Profit		90		64		144
Price Variances		–	F	40	F	42
		90		104		186
Expenses		50		60		80
Net Profits		40		44		106
By comparison the profits for: –						
AVCO		40		36		100
FIFO		50		34		120
LIFO		30		22		46
Replacement		40		20		64

The difference between the profits using standard costs and AVCO, FIFO and LIFO depends on the standard price and on the way the price variances are treated. In this example the variances on opening stock are dealt with at the beginning of the period. Often the standards are revised more frequently than annually and thus these variances would be spread through the year.

Assignment Exercises

Assignment Exercises followed by the letter x do NOT have answers shown at the back of the book.

13.1x Calculate the material variances from the following data, stating whether they are price variances or usage variances, and whether they are adverse or favourable.

(i)	Material A:	Standard price per ton	£40
		Standard usage per unit	11 tons
		Actual price per ton	£40
		Actual usage per unit	13 tons
(ii)	Material B:	Standard price per metre	£25
		Standard usage per unit	60 metres
		Actual price per metre	£28
		Actual usage per unit	60 metres
(iii)	Material C:	Standard price per lb.	£3
		Standard usage per unit	1,000 lb.
		Actual price per lb.	£3
		Actual usage per unit	973 lb.
(iv)	Material D:	Standard price per yard	£17
		Standard usage per unit	440 yards
		Actual price per yard	£14
		Actual usage per unit	440 yards

13.2x Draw graphs from the data in 13.1 letting a shaded area be the variance. Use lines drawn as ---------- to represent standard costs, lines drawn .... representing actual costs, and lines drawn _._._._ where standard costs and actual costs are the same.

13.3x Calculate the materials variances from the following data.

(i)	Material E:	Standard price per metre	£6
		Standard usage per unit	88 metres
		Actual price per metre	£6
		Actual usage per unit	85 metres
(ii)	Material F:	Standard price per ton	£117
		Standard usage per unit	30 tons
		Actual price per ton	£123
		Actual usage per unit	30 tons
(iii)	Material G:	Standard price per litre	£16
		Standard usage per unit	158 litres
		Actual price per litre	£16
		Actual usage per unit	165 litres
(iv)	Material H:	Standard price per foot	£16
		Standard usage per unit	92 feet
		Actual price per foot	£19
		Actual usage per unit	92 feet
(v)	Material I:	Standard price per ton	£294
		Standard usage per unit	50 tons
		Actual price per ton	£300
		Actual usage per unit	50 tons
(vi)	Material J:	Standard price per kilo	£27.5
		Standard usage per unit	168 kilos
		Actual price per kilo	£27.5
		Actual usage per unit	156 kilos

114

	(vii) Material K:	Standard price per barrel	£44	
		Standard usage per unit	23	barrels
		Actual price per barrel	£44	
		Actual usage per unit	25	barrels
	(viii)Material L:	Standard price per ton	£248	
		Standard usage per unit	40	tons
		Actual price per ton	£232	
		Actual usage per unit	40	tons

13.4x Using the same method as in 13.2 draw graphs of the data in 13.3.

13.5 Calculate the following materials variances:

	(i) Material Q:	Standard price per ton	£20	
		Standard usage per unit	34	tons
		Actual price per ton	£18	
		Actual usage per unit	37	tons
	(ii) Material R:	Standard price per yard	£17	
		Standard usage per unit	50	yards
		Actual price per yard	£19	
		Actual usage per unit	46	yards
	(iii) Material S:	Standard price per metre	£12	
		Standard usage per unit	15	metres
		Actual price per metre	£14	
		Actual usage per unit	18	metres
	(iv) Material T:	Standard price per roll	£40	
		Standard usage per unit	29	rolls
		Actual price per roll	£37	
		Actual usage per unit	27	rolls
	(v) Material U:	Standard price per kilo	£7	
		Standard usage per unit	145	kilos
		Actual price per kilo	£8	
		Actual usage per unit	154	kilos
	(vi) Material V:	Standard price per gallon	£25	
		Standard usage per unit	10,000	gallons
		Actual price per gallon	£22	
		Actual usage per unit	9,850	gallons

13.6x Using the same method as in 13.2 draw graphs of the data in 13.5.

13.7 Calculate the following materials variances:

	(i) Material AB:	Standard price per roll	£19	
		Standard usage per unit	500	rolls
		Actual price per roll	£17	
		Actual usage per unit	482	rolls
	(ii) Material CD:	Standard price per gallon	£50	
		Standard usage per unit	22	gallons
		Actual price per gallon	£54	
		Actual usage per unit	25	gallons
	(iii) Material EF:	Standard price per litre	£12	
		Standard usage per unit	180	litres
		Actual price per litre	£12	
		Actual usage per unit	191	litres

(iv) Material GH: Standard price per metre   £16
                Standard usage per unit   100 metres
                Actual price per metre   £18
                Actual usage per unit   107 metres

(v) Material IJ: Standard price per ton   £105
               Standard usage per unit   200 tons
               Actual price per ton   £99
               Actual usage per unit   200 tons

(vi) Material JK: Standard price per mile   £1,000
               Standard usage per unit   29 miles
               Actual price per mile   £1,022
               Actual usage per unit   27 miles

13.8x Using the same method as in 13.2 draw graphs of the data in 13.7.

Chapter Fourteen

Introduction to Variance Analysis II: Labour Variances

The computation of labour variances is similar to that of material variances. With labour variances the analysis can be broken down into:

(a) Wage rate variances.

(b) Labour efficiency variances.

Because the computation of labour variances is so similar to those of material variances only two examples will be given.

1. Labour Variances — Computations
(a) Wage Rate Variance

	Product A
Standard hours to produce	100
Actual hours to produce	100
Standard wage rate per hour	£0.9
Actual wage rate per hour	£1.0

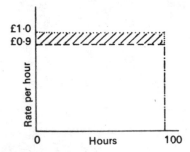

As the actual and standard hours are the same, then the only variance will be a wage rate variance, computed:

	£
Actual cost per unit 100 × £1.0	100
Standard cost per unit 100 × £0.9	90
Variance (adverse)	£10

The diagram illustrates this in that the variance is represented by the shaded area. This is £0.1 by a quantity of 100, therefore the variance is £10. The variance extends to the wage rate line and it is thus a wage rate variance, and as the shaded area is outside the standard cost lines, indicated by lines marked ------- then it is an adverse variance.

(b) Labour Efficiency Variance

Produce B

Standard hours to produce	400
Actual hours to produce	370
Standard wage rate per hour	£1.0
Actual wage rate per hour	£1.0

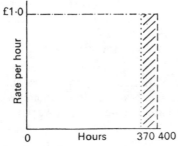

As the actual and standard wage rates are the same, then the only variance will be a labour efficiency variance, computed:

	£
Actual cost per unit 370 × £1.0	370
Standard cost per unit 400 × £1.0	400
Variance (favourable)	£30

The diagram illustrates this in that the variance is represented by the shaded area. This is a quantity of 30 by a rate of £1.0, therefore the variance is £30. The variance extends to the time line, therefore this is an efficiency variance, as the job has been completed in a different number of hours than standard. As the shaded area is inside the standard cost lines indicated by lines marked ------ then it is a favourable variance.

(c) Combined Wage Rate and Efficiency Variance

Product C

Standard hours to produce	500
Actual hours to produce	460
Standard wage rate per hour	£0.9
Actual wage rate per hour	£1.1

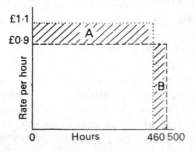

The net variance can be computed as:

$$
\begin{array}{lr}
 & \text{£} \\
\text{Actual cost per unit } 460 \times £1.1 & 506 \\
\text{Standard cost per unit } 500 \times £0.9 & 450 \\
\hline
\text{Variance (adverse)} & £56 \\
\end{array}
$$

The diagram shows that this is made up of two variances. The first variance, shown as the shaded portion A, is an adverse wage rate variance (it is outside the standard cost lines, therefore it is an adverse variance because actual cost for this has exceeded standard cost). The second variance, shown as the shaded portion B, is a favourable labour efficiency variance (it is inside the standard cost lines, therefore actual hours have been less than standard hours).

The adverse wage rate variance can, therefore, be seen to be £0.2 by a quantity of 460 = £92. The favourable efficiency variance is a quantity of 40 by a price of £0.9 = £36. The net adverse variance is, therefore, made up of:

$$
\begin{array}{lr}
 & \text{£} \\
\text{Adverse wage rate variance} & 92 \\
\text{Favourable labour efficiency variance} & 36 \\
\hline
 & £56 \\
\end{array}
$$

2. Labour Variances — Analysis

Labour wage rates will probably be set in conjunction with the trade unions involved, so that this variance may not really be subject to control at any other level other than at the bargaining table with the unions involved. Nevertheless such a variance could arise because a higher grade of labour was being used than was necessary, even taking into account trade union needs. It might reflect a job running behind schedule that had to be finished off quickly even though higher grade labour was used. It might have been a rush job that also meant bringing in a higher grade of labour as well. The staffing policy of the firm may have come adrift because they have not recruited sufficient numbers of the various grades of labour.

Labour efficiency variances can be caused by a great number of things. Using unsuitable labour, unsuitable machinery, workers trying to slow work up so that more overtime rates of pay are earned, the day after a bank holiday, or the day before it, can affect performance. The morale of workers, the physical state of workers, using poor materials which slows up production, hold-ups because of bottlenecks in production and so on. The possibilities are almost endless. At the same time if the variance was worth calculating then some form of action should follow, as otherwise there is no point at all in doing the accounting work of calculating such variances.

Appendix to Chapter Fourteen

Methods of Remunerating Labour

Wage Systems

The large majority of people are paid in accordance with rules which are a combination of two main alternative systems. These two alternatives are payment by results and payment for time spent at work.

Payment by results

In its starkest form this consists of paying according to the quantity of good output achieved and can be expressed graphically as in exhibit 14.1.

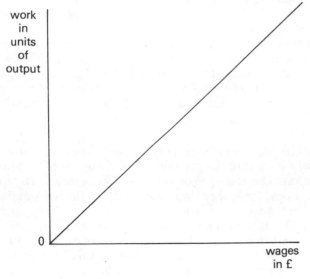

Exhibit 14.1   Payment at piece-work rates.

For each unit of work produced the same amount of money is added to the employee's wages. At its lowest point, this means no pay. As work is done the wages increase proportionately at a steady rate and the result is depicted on the graph as a straight line. In practice the disadvantages of such a systems are so great that it is virtually non-existent in industry today. It is restricted to special cases such as work sub-contracted to individuals working at home. The most obvious objection concern the fairness of such a method of calculation and the effect on the quality of work done.

The question of fairness arises because frequently the cause of employees' idle time is purely an external one. Thus, for example, nil output can be the result of a break in the supply of components. Under such circumstances it would not be fair to withold pay and clearly unacceptable to the trade unions. It is usual to find that piecework is underpinned by a guaranteed minimum wage for an agreed period. The length of the period varies according to the strength of the parties to the agreement.

As for the quality of work done under piecework agreements, this is always going to be a problem when people are encouraged to work at fast rates. Inspection and quality control can be emphasized, but even at its best, this cannot resolve all the difficulties.

Adapted piece-work systems

The great advantage which piecework systems attempt to gain is to motivate the operators to high levels of achievement. It is a matter of personal experience with most people that payment by results does urge them on from relatively low to higher levels of achievement. According to the type of production and factory organisation involved, it is frequently useful to introduce some variant of pure piecework. Differential rates per unit dependent upon the level of working can sometimes be introduced. These are useful when the work is highly repetitive and easily measured in terms of a standard time. In these circumstances the individual is always motivated by possibilities of higher pay and from the management's point of view the advantage is in reducing labour cost per unit. Such systems do not work without limits, as people involved set their own levels of pay requirements versus work effort and seldom go beyond these self-imposed boundaries.

Standards

The basis of control over labour costs is in knowing what a cost *ought* to be. Another way of saying this, is that work done needs to be expressed in standard terms. This is the job of Work Study Engineers. They perform two related functions. First, they study the nature of the work and the methods employed and attempt to improve on the work flow and layout of equipment. This is termed a method study. Second, they measure the time required to perform a task. The final result of this measurement is the standard time allowed. If the standard time allowed for a specified task is one hour, then the quantity of work done in completing the task is one standard hour. Somebody working at twice the standard rate and completing the task twice within one hour, would have done two standard hours of work. A standard hour of work is a measure of work done and not a measure of time. A standard hour may be defined as the amount of which should be performed in one hour by a normal operator working in reasonable conditions. Since these are not closely defined terms, if follows that there is some degree of averaging and estimating in setting standard times. The usual method employed for setting standards is to average a large number of readings involving different work study engineers, operators and times of day and week. In this way, personal factors are smoothed out. In addition to this averaging process, allowances are included in the time for personal requirements, fatigue and unavoidable delays.

Perhaps it should be emphasized that the average referred to above is one of measurement adjusted for the time-study engineers experienced opinion of the operators work rate. It is not a simple measurement of how long the job took. If that were the case, then there would be no defence against operators performing slowly when under observation.

Adapted piece work systems

In any system which is designed to increase productivity, the benefit to the employer comes from spreading the fixed overheads over a greater number of units produced. In straight piece work the increase in production results in higher wages to employees and a smaller share of overhead per unit. In time-rate systems, if production is increased the labour cost remains unaltered in total and the employer benefits from lower wage cost per unit as well as from lower overhead cost per unit. There are two variants in piece work which are designed to share the benefits in a way which falls between the two extremes outlined above. They are named after their developers, Halsey and Rowan.

The Halsey systems

Given a standard time for a unit of work done, it is possible to calculate how much time has been saved when the job is completed. It is this time saved, valued at the time-rate which is shared between employee and employer, according to some agreed proportion.

Example

Allowed time/unit:	1 hour
Rate/hour:	£2
Actual time taken:	45 minutes
Proportion:	50%

The rate of pay per unit is then calculated as:

Time rate £2 × ¾ =	£1.50
Bonus (1 − ¾) × £2 × 50% =	25
	£1.75

The bonus formula is:

(time allowed − time taken) × rate of pay × % share agreed for the employee.

In this example the rate/unit of output is £1.75 for labour, rather than £2 in piece work.

The Rowan system

Here the system is designed to dampen down the bonus at higher levels of output and appeals to employers in situations where there are severe reservations about the accuracy of the standards. As in the Halsey system as bonus is calculated, but this time the share is given by the ratio of time taken to time allowed.

Example

Using the same data as given for the Halsey example, the rate of pay is now calculated as:

Rate/unit,

Time rate £2 × ¾ =		£1.500
Bonus $(1 - ¾) × £2 × \frac{45}{60}$ =		.375
		£1.875

Time taken is 45 minutes compared to the allowed 60 minutes hence the share of $\frac{45}{60}$

As the time saved increases, the bonus also increases, the bonus also increases until the job is being performed at twice the standard rate. After which any further saving in time would actually reduce the bonus. This can be demonstrated easily:

Let X be the time taken.

Let Y be the time allowed.

Bonus, $B = (Y - X) × \frac{X}{Y} × £R$.

$B = (X - \frac{X^2}{Y}) × R$ where Y and R are constant.

Differentiating:

$\frac{dB}{dX} = (1 - \frac{2X}{Y}) × R$ and $\frac{dB}{dX} = 0$ when $X = \frac{1}{2} Y$.

At this point the bonus is a maximum. Note that $\frac{d^2B}{dX^2} = -\frac{2R}{Y}$ which is

negative, as it must be if the point $X = \frac{Y}{2}$ is to be a maximum.

For those whose mathematical ability is not their strongest point, this can be illustrated by using two cases where the time taken is (a) ½ hour, (b) ¼ hour.

(a) Time rate £2 × ½		1.00
Bonus $(1 - ½) × £2 × \frac{30}{60}$		.50
		£1.50
(b) Time rate £2 × ¼		.50
Bonus $(1 - ¼) × £2 × \frac{15}{60}$		.375
		£0.875

Group Bonus Schemes

Not all workers can be associated with individual piecework schemes, either because their work is not easily measured in terms of production or because they work in teams and individual effort cannot be measured. In such cases a gang or team or larger group can be associated and share a group bonus between them. Such bonuses are calculated according to output achieved. Clearly the output must be definitely associated with the group, to avoid the confusion that could result from overlap.

These group bonus schemes can be extended to include the associated indirect workers, such as supervisors and store-keepers. Without these extensions, unfortunate anomalies can occur which are certain to cause considerable labour problems. It is a central feature of incentive schemes that they inevitably have a ripple effect throughout the firm's labour force.

Profit Sharing and Co-Partnership Schemes

In the simplest version of profit sharing the firm issues a bonus to all its employees based on a formula involving profits and wages. The bonus usually takes the form of a percentage of the annual wage, paid in a lump sum. Such schemes are popular at pay-out time and create goodwill amongst employees, but they are remote from day to day working and are felt to have little influence on productivity.

Some schemes go further towards involving employees in the success of the company by encouraging the employees to become shareholders. This can be done either by issuing shares as a bonus or by offering shares at some discount rate. Again these schemes tend to be remote from the daily problems of the workforce. The size of an individual's shareholding is likely to be so small that it will not significantly alter his attitude to his firm as his employer. His theoretical position as shareholder and therefore part-owner is so weak in practice as to have no significance.

Trade Unions are fairly lukewarm about these share-owning schemes and prefer to concentrate on negotiated wages, manning levels and working conditions. It is possible that their attitude would change if there were a significant alteration in size of bonus share issues, but then existing shareholders would offer total resistance since they would be losing control of the company.

Measured Day Work

Despite the adaptations introduced in such systems as Rowan and Halsey, there is a steady present day movement towards paying a fixed wage based on time, with augmentation from group productivity schemes. There are two main sources of pressure, acting in this direction. Opposition to piecework schemes comes from Trade Unions, who traditionally are opposed to concentrating work into few hands whilst there is unemployment in the general economy. Trade Unions also resist the tendency to put their members into situations of risk of industrial injury. There is always the fear that people anxious to increase their wages are prone to take unnecessary risks and can become impatient with safety regulations and precautions.

124

Firms, too, find difficulties about piece rate systems. Their main objection is one of cost, since these schemes are costly to run, entailing as they do considerable requirements with regard to maintaining records of individual performance.

Measured Day Work is the result of these pressures. In essence the management and labour representative agree that for specified wage rates and manning levels, the labour force will achieve a certain level of output. Incentives are built in by agreeing bonuses for achievement over and above the agreed level of output.

Graphical Illustration

A summary of the different systems is presented in graphical form in exhibit 14.2. This shows the way in which weekly wages vary as productivity increases, according to the wage system used.

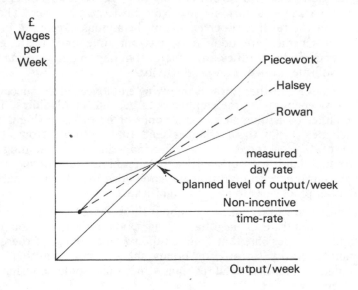

Exhibit 14.2

Whatever method of wage calculation is used, the management have a plan, usually in the form of an attainable target. Whichever incentive wage method is employed it will tend to give the same results around this planned level and will only deviate markedly when productivity is widely away from it.

Assignment Exercises

Assignment Exercises followed by the letter x do NOT have answers shown at the back of the book.

14.1x Calculate the labour variances from the following data, stating whether they are rate variances or efficiency variances, and whether they are favourable or adverse.

(i)	Standard hours to produce	20
	Actual hours to produce	22
	Standard wage rate per hour	£1.4
	Actual wage rate per hour	£1.4
(ii)	Standard hours to produce	150
	Actual hours to produce	150
	Standard wage rate per hour	£1.5
	Actual wage rate per hour	£1.6
(iii)	Standard hours to produce	67
	Actual hours to produce	67
	Standard wage rate per hours	£1.7
	Actual wage rate per hour	£1.5
(iv)	Standard hours to produce	200
	Actual hours to produce	189
	Standard wage rate per hour	£1.8
	Actual wage rate per hour	£1.8

14.2x Draw graphs from the data in 14.1 letting a shaded area be the variance. Use lines drawn as ------- to represent standard costs, lines drawn .... representing actual costs, and lines drawn _._._._._ where standard costs and actual costs are the same.

14.3x Calculate the labour variances from the following data:

		Standard hours	Actual hours	Standard wage rate	Actual wage rate
(i)	Job A	220	218	£2.1	£2.1
(ii)	Job B	115	115	£1.7	£1.9
(iii)	Job C	200	240	£1.8	£1.8
(iv)	Job D	120	104	£2.0	£2.0
(v)	Job E	68	68	£1.8	£1.5
(vi)	Job F	30	34	£1.7	£1.7
(vii)	Job G	70	77	£1.6	£1.6
(viii)	Job H	100	100	£1.9	£2.0

14.4x Using the same method as in 14.2 draw graphs of the data in 14.3.

14.5 Calculate the labour variances from the following data:

		Standard hours	Actual hours	Standard wage rate	Actual wage rate
(i)	Job I	150	142	£2.0	£2.2
(ii)	Job J	220	234	£1.9	£1.7
(iii)	Job K	50	48	£2.0	£1.9
(iv)	Job L	170	176	£2.0	£2.2
(v)	Job M	140	149	£2.1	£1.8
(vi)	Job N	270	263	£1.6	£2.0

14.6x Using the same method as in 14.2 draw graphs of the data in 14.5.

14.7x Calculate the labour variances from the following data:

		Standard hours	Actual hours	Standard wage rate	Actual wage rate
(i)	Job P	200	200	£1.9	£2.1
(ii)	Job Q	150	140	£2.0	£1.8
(iii)	Job R	175	169	£1.5	£1.9
(iv)	Job S	180	164	£2.2	£2.2
(v)	Job T	80	69	£2.5	£2.3
(vi)	Job U	70	74	£2.0	£2.1

14.8x Using the same method as in 14.2 draw graphs of the data in 14.7.

14.9 You are required to calculate the labour variances from the following data:

		Standard hours	Actual hours	Standard wage rate £	Actual wage rate £
(i)	Job A	136	136	3.6	3.0
(ii)	Job B	200	200	3.8	4.0
(iii)	Job C	140	154	1.6	1.6
(iv)	Job D	180	164	2.2	2.2
(v)	Job E	75	70	2.0	1.8
(vi)	Job F	540	526	1.6	2.0
(vii)	Job G	440	468	1.8	1.6
(viii)	Job H	70	74	2.0	2.1
(ix)	Job I	180	214	2.0	2.1

14.10 George Ltd. pays its labour force a guaranteed minimum wage of £120 a week. In addition it pays a bonus of £2 for each hour of production time saved. What amount would each of the following employees earn?

Employee	Hours Worked	Standard Output/ Hour Units	Actual Units Produced
A	40	60	3000
B	42	60	3300
C	40	60	2350

14.11x Graham Company Limited operates a Halsey type bonus with the time saved divided 60% to the employee and 40% to the employer. The hourly rate of pay is £4. Calculate the amounts of hours due to the following: –

Employee	Hours Worked	Standard time Per Unit	Units Produced
X	40	1 hour	80
Y	40	1 hour	60
Z	36	1 hour	48

14.12 Using the information in 14.11 what amounts would have been payable if the Company had used the Rowan system?

14.13x A team of workmen are paid a group bonus on top of their hourly rate. The bonus is calculated by working out the amount by which the group exceeds its standard, expressed as a percentage. Seventy five per cent of this calculated figure is then applied to the basic hourly rate to give the bonus rate. Details of the teams work is given below. Calculate the wages of M, N and P whose details of work are also given.

Group: –

Actual Hours Worked	Number of Units Produced	Standard Output per Hour
420	28,000	60

Individual	Actual Hours Worked	Rate of Pay per Hour £
M	42	3
N	44	3.40
P	40	2.80

Chapter Fifteen

Introduction to Variance Analysis III: Overhead Variances

Management Overheads

In Chapter 7 the problem of allocating manufacturing overheads to jobs or processes, was introduced. In the first instance the costs were collected in cost centres — normally recognisable departments of the organisation. The total costs of these centres is then applied to products or jobs as they pass through the operations of the cost centre.

Suppose that a firm collects costs into three manufacturing departments with these results: –

Department	A	B	C
	£	£	£
Fixed Overhead Cost	50,000	40,000	20,000
Variable Overhead Cost	30,000	35,000	40,000
Total Overhead	80,000	75,000	60,000
Direct Labour Hours	10,000	30,000	15,000
Direct Labour Cost	£22,000	£59,000	£35,000
Machine Hours	20,000	2,000	10,000

Exhibit 15.1

A decision has to be taken as to which activity, either labour or machine time, is the dominant factor in the department and will provide the most sensible basis for allocating the overhead.

In the case of Department A Machine Hours appear to be the major factor and therefore overheads will be charged on the basis $\frac{£80,000}{20,000}$ hours $= £4$ per machine hour. The firm will record for each job or process the number of machine hours taken and the overheads allocated on this total of hours at £4 per hour.

In Department B labour appears to be the dominant feature and therefore overheads will be charged on a labour hour rate calculated at $\frac{£75,000}{30,000}$ hours

$= £2.50$ per hour. Department C does not exhibit any dominant activity and could either be expressed in a machine hour rate or a labour hour rate. Some firms where rates of pay in a department are stable and the mix of labour at different rates of pay stays the same prefer to express the overheads as a percentage of labour cost. In department C it could be $\frac{£60,000}{£35,000} = 171\%$. Thus the labour cost for all work going through department C would be collected and overheads allocated at 171% of this labour cost figure.

Predetermined Rates

The usual procedure whether using standard costing or not is to predetermine the overhead absorption rates using budgeted figures both for the overhead costs and for the activity measure, whether machine or labour hours or cost. This process has a number of advantages – since not only does it allow proper current estimates to be made for things such as price quotations – but also it avoids the problem of fluctuating overhead rates at different times of the year due to seasonal variations. For example an ice cream manufacturer is likely to be much more active in the summer months than the winter. Because activity is low in winter the rate of absorption is likely to rise steeply since costs will not reduce proportionately. It makes more sense to view the overheads in this type of business on an annual cycle and recover the same amount of overhead in both summer and winter.

Variances in Overhead Recovery

As in all situations where budgeted figures are used there is almost certainly going to be variances at the end of a period. Take figures from Exhibit 15.1 for department A as the budget and compare them with actual performance: –

	Department A	
	Budget figures	Actual figures
	£	£
Fixed Overhead	50,000	52,000
Variable Overhead	30,000	37,000
Total Overhead	80,000	89,000
Machine Hours	20,000	25,000
Machine Hour Rate £4		

Exhibit 15.2

The actual machine hours worked of 25,000 will have been used to allocate overheads to production at the rate of £4 per hour and therefore £100,000 will have been allocated. Compared to actual overheads of £89,000 this represents an over-absorption of £11,000. Only if 22,250 machine hours had been worked would the recovery have been exactly equal to actual overhead costs.

In a cost accounting system not using standard costing the over or under absorption of overheads would be either: –

1) transferred wholly to cost of goods sold in the profit and loss account for the period.

2) allocated between closing inventories and cost of goods sold

3) carried forward to the next period.

The first choice would be used if the difference was felt to represent a shortfall in achievement for example if the number of hours worked had dropped due to bad management planning. The second would be applied if the differences were felt to be due to poor estimates of the original budgets. The third would only apply to interim accounts – not those at a year end.

Analysing the variances

The Variance between the amount recovered of £100,000 and the actual overhead cost of £89,000 can be analysed into a number of constituent variances in the normal manner of standard costing. In the example we have used the variance can be due to

1) the prices paid for goods and services being different from original estimates or standards.

2) the volume of activity during the period being different from the original estimate.

These are known as the budget or spending variance for the first and a volume variance for the second reason.

Budget or Spending Variance

This represents the difference between the actual cost of overhead and the budgeted overhead cost adjusted to the actual level of operational activity.

From Exhibit 15.2 the budget figures need to be increased to take account of the fact that actively measured in machine hours has increased from 20,000 to 25,000 hours. This will not of course increase the Fixed Overhead – only the variable overheads which we will assume increase by 25% in line with the hours.

	a Original Budget	b Adjusted Budget	c Actual	b – c Variance
Fixed Overhead	50,000	50,000	52,000	(2,000)
Variable Overhead	30,000	37,500	37,000	500
	80,000	87,500	89,000	(1,500)

Exhibit 15.3

The Actual Expenditure exceeds the Adjusted Budget by £1,500 which represents an adverse Budget or Spending Variance.

Volume Variance

The other factor apart from the cost of the overheads which was budgeted in developing the predetermined standard was the number of machine hours. In the example we estimated that 20,000 machine hours would be worked whereas 25,000 were actually worked. This difference would not matter if all the overheads were variable since the rate per hour would be constant at different activities. Where fixed costs are concerned however increasing the activity will increase the amount recovered above the level required, and if activity is below budget insufficient overhead will be recovered.

In the example the rate is split: —

$$\text{Fixed} \quad \frac{50,000}{20,000} = £2.50$$

$$\text{Variable} \quad \frac{30,000}{20,000} = \underline{£1.50}$$
$$£4.00$$

When the machine hours increase from 20,000 to 25,000 we recover $5,000 \times £2.50 = £12,500$ more than required.

An alternative way of viewing this is to compare the amount of overheads recovered at 25,000 hours with the flexible budget for this level of activity: —

Recovered 25,000 × £4	=	100,000
Budget Variable Cost 25,000 × 1.50	37,500	
Fixed Cost	50,000	87,500
Volume variance		12,500

This variance shows that by increasing the utilisation of the fixed resources in a business considerable savings are made. The £12,500 is a favourable variance in terms of the original standard.

Summary of Variances

The analysis so far shows: —

	£
Standard Overhead recovered at actual level of activity (25,000 × £4)	100,000
Budget or Spending Variance — adverse	1,500
	101,500
Volume Variance — favourable	12,500
Actual level of Manufacturing Overheads	89,000

Assessing Variances

In Standard Costing in an organisation where products are being manufactured it is common for the cost of the overheads to be related to the product. If in the example a Superwidgit is manufactured in department A which it is estimated requires 2 machine hours per widgit then the standard cost of overhead per Superwidgit will be $2 \times £4 = £8$.

If in the actual period a Superwidgit takes less than two hours to make there will be a favourable variance which will be costed at £4 per hour. Similarly if more than two hours are taken there will be a unfavourable variance.

Using the example and assuming Department A exclusively manufactures Superwidgits, the Original Budget is to make 10,000 Superwidgits and the actual production of Superwidgits in 12,000.

	Department A Original Budget	Actual
	£	£
Total overhead	80,000	89,000
Machine Hours	20,000	25,000
Hours per Superwidgit	2	
Number of Units	10,000	12,000

To produce 12,000 widgits should take 24,000 hours at the standard rate. Since the actual hours are 25,000 there is an adverse variance of 1,000 hours which costs £4 per hour (note this is both fixed and variable overhead in effect being wasted through operating at below expected efficiency). Relating this adverse £4,000 variance to the other overhead variances we get: —

	£
Standard Cost of Overheads for 12,000 Actual Superwidgits produced $\times$ £8 =	96,000
Efficiency Variance — adverse	4,000
Standard Overhead recovered at Actual Level of Activity	100,000
Budget Variance — adverse	1,500
	101,500
Volume Variance — favourable	12,500
Actual level of Manufacturing Overhead	89,000

A Comprehensive Example

The data set out below refers to a cost centre for a particular period of time:

Budget

Variable Overheads (extract)

	Output		Cost
in units	in standard hours		£
9,800	49,000		98,000
9,900	49,500		99,000
10,000	50,000		100,000
10,100	50,500		101,000
10,200	51,000		102,000

Fixed overheads 150,000

Budgeted volume of production 10,000 units

Standard Labour Hours/Unit = 5

Actual

Variable overhead	£104,000
Fixed overhead	£160,000
Direct labour hours worked	49,000 hours
Units of production	9,900 units

9,900 units of production is the equivalent of 9,900 × 5 = 49,500 standard direct labour hours.

Before making the variance calculations it will be helpful to make some observations on the data given. The flexible budget shows that each unit of production has a standard variable overhead cost of £10. Alternatively, this can be expressed as £10 ÷ 5 = £2 per standard hour of labour. It should not be assumed that this rate of £2 would also apply to levels of production outside the range shown. These may well be step costs, such as additional supervision, which would alter the standard variable overhead rate at higher levels of output.

The fixed costs are thought likely to remain fixed provided the range of output does not extend too far above or below the budgeted volume of production. The fixed standard rate is £150,000 ÷ 50,000 = £3 per standard hour of labour, or £150,000 ÷ 10,000 = £15 per unit.

The Standard Unit Cost for Overhead is thus £10 + £15 = £25 per unit and £2 + £3 = £5 per labour hour.

This budgeted volume of production is likely to be the level of output thought of as being normal and acceptable in the long run. It is frequently referred to as the normal volume of production.

Calculation of variances

Firstly it is helpful to calculate the net variance which is to be analysed. This is developed from the standard cost of the actual units produced: —

Standard Cost of Actual Production 9,900 × £25 =	£247,500
Actual Overhead Costs Total	£264,000
Total Variance —	Adverse 16,500

This is broken down into: —

Efficiency Variance

Actual Units Produced 9,900 × 5 hours =	49,500	(standard labour hours)
Actual labour Hours	49,000	

Labour Hours Saved	500		
Efficiency variance at the overhead rate per labour hour £5		Favourable	2,500

Budget Variance

Budgeted Overheads at Actual Labour Hours worked of 49,000 —	Variable	98,000		
	Fixed	150,000		248,000
Actual Overheads				264,000
Budget Variance —			Adverse	16,000

Volume Variance

Budgeted Recovery of Fixed Overheads at standard activity 50,000 hrs × £3		150,000
Actual Recovery of Fixed Overheads at actual activity 49,000 hrs × £3		147,000
Volume Variance —	Adverse	3,000

Summary of Variances

		£
Efficiency	Favourable	2,500
Budget	Adverse	16,000
Volume	Adverse	3,000
	Net Adverse	16,500

Reconciliation of Standard and Actual Cost

Standard Cost of Actual Production 9,900 units × £25	247,500
Efficiency Variance — favourable	2,500
Budgeted Level of Overhead Cost on Actual Labour Hours at Standard 49,000 × £5	245,000
Budget Variance — adverse	16,000
	261,000
Volume Variance — adverse	3,000
Actual Cost of Overheads	264,000

Variances and Management Action

The calculation of variances and their explanation to managers is of no value unless the information so revealed is put to use in making decisions which changes subsequent activities. The question then arises as to whether every variance needs some form of action. It is not possible to be dogmatic here, it really does depend on circumstances. With some variance a fairly large variance may be fairly insignificant, whereas with others even a small amount may call for urgent action.

There is no doubt that variance calculations of the right type, transmitted to the right people at the right time, and which have an effect upon subsequent operations, can be of immense use. On the other hand much of the effort put into variance calculation in many firms just goes to waste, as managers do not act on the information. This is very often because a poor "selling" job has been done by the accounting staff to the managers concerned, in that they have not either been able to convince the manager that variance analysis is worthwhile, or possibly that the information provided is not really what the managers requires to enable him to tackle his job properly.

Assignment Exercises

Assignment Exercises followed by the letter x do NOT have answers shown at the back of the book.

15.1   Calculate the overhead variances from the following data.

   (a)   Budgeted for £6,000 variable overhead and 1,000 machine hours.

           Actual overhead   £5,840

           Actual machine hours   1,000

   (b)   Budgeted for £20,000 variable overhead and 5,000 machine hours.

           Actual overhead   £21,230

           Actual machine hours   5,000

   (c)   Budgeted for £12,000 Fixed overhead and the actual overhead is found to be £11,770.

   (d)   Budgeted for £40,000 Fixed overhead and the actual overhead is found to be £41,390.

   (e)   Budgeted production of 2,000 units in 8,000 hours. Standard variable overhead rate is £3 per hour.

         In fact 2,000 units are produced in 7,940 hours.

   (f)   Budgeted production of 5,000 units in 15,000 hours. Standard variable overhead rate is £4 per hour.

         In fact 4,860 units are produced in 15,000 hours.

15.2 Calculate the overhead variances in the following cases:

(a) Budgeted for £37,000 fixed overhead. The actual fixed overhead turns out to be £36,420.

(b) Budgeted for production of 500 units in 250 hours. The variable overhead rate is £6 per hour. In fact 500 units are produced in 242 hours.

(c) Budgeted for £18,000 variable overhead and 9,000 machine hours. Actual overhead is £18,000 and actual machine hours 8,820.

(d) Budgeted for £9,000 variable overhead and 3,000 machine hours. Actual overhead is £8,790 and actual machine hours 3,000.

(e) Budgeted for £120,000 fixed overhead. The actual fixed overhead turns out to be £129,470.

(f) Budgeted for production of 10,000 units in 30,000 hours. Standard variable overhead rate is £8 an hour. In fact 9,880 units are produced in 30,000 hours.

15.3 Calculate the following overhead variances:

(a) Budgeted fixed overhead is £30,000 and budgeted hours 10,000. Actual fixed overhead turns out to be £30,000 but actual hours were 10,320.

(b) Budgeted fixed overhead is £40,000 and budgeted hours 20,000. Actual overhead turns out to be £39,640 and actual hours worked 20,000.

(c) Budgeted fixed overhead is £5,000 and budgeted hours 10,000. Actual overhead turn out to be £5,000, but the actual hours are 9,600.

(d) Budgeted fixed overhead is £60,000 and budgeted hours 15,000. Actual fixed overhead turns out to be £62,390 and actual hours 15,000.

15.4x You are required to calculate the overhead variances of Joseph Ltd. The budget is prepared as:

(a) Total budgeted variable overhead £400,000.

(b) Total budgeted fixed overhead £160,000.

(c) Budgeted volume of production 80,000 direct labour hours for 40,000 units.

The actual results turn out to be:

(d) Actual variable overhead £403,600.

(e) Actual fixed overhead £157,200.

(f) Actual volume 78,500 direct labour hours which resulted in 42,000 units of production.

15.5x You are required to calculate the overhead variances of Raymond Ltd. The budget is prepared as:

(a) Total budgeted variable overhead £100,000.

(b) Total budgeted fixed overhead £125,000.

(c) Budgeted volume of production 50,000 direct labour hours of 250,000 units.

The actual results turn out to be:

(d) Actual variable overhead £96,500.

(e) Actual fixed overhead £129,400.

(f) Actual volume 52,000 direct labour hours which resulted in 244,000 units.

15.6x You are required to calculate the overhead variances of Edward Ltd. The budget is prepared as:

(a) Total budgeted variable overhead £500,000.

(b) Total budgeted fixed overhead £200,000.

(c) Budgeted volume of production 200,000 direct labour hours or 100,000 units.

The actual results turn out to be:

(d) Actual variable overhead £508,000.

(e) Actual fixed overhead £211,600.

(f) Actual volume 196,000 hours which resulted in 92,000 units of production.

Chapter Sixteen

Introduction to Variance Analysis IV

Sales Variances

The analysis of the difference between budgeted sales levels and actual levels can have an important bearing on the understanding of results. The main factors which are important in analysing sales are

(*a*) selling price variances

(*b*) volume variances

(*c*) mix variances.

The selling price variance measures the overall profit difference caused by budgeted unit selling price and actual unit selling price being different. If the budget was to sell 100 widgits at £5 each and the actual sales were 100 widgits of £4.50 each, there will be a profit reduction of £50 due to the adverse selling price variance of 50p per unit on the 100 units sold.

The Volume Variances in Sales will be measured in terms of the difference in the total quantity being sold between budget and actual. The impact of changes in volume of sales on profit can only be measured if we know the profitability of the sales. This will be dealt with at gross profit level. Thus if the budget is to sell 100 widgits with a unit gross margin of £2 and the actual sales achieved are only 90 widgits then there is an adverse variance of 10 units at the margin of £2 which represents a loss of profit of £20. If several products are being sold the variance will be worked on total units actually sold in the proportion originally budgeted.

Example

Product	Budget Sales Units	%	Budget Gross Margin £	Total Budget Margin £	Actual Sales Units	Actual Sales in Budget %
X	200	33.3	1	200	250	240
Y	200	33.3	1.50	300	190	240
Z	200	33.3	3.50	700	280	240
	600	100.0		1,200	720	720

The Volume Variance is calculated by Company Actual Sales in budget percentage mix with the original budget at budget margins: –

Product	Budget Sales Units	Actual Sales in Budget % Units	Variance Units	Budget Margin £	Volume Variances
X	200	240	40	1.00	40.00
Y	200	240	40	1.50	60.00
Z	200	240	40	3.50	140.00
	600	720	120		240.00

The Mix Variance arises where more than one product is being sold and the different products have differing profit margins. If the proportions in which the actual sales of the products varies from budget then the overall profit will vary as a consequence.

In the example on volume variance the original budget was compared with actual sales split in the budget mix. For the mix variance these figures of actual sales in budget mix are compared with the actual sales and the differences evaluated at the budgeted gross profit margin.

	Actual Sales Budget % Units	Actual Sales Units	Variance Units	Budget Gross Margin £	Mix Variance
X	240	250	+ 10	1.00	+ £10
Y	240	190	− 50	1.50	− £75
Z	240	280	+ 40	3.50	+£140
	720	720	−		+ £75.0

The difference in mix between budget and actual has increased profit by £75 due to the influence of more sales of product Z i.e. there is a favourable mix variance of £75.

Example

Product	%	Units	Budget Unit Selling Price £	Budget Unit Gross Profit £	Budget Total Profit £	Units	Actual Unit Selling Price £	Actual Unit Gross Profit £	Actual Total Profit £
A	16.7	100	20	5	500	90	21	6	540
B	33.3	200	25	10	2,000	220	24	9	1,980
C	50	300	10	2	600	350	10	2	700
	100	600			3,100	660			3,220

Total Variance = Actual Profit   3,220
       Budget Profit   3,100

       Favourable Variance   120

Firstly eliminate the price variance using the actual units sold as the basis.

	Actual Units Sold	Budget Price	Actual Price	Unit Variance	Total Price Variance
	1	2	3	$3 - 2 = 4$	$1 \times 4 = 5$
		£	£	£	£
A	90	20	21	+ 1	+ 90
B	220	25	24	− 1	− 220
C	350	10	10	−	−
				Adverse Price Variance	. − 130

Secondly eliminate the volume variance using the unit budgeted gross profit to evaluate the variance.

	Actual Units Sold	Actual Units in Budget %	Budget Units Sold	Variance in Units	Budget Unit Gross Profit	Total Value Variance
	1	2	3	$2 - 3 = 4$	5	$4 \times 5 = 6$
					£	£
A	90	110	100	+ 10	5	+ 50
B	220	220	200	+ 20	10	+ 200
C	350	330	300	+ 30	2	+ 60
	660	660	600	+ 60		+ 310
				Favourable Volume Variance		

Finally eliminate the mix variance. This is done by comparing the actual total units sold in the mix as originally budgeted with the actual sales.

	Budget %	Actual Total Sales Split in Budget %	Actual Sales Units	Difference $3 - 2 = 4$ Units	Budget Unit Gross Profit	Mix Variance
	1	2	3		5	$4 \times 5 = 6$
					£	
A	16.7	110	90	− 20	5	− 100
B	33.3	220	220	−	10	−
C	50.0	330	350	+ 20	2	+ 40
		660	660			
			Adverse Mix Variance			− 60

Summary of Variance

Adverse Price Variance		− 130
Favourable Volume Variance		+ 310
Adverse Mix Variance		− 60
Favourable total Sales Variance		+ 120

The Gross Profit Margin may change for reasons other than changes in Sales — for example if the cost of materials varies from budgets or wage rates change. This type of variance has however already been dealt with under Material and Labour Variances.

Assignment Exercises

Assignment exercises followed by the letter x do NOT have answers shown at the back of the book.

16.1 The Grange Company had the following results for the year to 31 March 19-1. A single product — a toggle was made by the Company.

	Budget	Actual
Sales in units	125,000	150,000
Sales in £	312,500	356,250

The Standard cost of manufacturing each unit was £1.50.

What are the price and volume variances on sales in 19-1.

16.2x Corporec PLC manufactures a detergent in one of its plants. The information for the year to 30 September 19-2 was as follows: —

	Budget	Actual
Sales in gallons	180,000	170,000
Sales in £	540,000	527,000

The Standard Cost of manufacturing a gallon was £2.

Calculate the price and volume variances for 19-2.

16.3 The following data was collected for Molton Ltd. for the year ended 31 March 19-3.

Product	Budget Selling Price	Budget Sales Units	%	Budget Gross Profit per Unit	Budget Gross Profit Total	Actual Selling Price	Actual Sales Units	%	Actual Gross Profit per Unit	Actual Gross Profit Total
	£			£	£	£			£	£
M	5	800	25	1.00	800	5.10	840	30	0.90	756
N	8	1,600	50	1.50	2,400	7.90	1,680	60	1.40	2,352
P	7	800	25	1.20	960	7.30	280	10	1.20	336
		3,200	100		4,160		2,800	100		3,444

Calculate price, volume and mix variances for 19-3.

16.4x The following information relates to Burton Company for the year to 30 June 19-6.

Product	Budget Units	Sales %	Budget Selling Price Unit	Budget Gross Profit per Unit	Actual Units	Sales %	Actual Unit Selling Price	Actual Unit Gross Profit
			£	£			£	£
A	400	14.3	30	5	500	20.8	29	4
B	600	21.4	25	4	400	16.7	27	5
C	1,800	64.3	40	10	1,500	62.5	39	9
	2,800	100.0			2,400	100.0		

Calculate price, volume and mix variances for 19-6.

Chapter Seventeen

Introduction to Break-Even Analysis: Part I

The level of activity achieved by a firm is of paramount importance in determining whether the firm is making a profit or loss, and the size of such profits or losses. Let us take an example to which the answer is obvious. If a firm has fixed costs of £10,000 and its total revenue is £8,000, then, no matter how much the variable costs are, the firm is bound to make a loss. A firm has to cover both its fixed costs + its variable costs before it can make a profit. With very low revenue, as in the case already stated, a loss would be bound to be incurred.

There is, therefore, a great deal of interest in exactly how much revenue (i.e. sales) has to be earned before a profit can be made. If revenue is below fixed costs then a loss will be incurred: if revenue is below fixed costs + variable costs then a loss will still be incurred. Where revenue is greater than fixed costs + variable costs then a profit will have been made. The question then arises — at what point does the firm stop incurring a loss and with the next unit of revenue it will make a profit, i.e. at what point does the firm break-even or make neither a profit nor a loss?

Fixed costs stay unchanged over stated ranges in the volume of production, but variable costs are those that change with volumes in production. As revenue increases so do variable costs, so that the only item that remains unchanged is that of fixed costs. Let us look at an example of a firm showing the changing costs and revenue over differing volumes of production.

Apollo Ltd. has fixed costs of £5,000. The variable costs are £2 per unit. The revenue (selling price) is £3 per unit. Looking at production in stages of 1,000 units we can see that the figures emerge as in Exhibit 17.1.

Exhibit 17.1

No. of Units	Fixed Cost £	Variable Cost £	Total Cost: Variable + Fixed £	Revenue (Sales) £	Profit £	Loss £
0	5,000	Nil	5,000	Nil		5,000
1,000	5,000	2,000	7,000	3,000		4,000
2,000	5,000	4,000	9,000	6,000		3,000
3,000	5,000	6,000	11,000	9,000		2,000
4,000	5,000	8,000	13,000	12,000		1,000
5,000	5,000	10,000	15,000	15,000	Nil	Nil
6,000	5,000	12,000	17,000	18,000	1,000	
7,000	5,000	14,000	19,000	21,000	2,000	
8,000	5,000	16,000	21,000	24,000	3,000	
9,000	5,000	18,000	23,000	27,000	4,000	

With activity of 5,000 units the firm will break-even, it will make neither a profit not a loss. Above that the firm moves into profit, below that the firm would never make a profit.

We could have calculated the break-even point without drawing up a schedule of costs etc. as in Exhibit 17.1. Instead we could have said that for one unit the revenue is £3 and the variable cost is £2, so that the remainder of £1 is the amount out of which the fixed costs have to come and anything left over would be profit. The £1 is thus the "contribution" towards fixed costs and profit. Now if the contribution was only just enough to cover fixed costs then there would be no profit, but neither would there be any loss. There are £5,000 fixed costs, so that with a contribution of £1 per unit there would have to be 5,000 units to provide a contribution of £5,000 to cover fixed costs. It could be stated as:

$$\text{Break-even Point} = \frac{\text{Fixed Costs}}{\text{Selling price per unit} - \text{Variable Costs per unit}}$$

i.e. in the case of Apollo Ltd. $\dfrac{£5,000}{£3 - £2} = \dfrac{5,000}{1} = 5,000$ units.

The Break-Even Chart

The information given in Exhibit 17.1 can also be shown in the form of a chart. Many people seem to grasp the idea of break-even analysis rather more easily when they see it in chart form. This is particularly true of people who are not used to dealing with accounting information. We will, therefore, plot the figures from Exhibit 17.1 on a chart which is shown as Exhibit 17.2.

The use of the chart can now be looked at. It would be extremely useful if you could draw the chart as shown in Exhibit 17.2 on a piece of graph paper. The larger the scale that you use the easier it will be to take accurate reading. Plot the lines from the figures as shown in Exhibit 17.1.

To find the break-even point in terms of units of product, draw a line straight down from the break-even point so that it meets the base line at right-angles. This is shown in Exhibit 17.3 as line A, which when read off on the base line gives units of products and Sales as 5,000 units. Now draw a line direct to the vertical £'s line so that it meets that at a right-angle. This is line B and shows £15,000. This means that according to the chart the break-even point is shown at 5,000 units where both costs and revenue are equal at £15,000. This is naturally the same answer as given by ordinary means in Exhibit 17.1.

As production and sales goes above 5,000 units then the firm makes profits. When production and sales is above 5,000 units then the difference represents the "safety margin" as this is the number of units in excess of the break-even point, below which the firm would incur losses.

Look at the chart again, and without consulting the book attempt to answer the following; answer by taking readings off your chart:

(i) What would the total costs of the firm be at (a) 2,000 units, (b) 7,000 units, (c) 8,500 units.

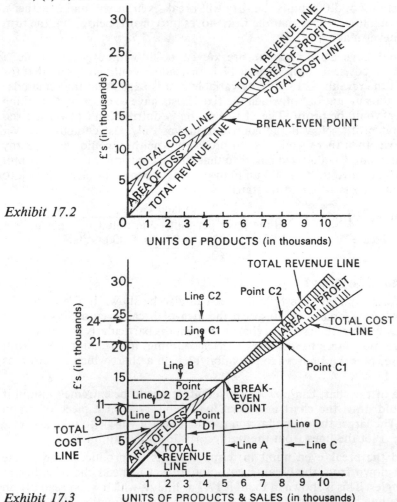

Exhibit 17.2

Exhibit 17.3

(Remember: take a line up from the product line for the figure needed, then from where the cost line is bisected draw a line to the £'s line to meet it at right angles.)

(ii) What is the revenue for (a) 3,000 units, (b) 6,000 units, (c) 7,500 units.

Before proceeding further now look at the answers which are shown at the end of this chapter.

Now we will try to find the amount of profit or loss at various levels by looking at the chart in Exhibit 17.3. First let us calculate the profit made if 8,000 units are going to be made and sold. Draw a line up from the product line at right angles (shown as line C) until it bisects both the Total Cost line and the Total Revenue line, the points of intersection being shown as C1 for the Total Cost line and C2 for the Total Revenue line. Read off the amounts in £'s by taking lines across to the £'s vertical line until they meet it at right angles. These are shown as lines C1 and C2. The line from C1 will give a reading of £21,000 and from C2 of £24,000. As the Total Revenue exceeds the Total Costs there is a profit, and in this case the profit is £3,000. If we now try for 3,000 units showing the line drawn up from the product line will be at point D1 and of the Total Cost line as D2. Reading off to the £'s line D1 shows as £9,000 whilst D2 shows as £11,000. In this case the Total Cost exceeds the Total Revenue by £2,000 and there is, therefore, a loss of £2,000.

Before you proceed further, attempt to find from your own chart the profit or loss recorded at (i) 1,000 units, (ii) 4,000 units, (iii) 6,500 units and (iv) 8,500 units.

The answers can be checked by looking at the end of this chapter.

Answers

(i) (a) £9,000 (b) £19,000 (c) £22,000
(ii) (a) £9,000 (b) £18,000 (c) £22,500
(i) Loss £4,000 (ii) Loss £1,000
(iii) Profit £1,500 (iv) Profit £3,500

Assignment Exercises

Assignment Exercises followed by the letter x do NOT have answers shown at the back of the book.

17.1x Hedges Ltd. has fixed costs of £8,000. The variable costs are £4 per unit. The revenue (selling price) is £6 per unit. You are required (i) to draft a schedule as follows filling in the columns (a) to (f) for each stage of 1,000 units up to 10,000 units.

No. of units	*(a)* Fixed Cost £	*(b)* Variable Cost £	*(c)* Total Cost £	*(d)* Revenue £	*(e)* Profit £	*(f)* Loss £
0						
1,000						
2,000						
3,000						
4,000						
5,000						
6,000						
7,000						
8,000						
9,000						
10,000						

(ii) You are also required to draw a break-even chart from the data in this schedule. Draw it carefully to scale on a piece of graph paper. Retain your answer, you will need it for some questions which follow later.

17.2x Cover up the schedule you constructed as your answer to 17.1(i) and look instead at the break-even chart constructed as the answer to 17.1(ii). Answer the following:

(a) What are the total costs at production levels of (i) 4,000 units, (ii) 7,000 units, (iii) 9,000 units, (iv) 5,500 units.

(b) What is the total revenue at (i) 3,000 units, (ii) 8,000 units, (iii) 5,500 units.

17.3x Look at your schedule in answer to 17.1(i) and answer the following:

(a) What are the total costs at production levels of (i) 4,000 units, (ii) 7,000 units, (iii) 9,000 units, (iv) 5,500 units — you will have to deduce this amount as it is not shown as a figure on the schedule.

(b) What is the total revenue at (i) 3,000 units, (ii) 8,000 units, (iii) 5,500 units.

17.4x From your break-even chart per 17.1(ii) calculate the profit or loss that will be made at levels of (i) 3,000 units, (ii) 10,000 units, (iii) 4,000 units, (iv) 7,000 units, (v) 8,500 units.

17.5x From the schedule in 17.1(i) calculate the profit or loss that would be made at levels of (i) 3,000 units, (ii) 10,000 units, (iii) 4,000 units, (iv) 7,000 units, (v) 8,500 units (this last figure will have to be deduced as it is not a figure on the schedule).

17.6x Carlos Ltd. has fixed costs of £6,000 and variable costs of £6 per unit. Revenue is £7 per unit. (i) You are required to draw up a schedule as follows, filling in the columns (a) to (f) for each stage of 1,000 units of production up to 10,000 units.

No. of units	(a) Fixed Cost £	(b) Variable Cost £	(c) Total Cost £	(d) Revenue £	(e) Profit £	(f) Loss £
0						
1,000						
2,000						
3,000						
4,000						
5,000						
6,000						
7,000						
8,000						
9,000						
10,000						

(ii) You are required to draw a break-even chart from the data in this schedule. Draw it carefully on a piece of graph paper. Retain your answer, you will need it for some questions which follow later.

17.7x Cover up the schedule you constructed as your answer to 17.6(i) and look instead at the answer to 17.6(ii). Answer the following:

(a) What are the total costs at production levels of (i) 3,000 units, (ii) 5,000 units, (iii) 8,000 units, (iv) 9,500 units.

(b) What is the total revenue at (i) 2,000 units, (ii) 7,000 units, (iii) 8,500 units.

17.8x Look at your schedule in answer to 17.6(i) and answer the following:

(a) What are the total costs at levels of (i) 3,000 units, (ii) 5,000 units, (iii) 8,000 units, (iv) 9,500 units.

(b) What is the total revenue at (i) 2,000 units, (ii) 7,000 units, (iii) 8,500 units — you will have to deduce this amount as it is not shown as a figure on the schedule.

17.9x From your break-even chart per 17.6(ii) calculate the profit or loss that will be made at levels of (i) 4,000 units, (ii) 6,000 units, (iii) 7,500 units, (iv) 9,000 units.

17.10x From the schedule in 17.6(i) calculate the profit or loss that would be made at levels of (i) 4,000 units, (ii) 6,000 units, (iii) 7,500 units, (iv) 8,000 units.

17.11 Carol Ltd. has fixed costs of £20,000. Variable costs are £8 per unit, and Revenue £12 per unit.

(a) What are the total costs at production levels of:
(i) 3,000 units, (ii) 5,000 units, (iii) 7,000 units.

(b) Calculate the profit or loss that would be made at levels of
(i) 4,000 units, (ii) 6,000 units, (iii) 9,000 units, (iv) 7,500 units.

(c) At what level would the firm break even?

17.12 Wilkes Ltd. has fixed costs of £150,000. Variable costs are £20 per unit, and revenue £26 per unit.

(a) What are the total costs at production levels of:
(i) 15,000 units, (ii) 22,000 units, (iii) 44,000 units.

(b) Calculate the profit or loss that would be made at levels of:
(i) 20,000 units, (ii) 29,000 units, (iii) 38,000 units, (iv) 48,000 units.

(c) At what level would the firm break even?

Chapter Eighteen

Introduction to Break-Even Analysis: Part II

Changes and Break-Even Charts

The effect of changes on profits can easily be shown by means of drawing fresh lines on the chart to show the changes, or intended changes, in the circumstances of the firm. Let us first of all consider what factors can bring about a change in the profits of a firm. These are:

(a) The selling price per unit could be increased (or decreased).

(b) A possible decrease (or increase) in fixed costs.

(c) A possible decrease (or increase) in variable costs per unit.

(d) Increase the volume of production and sales.

We will investigate these by starting with the same basic information for a firm and then seeing what would happen if each of the changes (a) to (d) were to happen.

The basic information, before suggested changes, is as follows:

			Total Costs:			
No. of Units	Fixed Cost	Variable Cost	Variable + Fixed	Revenue (Sales)	Profit	Loss
	£	£	£	£	£	£
100	2,000	400	2,400	900		1,500
200	2,000	800	2,800	1,800		1,000
300	2,000	1,200	3,200	2,700		500
400	2,000	1,600	3,600	3,600	Nil	Nil
500	2,000	2,000	4,000	4,500	500	
600	2,000	2,400	4,400	5,400	1,000	
700	2,000	2,800	4,800	6,300	1,500	
800	2,000	3,200	5,200	7,200	2,000	
900	2,000	3,600	5,600	8,100	2,500	

The above information shows that variable costs are £4 per unit and selling price £9 per unit. We can draw a chart to incorporate this information before considering the changes being contemplated. This is shown as Exhibit 18.1 on the next page.

(a) Increase Selling Price

Taking a copy of the old chart as a base we can now draw an extra line on it to represent an increase in selling price. Let us suppose that the selling price could be increased by £2 per unit. This can now be shown on a Break-Even chart, see Exhibit 18.2. The line shown as "New Total Revenue" could then be added. This would mean that the break-even point would change as the increased revenue would mean that costs were covered sooner. The dotted area shows the reduction in the loss area that would be incurred at the same volume of sales, whilst the shaded area shows the increase in profit at the various volumes of sales.

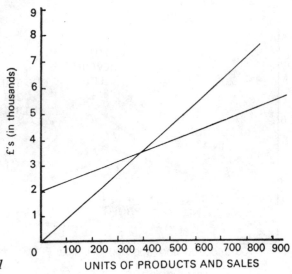

Exhibit 18.1

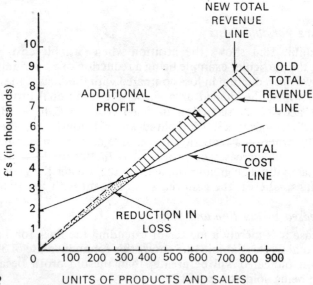

Exhibit 18.2

150

(b) Reduce Fixed Costs

Again taking a copy of the old chart we can now draw extra lines etc. on it, see Exhibit 18.3. The reduction of £800 in fixed costs results in a new line being drawn for New Total Costs. The reduction in loss if sales were at a low volume is represented by the dotted area whilst the shaded area shows the additional profit at various volumes of activity. The change in profit or loss will be constant at £800 over these volumes.

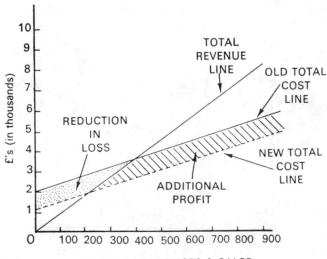

Exhibit 18.3 UNITS OF PRODUCTS & SALES

(c) Reduce Variable Costs

Here Exhibit 18.4 shows the position when variable costs per unit are reduced, the particular example being a reduction of £2 per unit. The dotted area shows the reduction in loss compared with the facts if the costs had not changed, whilst the shaded area shows the additional profit at different levels of activity. A reduction in fixed costs in Exhibit 18.3 showed a constant difference of £800 compared with previously over the whole range of activity, whereas a reduction in variable costs as in Exhibit 18.4 brings about different increases of profit, or reduction of loss, over the whole range of activity. The greater the activity the greater the gain with variable cost savings, whereas the gain remains constant with fixed cost savings.

(d) Increased Production and Sales

In this case it is merely a matter of extending the lines for Total Revenue and of Total Costs. Exhibit 18.5 shows this for an increase of 300 units. The new profit indicated will be greater than the old profit because all extra units are being sold at a profit.

The Limitations of Break-Even Charts

In each of the cases looked at it has been assumed that only one of the factors of variable cost, fixed cost, selling price, or volume of sales has in fact altered. Usually this is not the case. An increase in price may well reduce the number sold. There may well be an increase in fixed cost which has an effect which brings down variable costs. The changes in the various factors should, therefore, be studied simultaneously rather than separately.

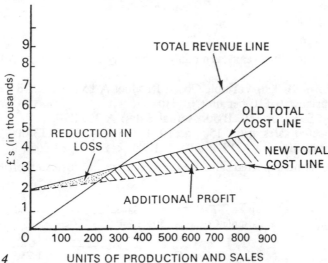

Exhibit 18.4

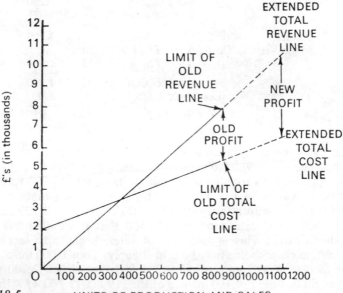

Exhibit 18.5

In addition where there is more than one product, the proportions in which the products are sold, i.e. the product mix, can have a very important bearing on costs. Suppose that there are two products, one has a large amount of fixed costs but hardly any variable costs, and the other has a large amount of variable costs but little fixed costs. Therefore if the proportions in which each are sold change very much this could mean that the costs and profit could vary tremendously, even though the total figures of sales stayed constant. An illustration of this can be seen in Exhibit 18.6.

Exhibit 18.6

In considering the break-even analysis we may expect that the following will occur.

Fixed Costs £1,000, Variable Costs: Product A £5 per unit, B £20 per unit.
Selling prices: A £10 per unit, B £30 per unit.
Expected Sales: A 150, B 50. Actual Sales: A 30, B90.
The expected sales are A 150 × £10 + B 50 × £30 = £3,000.
The actual sales are A 30 × £10 + B 90 × £30 = £3,000.

The actual and expected sales are the same, but the costs and profit are quite different.

			£
Expected:	Sales		3,000
Less Variable Costs: A 150×£5 =		750	
B 50×£20 =		1,000	1,750
	Contribution		1,250
	Less Fixed Costs		1,000
	Net Profit		£250

			£
Actual:	Sales		3,000
Less Variable Costs: A 30×£5 =		150	
B 90×£20 =		1,800	1,950
	Contribution		1,050
	Less Fixed Costs		1,000
	Net Profit		£50

Variable costs are usually taken to be in direct proportion to volume, so that 1,000 units means (say) £5,000 variable costs and therefore 2,000 units would mean £10,000 variable cost, 3,000 units equal £15,000 variable cost and so on. This is often a reasonable estimation of the situation, but may well hold true only within fairly tight limits. For instance 3,100 units could mean £16,000 costs instead of the £15,500 that it would be if a linear relationship existed. This is also true of sales, because to increase sales beyond certain points some may be sold cheaply. Thus 1,000 units might be sold for £9,000; 2,000 units sold for £18,000; but to sell 2,200 units the revenue might be only £19,100 instead of the £19,800 (2,200×£9) that might be expected if a linear relationship existed over all ranges.

It is assumed that everything produced is sold, and that stocks-in-trade remain constant. It would be difficult to do otherwise as both sales revenue and costs relate to one and the same measure of volume.

Assignment Exercises

Assignment Exercises followed by the letter x do NOT have answers shown at the back of the book.

Table A. This table consists of data on which questions 18.1 to 18.6 inclusive are based.

No. of units	Fixed Costs £	Variable Costs £	Total Costs £	Revenue £	Profit £	Loss £
0	800	nil	800	nil		800
100	800	300	1,100	500		600
200	800	600	1,400	1,000		400
300	800	900	1,700	1,500		200
400	800	1,200	2,000	2,000	nil	nil
500	800	1,500	2,300	2,500	200	
600	800	1,800	2,600	3,000	400	
700	800	2,100	2,900	3,500	600	
800	800	2,400	3,200	4,000	800	
900	800	2,700	3,500	4,500	1,000	

18.1x (a) What was the break-even point from the data in Table A.

(b) It is suggested that selling price be increased by 10 per cent. What would the new break-even point be if this was adopted and the other data remained constant?

(c) Draw a break-even chart on graph paper showing: (i) The original data in Table A, (ii) A line superimposed on it to show the selling price increase by 10 per cent per unit, (iii) Put a dotted area on the chart to represent the reduction of the loss area, (iv) Put a shaded area on the chart to represent the increase in profit at the various volumes of sales.

18.2x (This question does NOT link up with 18.1.)

Fixed costs can possibly be reduced to £500.

(a) Assuming the other data in Table A remains constant, what would the new break-even point be?

(b) Draw a break-even chart on graph paper showing: (i) The original data in Table A, (ii) The new data re-fixed costs superimposed on it, (iii) Put a shaded area to represent the additional profits that would be made, (iv) Put a dotted area to represent the reduction in the loss area.

18.3x (This question does NOT link up with 18.1 or 18.2)

Variable costs may be reduced to £2 per unit.

(a) Assuming that the other data in Table A remains constant what would the new break-even point be?

(b) Draw a break-even chart on graph paper showing: (i) The original data from Table A, (ii) The new data re variable costs superimposed on it, (iii) Put a shaded area to represent the additional profits that would be made, (iv) Put a dotted area to represent the reduction in the loss area.

18.4x (This is not linked up with 18.1, 18.2 or 18.3.)

Production and Sales may be increased to 1,100 units without any increase in fixed Costs. Assuming that the increase in variable costs and revenue per Table A is extended in the same ratio as shown throughout the table, then:

(a)   What would the profit be at the volume of 1,100 units?

(b)   Draw a break-even chart showing the original data from Table A with the new data extended on it.

18.5x (This is not linked up with 18.1; 18.2; 18.3 or 18.4.)

If variable costs are increased to £4 per unit, but all the other items in Table A remain constant then:

(a)   What would the new break-even point be?

(b)   Draw a break-even chart showing (i) The original data from Table A, (ii) The new data re variable costs superimposed on it, (iii) Put a shaded area showing the reduction in profit, (iv) Put a dotted area showing the increase in loss.

18.6x (This is not linked up with 18.1; 18.2; 18.3; 18.4 or 18.5.)

If revenue is reduced to £4.5 per unit, but all the other items in Table A remain constant, then:

(a)   What would the new break-even point be?

(b)   Draw a break-even chart showing (i) The original data from Table A, (ii) The new data about revenue superimposed on it, (iii) Put a shaded area showing the reduction in profit, (iv) Put a dotted area showing the increase in loss.

Table B. This table consists of data on which questions 18.7 to 18.10 are based.

No. of units	Fixed Costs £	Variable Costs £	Total Costs £	Revenue £	Profit £	Loss £
0	16,000	—	16,000	—		16,000
1,000	16,000	7,000	23,000	9,000		14,000
2,000	16,000	14,000	30,000	18,000		12,000
3,000	16,000	21,000	37,000	27,000		10,000
4,000	16,000	28,000	44,000	36,000		8,000
5,000	16,000	35,000	51,000	45,000		6,000
6,000	16,000	42,000	58,000	54,000		4,000
7,000	16,000	49,000	65,000	63,000		2,000
8,000	16,000	56,000	72,000	72,000	nil	nil
9,000	16,000	63,000	79,000	81,000	2,000	
10,000	16,000	70,000	86,000	90,000	4,000	

18.7x (a)   What was the break-even point from the data in Table B?

(b)   It is suggested that selling price be increased by £2 per unit. What would the new break-even point be if this was adopted and the other data remained constant?

(c)   Draw a break-even chart on graph paper showing (i) The original data in Table B, (ii) A line superimposed on it to show the selling price increased by £2 per unit, (ii) Put a dotted area on the chart to represent the reduction of the loss area, (iii) Put a shaded area on the chart to represent the increase in profit at the various volumes.

18.8   (This question does NOT link up with 18.7.)

Variable costs may be reduced to £6.5 per unit. Assuming that the other data in Table B remained constant would the new break-even point be?

18.9   (This question does not link up with 18.7 or 18.8.)

Fixed costs can be reduced to £13,000. Assuming the other data in Table B remains constant, what would the new break-even point be?

18.10   (This question does not link up with 18.7; 18.8 or 18.9.)

Production and Sales may be increased to 12,000 units. This can be accomplished without any increase in fixed costs. Other costs and revenue will move in the same ratio as previously. What would the profit be at a volume of 12,000 units.

18.11

No. of units	Fixed Costs	Variable Costs	Total Costs	Revenue	Profit	Loss
0	£	£	£	£	£	£
100						
200						
300						
400						
500						
600						
700						
800						
900						

(a)   Complete the above table if Fixed Costs are £1,400, Variable Costs £6 per unit, and Revenue £10 per unit.

(b)   What was the break even point.

(c)   What would be the new break even point in each of the following situations assuming in each case that the other data remained constant:

(i)   Selling price increased by 10 per cent.

(ii)   Selling price reduced by 20 per cent.

(iii)   Fixed costs rose to £2,000.

(iv)   Fixed costs fell to £1,200.

(v)   Variable costs rose to £8 per unit.

(vi)   Variable costs fell to £5 per unit.

Chapter Nineteen

Introduction to Pricing Policy

One thing is clear — that in the long term the revenues of a firm must exceed its costs or else the firm will go out of business. If it was a company it would have to be liquidated, if it was a firm run by a sole trader he might conceivably become bankrupt. On the other hand firms may find that in the short term costs sometimes exceed revenues, in other words the firm makes a net loss. Many firms do make losses from time to time without being forced out of business.

This being so, the way in which the prices are determined of the goods sold by the firm is of paramount importance. You may well expect that there are some definite rules which will be observed by a firm when it fixes its prices, and that these rules are followed by all businesses. Your expectations would, however, be quite wrong.

With pricing, each firm has certain features which may not apply to other firms, and this will affect its pricing policy. For instance, taking a simple illustration, let us look at the price of sugar sold by three different businesses dealing in groceries. The first business (A) is a grocer's shop in a village, it is the only grocer's shop, and the next shop at which the villagers can buy sugar is thirty miles away. The second shop (B) is also a grocer's shop in a town where there are plenty of other shops selling sugar. The last business (C) is a very large supermarket in a city, in a street where there are other large supermarkets. For a bag of sugar you might have to pay, at (A) 20p, (B) 18p, (C) 14p. The sugar may well be of exactly the same quality and be manufactured by the same firm. Firm (A) buys in small quantities, subsequently it pays a higher price than (B) or (C) for its sugar, but it knows that none of its customers want to go thirty miles for sugar. The owner does not want to lose the self-respect by over-charging anyway, so he settles for 20p. He always remembers that if he charged more, then his customers might well buy sugar in large quantities when they went to the market town to shop. Firm (B) makes hardly any profit at all out of his sugar sales, he fears that if his regular customers go elsewhere for their sugar they may well decide to buy other things as well, so that not only would he lose his sugar sales he may lose a great deal of his other sales. Supermarket (C) sells sugar at a loss — it does this quite deliberately to tempt in customers who come to buy cheap sugar, and then buy other items on which the supermarket makes reasonable profits.

If there can be such differences in the selling price of a bag of sugar sold by three firms, none of whom had in fact produced the sugar, then how much more complex is the position where firms manufacture goods and then have to fix prices. This is where study of economics helps one to get this in better perspective. The elasticity of demand must be considered as well as whether or not the firm has a monopoly, and other factors so that economics gives you a framework in which your thinking can be carried on. It is not the purpose of this book to be an economics text, but you can well see that really the thinking behind pricing relies on economic analysis. We will content ourselves with accepting that this is so, and will merely look at how accounting portrays it.

Although there may be no clearly defined rules on pricing, it can at least be said that views of pricing can be traced to one of two attitudes. These are:

1. Ascertain the cost of the product and then add something to that for profit, the sum being the selling price. This is usually known as "Full-Cost Pricing".

2. Ascertain the price at which similar products are selling, and then attempt to keep costs below that level so as to make a profit.

Many of the problems connected with full-cost pricing are those concerned with absorption costing and marginal costing. In absorption costing the whole of the fixed costs were allocated to products, whereas in marginal costing the "contribution" was found out of which fixed costs would have to come leaving the profit as the difference. The information shown in Exhibit 19.1 has been drawn up on a full-cost basis, using the following philosophy.

A considerable number of firms use the full-cost basis, very likely because it is easy to apply. This is of itself not meant as a criticism — after all the accounting that is used should be the simplest method of achieving the desired ends. There is certainly no virtue at all in using complicated methods when simple ones would be sufficient. Complicated methods means that the accounting system costs more to operate, and if the benefits are no greater than those derived from the simple system, then the accounting system should be scrapped and replaced by the simple system. Using methods just because they are simple can, however, be harmful if they give the wrong data, whereas a more complex system might give the right data. The simple system of full-cost pricing is to find the cost of direct materials and direct labour and then add relevant amounts to represent overheads and profit. The selling price is calculated in a manner similar to the following:

	£
Cost of Direct Materials and Direct Labour	10
Add Variable Manufacturing Overhead	5
Add Share of fixed manufacturing overhead	1
	16
Add Percentage (say 50 per cent in this case) for Selling Administration and Finance Costs	8
	24
Add Percentage for profit (in this case say 25 per cent)	6
	30

The percentage of 50 per cent for selling, administration, and finance costs is probably based on the figures for the previous year, where as a total for the year these figures would have approximated to 50 per cent of the total of direct materials + direct labour + variable manufacturing overhead + fixed manufacturing overhead (i.e. in this case this would have amounted to £16 for one unit). Therefore taking 50 per cent as an addition is really saying that the basic situation is similar to the previous year.

Remember that this was an example, full-cost pricing is not always done in exactly the same manner, but the example just shown is a typical one. As we have seen already in chapter seven the allocation of fixed costs is very arbitrary, yet here the selling price is based upon figures produced as a direct consequence of such arbitrary allocation.

We can now look at Exhibit 19.1 where three firms are making identical products, and for the purpose of illustration we will assume that the variable and fixed costs for each firm are the same. Different accountants use different methods of allocating fixed overhead between products, even though in each case the allocation may seem to be quite rational. There is usually no one "right" way of allocating fixed overhead, instead there are "possible" ways. In this Exhibit each of the three firms manufactures two products, and because of the different ways in which they have allocated fixed overhead they have come up with different selling prices for their products.

Exhibit 19.1

	Blue Ltd. Products		Green Ltd. Products		Red Ltd. Products	
	B	A	B	A	B	A
	£	£	£	£	£	£
Direct Labour and Materials	10	12	10	12	10	12
Variable Overhead	16	10	16	10	16	10
Marginal Cost	26	22	26	22	26	22
Fixed Overhead	6	26	22	10	14	18
Full Cost	32	48	48	32	40	40
Add Profit: 12.5 per cent of Full Cost	4	6	6	4	5	5
	36	54	54	36	45	45

In real life once the selling prices have been calculated the market prices of similar goods are looked at, and the price fixed on the basis of competition etc. In this case the price might well be adjusted to £45 for both products A and B. In this case, by a coincidence — after all the allocation of fixed overhead has been done on an arbitrary basis — Red Ltd. has managed to get its selling prices calculated to exactly the general market price.

Suppose that the firms had really placed their faith in their selling price calculations. Blue might think that as the full cost of product B was £48 then it would lose £3 for every unit sold of product B. Green Ltd. might, on the other hand, think that as the full cost of Product A is £48 then it would lose £3 on every unit sold of product A. Blue Ltd. might decide to cease production of B, and Green Ltd. decide to cease production of A. If the plans had been for each firm to sell 100 of each of products A and B, then the plans have now altered to Blue Ltd. to produce and sell 100 of A only, Green Ltd. to sell 100 of B only, and Red Ltd. to sell both 100 of A and 100 of B. The summarised profits will now be as shown in Exhibit 19.2.

Exhibit 19.2	*Blue Ltd.*	*Green Ltd.*	*Red Ltd.*
	£	£	£
Sales: 100 of A × £45	4,500		4,500
100 of B × £45		4,500	4,500
Total Revenue	4,500	4,500	9,000
Less Costs: Direct Labour and Materials			
Product A 100 × £10	1,000		1,000
Product B 100 × £12		1,200	1,200
Variable Overhead:			
Product A 100 × £16	1,600		1,600
Product B 100 × £10		1,000	1,000
Fixed Overhead: does not change because of cessation of production in Blue Ltd. and Green Ltd. (see text)	3,200	3,200	3,200
Total Costs	5,800	5,400	8,000
Net Profit			1,000
Net Loss	1,300	900	

Exhibit 19.2 shows that Blue Ltd. and Green Ltd. would incur losses if they ceased production of product B and product A respectively. Yet if they had not ceased production they would both have made profits of £1,000 as Red Ltd. has done. After all they are similar firms with exactly the same costs — the only difference was the way they allocated fixed costs. The fixed costs in each firm totalled £3,200. Blue allocated this between products as A £6: B £26: Green allocated it A £22: B £10: C allocated it A £14: B £18. With 100 units of each product this amounted to an allocation of £3,200 for each firm. Fixed overhead does not change just because of ceasing production of one type of product. The factory rent and rates will remain the same, so will the typists' salaries and other fixed costs.

The question, therefore, arises as to which figure is relevant in deciding whether to continue the manufacture of a certain product or to cease production. The answer to this is that the marginal cost figure is the one that is relevant. If this is less than the selling price, then the difference will be the contribution towards fixed overhead, thus reducing the burden of the fixed overhead on the other products. This can be shown as:

	Product A	Product B
	£	£
Selling Price	45	45
Marginal Cost	26	22
Contribution towards fixed overhead and profit	£19	£23

Just let us test this out with another firm in Exhibit 19.3 which has the following cost and selling information. The firm would sell 100 of each product it manufactured. Total fixed overhead is £4,800 − allocated A £5 (100), B £7 (100), C £11 (100), D £15 (100), E £10 (100), i.e. £4,800 total.

Exhibit 19.3

Violet Ltd.

Products	A	B	C	D	E
Cost: (per unit)	£	£	£	£	£
Direct Labour and Materials	8	9	16	25	11
Variable overhead	7	8	10	13	14
Marginal Cost	15	17	26	38	25
Fixed Overhead	5	7	11	15	10
Full Cost	20	24	37	53	35
Selling Price per unit	30	21	31	80	20

On the full-cost basis only A and D would seem to be profitable. Should therefore, production of B, C and E be discontinued? According to what has been said production should cease only when the selling price is less than marginal cost. In Exhibit 19.4 we will see if following our own advice brings about the greatest profit. We will also see at the same time what would have happened if production was not cut at all.

Exhibit 19.4

	(1) *Following full-cost pricing, cease producing B, C and E*	(2) *Using marginal costing, cease producing E only*	(3) *Ignore costing altogether and produce all items*
	£	£	£
Sales: A 100×£30	3,000	3,000	3,000
B 100×£21		2,100	2,100
C 100×£31		3,100	3,100
D 100×£80	8,000	8,000	8,000
E 100×£20			2,000
Total Revenue:	11,000	16,200	18,200
Less Costs:			
Direct Labour and Materials: 100×cost per product	(£33) 3,300	(£58) 5,800	(£69) 6,900
Variable Cost: 100×cost per product	(£20) 2,000	(£38) 3,800	(£52) 5,200
Fixed Overhead (does not change)	4,800	4,800	4,800
Total Costs	10,100	14,400	16,900
Net Profit	£900	£1,800	£1,300

The £'s figures in brackets show the cost of each product, e.g. in (1) the Direct labour and Materials are A £8 + D £25 = £33.

As you can see in Exhibit 19.4 it would be just as well if we followed our own advice. This would give a profit of £1,800 compared with £900 using the full-cost method or £1,300 if we disregarded costing altogether. Sometimes the full-cost method will give far better results than ignoring costing altogether, but this case shows that in fact the wrong kind of costing can be even worse than having no costing at all! The marginal costing approach will, however, give the better answer in this sort of situation.

There is, however, a danger in thinking that if the marginal cost of each product is less than the selling price then activities will be profitable. This is certainly not so, and full consideration must be given to the fact that the total contributions from all the products should exceed the fixed costs otherwise the firm will incur an overall loss. Different volumes of activity will affect this. Let us look in Exhibit 19.5 with a two product firm making products A and B given different volumes of activity. Product A has a marginal cost of £10 and a selling price of £14. Product B has a marginal cost of £6 and a selling price of £8. Fixed costs are £1,400.

Exhibit 19.5   *Profit, or loss, at different volumes of activity*

	A	B	A	B	A	B	A	B
Units sold	100	100	200	200	300	300	400	400
	£	£	£	£	£	£	£	£
Contribution (Selling Price less Marginal cost) A £4 per unit, B £2 per unit	400	200	800	400	1,200	600	1,600	800
Total Contributions		600		1,200		1,800		2,400
Fixed Overhead		1,400		1,400		1,400		1,400
Net Loss		£800		£200				
Net Profit						£400		£1,000

Here the selling price always exceeds marginal cost, but if activity is low the firm will incur a loss.

The main lessons to be learned about selling prices is that:

(a) Selling prices should exceed marginal costs.

(b) In the long term the total contributions at given volumes must exceed the fixed costs of the firm.

Maximisation of Total Contribution

It should be stressed that it is the maximisation of the total contribution from a product that is important. In this the volumes of activity cannot be disregarded. Suppose for instance that a firm could only manufacture two products in future, whereas to date it had manufactured three. It may well be that per unit the contribution may well have been (A) £10, (B) £8 and (C) £6. If a decision was made on this basis only then (C) would be discontinued. However, if the volumes were (A) 20, (B) 15 and (C) 30, then the total contributions would be (A) $20 \times £10 = £200$: (B) $15 \times £8 = £120$: (C) $30 \times £6 = £180$. As (B) has the lowest *total* contribution it should be (B) that is discontinued, not (C).

162

Assignment Exercises followed by the letter x do NOT have answers shown at the back of the book.

19.1x Glasses Ltd. make four different products, Q, R, S and T. They have ascertained the cost of direct materials and direct labour and the variable overhead for each unit of product. An attempt is made to allocate the other costs in a logical manner. When this is done 10 per cent is added for profit.

The cost of direct labour and materials per unit is Q £14; R £28; S £60; T £32.

Variable overheads per unit are Q £4; R £8; S £13; T £12.

Fixed overhead of £1,900 is allocated per unit as Q £2; R £4; S £7; T £6.

You are required:

(a)   Calculate the prices at which the units would be sold by Glasses Ltd. if the full-cost system of pricing was adhered to.

(b)   What would you advise the company to do if, because of market competition, prices had to be fixed at Q £33; R £39; S £70; T £49?

(c)   Assuming production of 100 units of each item per accounting period, what would be the net profit (i) if your advice given in your answer to (b) was followed, (ii) if the firm continued to produce all of the items?

(d)   What would you advise the company to do if, because of market competition, prices had to be fixed at Q £17; R £48; S £140; T £39?

(e)   Assuming production of 100 units of each item per accounting period, what would be the net profit (i) if your advice given in your answer to (d) was followed, (ii) if the firm continued to produce all of the items.

19.2x Bottles Ltd. makes six different products, F, G, H, I, J and K. An analysis of costs ascertains the following:

Per Unit	F	G	H	I	J	K
	£	£	£	£	£	£
Direct labour and direct materials	15	17	38	49	62	114
Variable cost	6	11	10	21	22	23

Fixed costs of £11,400 are allocated per unit as F £4; G £7; H £7; I £10; J £16 and K £13.

Using full-cost pricing 20 per cent is to be added per unit for profit.

You are required to:

(a)   Calculate the prices that would be charged by Bottles Ltd. if the full-cost pricing system was adhered to.

(b)   What advice would you give the company if a survey of the market showed that the prices charged could be F £26; G £26; H £66; I £75; J £80; K £220?

(c)   Assuming production of 200 units per period of each unit manufactured what would be the profit of the firm (i) If your advice in (b) was followed, (ii) if the firm continued to produce all of the items?

(d)   Suppose that in fact the market survey had revealed instead that the prices charged could F £30; G £33; H £75; I £66; J £145 and K £130, then what would your advice have been to the company?

(e)   Assuming that production of each item manufactured was 200 units per month, then what would have been the profit (i) If your advice in (d) had been followed, (ii) if the company chose to continue manufacturing all items?

19.3   Jugs Ltd. make five different products — A, B, C, D and E. These have been costed per unit as:

Direct Materials and Direct Labour: A £16; B £19; C £38; D £44; E £23.

Variable overhead: A £11; B £17; C £23; D £14; E £9.

Fixed overhead totalling £3,600 per period is allocated per unit, on a basis of a production of 100 units of each item per period, as A £3; B £4; C £9; D £12; E £8.

When the total cost is found 10 per cent is added for profit.

You are required to:

(a)   Ascertain the selling prices of each item if the full-cost pricing system is used.

(b)   Owing to competition and the general state of the market, if prices had to be fixed at A £32; B £49; C £56; D £66; E £48; what would be your advice to the directors of Jugs Ltd?

(c)   Assuming production of 100 units per item would what be the net profit or loss (i) If your advice under (b) was adhered to by the company, (ii) If the company continued to produce all the items?

(d)   Suppose instead that the state of the market was different, and that the prices had to be fixed at A £24; B £38; C £68; D £64; E £29; what would be your advice to the directors?

(e)   Assuming production of 100 units per item, what would be the net profit or loss (i) If your advice under (d) was adhered to by the company, (ii) If the company continued to produce all the items?

19.4   Bunghole Ltd. make four different products: Cork, Plastic, Screwtop and Wedge. They have ascertained the cost of direct materials and direct labour and variable overhead which they state to be: Direct Labour and Materials: Cork £14, Plastic £5, Screwtop £37 and Wedge £23; Variable Overhead: Cork £22, Plastic £13, Screwtop £9 and Wedge £17.

The fixed expenses totalling £3,000 have been allocated between the products per unit produced as: Cork £4, Plastic £2, Screwtop £14 and Wedge £10. When this has been done a figure equal to 10 per cent of the total cost is added for profit.

You are required to:

(a)   Calculate the prices at which the products would be sold by Bunghole Ltd. if the full-cost system of pricing was adhered to.

(b)   What would you advise the company to do, if, because of competition, prices had to be fixed at: Cork £43, Plastic £16, Screwtop £58, and Wedge £59?

(c)   Assuming production and sales of 100 units of each product per period, taking the selling prices in (b) above, find what would be the net profit or loss if the firm followed your advice.

(d)   What would you advise the company to do, if because of competition prices had to be fixed at: Cork £49, Plastic £20, Screwtop £55 and Wedge £37?

(e)   Assuming production of 100 units of each item per accounting period, what would be the net profit or loss (i) if your advice given in your answer to (d) was followed, (ii) if the firm continued to produce all of the items.

Chapter Twenty

Introduction to Relevant Costs

One of the most difficult decisions facing a manager is to choose between alternative courses of action where there are a variety of complex issues involved. Usually one of the key issues he will have to face is one involving costs in which case it is important to make use of the available cost information correctly. Wrong conclusions can easily be drawn from cost information which is presented in ways that do not make clear the assumptions underlying the preparation of those costs. This was clearly seen in Chapter 19 on Pricing Policy.

For example if the estimated costs of Product X next period are:

	£
Variable Cost	10,000
Fixed Cost	20,000
Total Cost	30,000 ÷ estimated production of 15,000 units
	= £2 per unit.

Simply to state that the cost is £2 may be misleading since the decision may involve changing the number of units produced to 18,000 units and the costs would therefore be

	£
Variable Cost	12,000 (+ 20%)
Fixed Cost	20,000 (no change)
Total Cost	32,000 ÷ estimated production of 18,000 units
	= £1.78 per unit

In other words costs figures are usually only valid at certain assumed levels of production and cannot be used outside that level.

One of the hardest things to do in practice is to define the problem properly. A manager may be aware of a particular difficulty — for example a component may always cause difficulty through delayed production — but the solution may not always be obvious. The manager may think that the reason for delayed production is faulty machinery which frequently breaks down — in fact the difficulty may lay with the workforce which is inadequately trained — which is the real reason for machine breakdowns and therefore the basic problem. Not only is the definition of the real problem often difficult but also finding the full range of solutions to the problem.

Clearly considering all the possibilities to solve any problem is likely to involve too much work. Some judgement often has to be used to select the most likely winners. Very often what goes on at the present time is used as a basis for comparison with the alternatives to see if a change is worthwhile i.e. cost effective.

Having collected together the alternative courses of action that look feasible the next stage is to evaluate all the factors capable of being measured. If machinery is involved — how much will it cost to buy or rent? how much power will it use and therefore cost to operate? what will the cost of wages be? and so on. All of these costs can be totalled for each alternative to provide comparative costs of the choices.

In any set of alternatives it should not be forgotten that there are many things that cannot be expressed in quantitative and therefore cost terms. For example the attitude of employees towards new equipment may be crucial — in extreme cases they may refuse to operate it. The benefits of new equipment may be hard to evaluate because they are intangible — though nonetheless real. A new computer may speed up information flows and increase the total available sources of information — but what is this worth? Probably only a guess can be made in advance of the decision — however this type of judgement should always be made together with all the hard facts that can be collected in evidence. The cost consequences of decisions should always be considered even though they do not give the complete picture.

The use of marginal costs on decisions about pricing and whether a product line should be dropped or continued was considered in the previous chapter. Another typical example of using cost information in this way is a decision about whether a product should be manufactured internally or bought in from an outside supplier.

Example: A company currently manufactures a valve which is incorporated in another product. The valve costs are as follows:

Unit Cost

	£
Direct Material	1.50
Direct Labour — variable	2.50
Manufacturing Overheads:	
Variable	0.50
Fixed	1.50
	6.00

The fixed costs are based on a total cost estimate of £150,000 with 100,000 valves produced.

The company discovers that it could buy the valve outside for £5.00 — should it therefore discontinue manufacture?

We know that the unit variable cost is £4.50 which is below the price of £5.00 we can buy at from outside. The decision is thus not straightforward

— it would only be definite if the variable costs were more than £5.00 — when it would clearly pay as to buy in.

The question therefore is whether the 50p per unit difference between the variable cost of £4.50 and the buying price of £5 is in fact a worthwhile contribution to our fixed overheads of £150,000. Often it is useful to express the options in total cost terms rather than in unit costs: —

Producing 100,000 Units: —	£	Buying in 100,000 units	
Direct Material	150,000	Supplier	500,000
Direct Labour	250,000		
Variable Overhead	50,000		
	450,000		500,000
Fixed Overhead	150,000		?
	600,000		?

The query is how much of the Fixed Overhead will remain to be carried by the firm if manufacture is ceased and the valves bought in. If all the cost remains then the total cost of buying in would be £500,000 + £150,000 = £650,000 which is more than the costs of making ourselves. It is likely however that some element of the Fixed Overhead could be absorbed by expanding some other activity or by economy measures. If the remaining unabsorbed fixed costs fall below £100,000 then it would be worth considering the proposal to buy in.

Cost will not be the only consideration however since once manufacture is ceased the firm may lose control of essential things like quality and reliability of supply. The supplier may quickly put up his price if there is limited competition. These and other non-financial considerations may override the purely financial out-turn.

Scarce Resources

If a firm is operating in circumstances where one or more of its resources are limited — then to produce the maximum contribution the unit contribution for each product must be related to the scarce resource.

Illustration

A firm produces two products A and B. The firm can sell as many units as it can make and neither product is dependent for its market on the other. However the manufacture requires skilled labour and the firm only has 400 labour hours at its disposal. The details of the two products are as follows: —

	A £	B £
Unit Selling Price	40	20
Unit Variable Cost	36	18
Contribution per unit	4	2
Labour Hours per unit	4	1

At first glance product A with a unit contribution of £4 appears to be more attractive than B which has a unit contribution of £2. However A needs 4 hours of scarce labour whilst B only requires 1 hour. The contribution per labour hour for A is therefore £1 (£4 ÷ 4 hrs) whilst for B it is £2 (£2 ÷ 1 hr). Thus B appears better in terms of contribution per labour hour. This can also be shown in total terms as follows: −

Total
Contribution

If total hours are used to produce all A then the units produced

will be $\frac{400}{4}$ = 100 units × £4 per unit   £400

If total hours are used to produce all B then the units produced

will be $\frac{400}{1}$ = 400 units × £2 per unit   £800

The problem becomes more complex if the firm faces scarce resources in more than one input. For example if both labour and machine time are scarce then it is probably no longer possible to rank the products on the sample basis of contribution per hour since there are both labour and machine hours involved which may give different results. These problems can however be solved using linear programming techniques − but are not developed in this book.

Opportunity Costs

The real problem we are examining in evaluating decisions is to estimate the influence of the decision on resources available to the firm. Where the resources involved are variable costs like direct materials in current and continual use then the impact of the decision is usually clear − we can measure how much material is being used and what its current market price is. Where however the resource involved is in some old little used asset how do we assess its value? The only way this can be done is to assess the impact of a particular decision. For example a decision which makes use of an asset should bear the cost of the impact of the decision on the asset. If using it reduces its value because of the wear and tear or usage involved then the cost is the loss in value. The same decision may prevent the asset being sold − since it is not required for any other purpose − the cost of the decision is therefore the price that could be obtained from selling the asset.

The reasoning is: —

1) Establish the things which will be required as a consequence of your decision.

2) Determine what the business would do with the things required in 1) in the best available alternative.

3) The cost of the decision can now be assessed since it is the value of the items concerned evaluated by reference to the best alternative use in 2) (Which the business cannot undertake because of its decision).

Example

A business has in stock two raw materials which are suitable for an order enquiry it has just received. Material M of 10 tons originally cost £50 per ton. It costs £60 per ton to replace but has a scrap value if sold of only £20 per ton. Material Q of 8 tons originally cost £30 a ton. It has a replacement cost of £80 per ton and a scrap value of £5 per ton.

The order enquiry involves using 5 tons of M and 6 tons of Q. Material M is in continuous use and on use it is always replaced. Material Q is old stock left over from discontinued processes and if used would not be replaced. It is likely to be scrapped in the near future to release storage space.

Stages 1 and 2 of the decision are clearly set out above. the cost of the decision to take the order would be — for Material M the use of 5 tons at a value of £60 per ton = £300. This must be the cost of the decision since if used the material is replaced. For Material Q the decision is different because the best alternative use is scrap which has a value of £5 per ton which for 6 tons is worth £30. The replacement cost is not relevant since there is no intention to replace this item.

The value of materials implied by the order is therefore £330 and if the price is sufficient to cover this the business should consider it. Notice that the historic cost which for M is £250 (5 × £50) and for Q is £180 (6 × £30) is not relevant to the decision.

The idea of valuing a resource in terms of its alternative best use is often called opportunity costing, — a concept frequently used in economics. It of course presupposes that the decision taker knows what the best alternatives are.

Management in practice often has to take decisions with very inadequate information. Nonetheless it is better to try to approximate through the correct approach than not to attempt an assessment of this type at all — since a purely historic cost approach is likely to be very misleading.

Assignment Exercises

20.1 Thomas Machines Ltd produces a part used in large assemblies in a special department. The current years' costs have been as follows: –

	£
Direct Materials	100,000
Direct Labour	60,000
Variable Overhead	55,000
Fixed Overhead	95,000
	310,000

During the year 1000 parts have been produced. A new contract for the company would involve increasing output to 1,500 parts. This could be done by introducing a work system which would increase direct labour costs by 10%. The cost control department has recently obtained a quotation from an outside supplier to supply the part for £240 each, which is considerably less than the £310 it costs Thomas Machines to manufacture. If the part was sub contracted £40,000 of fixed overhead could be removed, the balance would remain.

What would you recommend the company to do?

20.2 Zebrite Productions Company produces three products X, Y, and Z all of which use a material called Zebo which is in short supply.

Faced with prospects of further cuts in material supplies with only 1,000 lbs being available it wants to know which products to concentrate on. The products are independent of each other and have market demands well in excess of available supplies.

Product		X		Y		Z
Direct Material	lbs	£	lbs	£	lbs	£
Zebo	20	200	10	100	5	50
Direct Labour and						
Variable Overhead		50		40		30
Fixed Overhead		30		30		30
Total Unit Cost		280		170		110
Selling Price		560		340		220

20.3 For a special short term project Alexit PLC wants to use the following items: –
1. Material 105 which originally cost £5,000 but is no longer used. Its replacement cost would be £10,000 but its realisable value if sold £1,000.
2. A machine originally costing £40,000 now depreciated by £25,000 to a book value of £15,000. If not used on the project the machine would be sold for £3,000. Its replacement cost is £50,000. At what value should they be charged to the project?

20.4x The managers' of the Tenco Company are considering whether to continue the manufacture of a sub-assembly or whether to buy it in from another firm. The costs related to the annual usage of 50,000 are as follows: –

	£
Direct Material	150,000
Direct Labour	200,000
Variable Overheads	50,000
Fixed Overhead	300,000
	700,000

If the sub assembly is bought in the variable costs would be expected to reduce by 90% and the fixed costs to reduce by 20%. The quoted price for buying in is £10 per unit.

Should the sub-assembly be bought-in or continue to be manufactured by the company?

20.5x Ace Zoots Company manufactures a cutting tool assembled from one each of two components A and B. The machinery in use in the workshop can be used to make either component. The workshop currently is working at full capacity – which is determined by the machine time available. 1200 machine hours are available. The details of manufacture are as follows: –

	Machine Hours Used	Unit Variable Cost £	Unit Fixed Cost £	Total Cost £
Component A	10	50	20	70
B	20	60	60	120
Assembly Cost		100	40	140
	30	210	120	330
Selling price				500

At the present time the company manufactures 40 units which uses all the machine time (40 units × 30 hours per unit = 1200 hrs). There has been a considerable increase in demand however and the company could sell up to 120 units per annum at the existing price. It can sub-contract Component A at a cost of £80 per unit and Component B at £90 per unit.

Which course of action would you recommend?

20.6x Alberta Company operates a department producing wooden boxes for packing purposes. It is considering buying the boxes from a specialised supplier. The costs of the department which produces 10,000 boxes per annum are as follows: –

	£
Timber at cost	1,000
Nails, Wire etc. at cost	500
Rent of premises	1,500
Depreciation of machine	800
Direct Labour	5,000
Allocated Fixed Cost	2,000
	10,800

The following explanations are related to the costs of the department: –

(a) Timber is valued at the current market replacement price for the material used.

(b) Nails, wire etc represents a proportion of the original price paid two years ago for a large supply bought at a liquidation sale. It cost £5,000 and was expected to last for 10 years. Five years supply is left and this at replacement price would cost £4,500. However the current supplies left in stock if sold off would only raise £500.

(c) Rent of premises represents the rent paid on a lease obtained some years ago. The equivalent market rental for similar space is now £2,500 per annum. The company is currently looking for space to rent similar to that occupied by the box department, in order to expand another department.

(d) Depreciation of machine represents the straight line depreciation charge on a machine bought 3 years ago. It cost £8,000 and had an expected life of 10 years and nil scrap value. Its current book value is therefore £5,600 i.e. Cost of £8,000 less Aggregate Depreciation of 3 × £800 = £2,400. If the department no longer needs the machine it would be sold at an expected price of £2,000.

(e) Direct Labour is the wages of the operatives in the department. Other departments would take over any operatives if the department shut.

(f) Allocated fixed costs represent general overheads which would not reduce if the department closed.

The company could buy the boxes for 95p each from an outside supplier. This cost amounting to £9,500 appears cheaper than continuing to manufacture itself.

Should it manufacture or buy in?

Chapter Twenty One

Responsibility Accounting

The development of modern organisations employing many people involves the creation of a management structure which delegates responsibility from one manager to several lower level employees called subordinates. In its simple basic form this type of management structure forms a pyramid with lower levels of management made responsible for limited areas of activity and responding upwards to senior managers for guidance and support where it is required.

Organisation Chart for Part of an Organisation

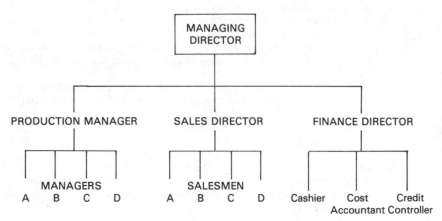

Exhibit 21.1

Exhibit 21.1 is a simplified organisation chart which shows that the Managing Director is the top level of management who delegates responsibility to three specialised directors in the areas of Production, Sales and Finance. They in turn delegate to lower levels of management. In a large organisation there can be many levels of delegation and in consequence a very complex organisation chart of relationships. The type of structure shown is called hierarchical because authority is passed down from the top to lower management levels. With the authority goes responsibility — those who are given the power implied by a particular management job are also required to account for how well they perform the job to those above them. Even the managing director will usually have to account for the whole organisation's performance to a board of directors acting for the shareholders.

Some different forms of organisation have evolved to meet the needs of different industries. For example a matrix form of relationship has been evolved in some aerospace industry organisations. The management is organised on one side by functions as in the traditional hierarchical structure i.e. a sales manager responding to a director in charge of sales. A team of people from different functions are allocated to the firms major projects each under the direction of a project director or leader. Thus the sales manager in addition to responding to his sales director will also respond to the project leader to which he is assigned.

Thus the actual way an organisation is structured will vary considerably in practice. Some will be very formal and hierarchical — others much more informal with authority being shared on a broader basis. The important thing is that in all organisations there needs to be control whatever the actual structure adopted and the basic features of control will remain the same.

Control in this context means influencing people to behave in the way you want them to, rather than in a way that they would themselves prefer. Absence of control means that everybody in the organisation would have complete autonomy — to come and go as they wished, to work hard or not at all. The extremes of absolute control where everyone behaves like a programmed machine and total anarchy where everyone does their own thing are not normally found. Most organisations have to find the right level of control which the people in the organisation respond to best. Too much control and people will lose motivation because they feel they are only cogs in a huge machine and are dehumanised. Too little control and there will be waste of resources with no proper coordination of effort.

It is always important to realise that an organisation is nothing other than a collection of people. Organisations do not think — only the people who work in them can do that. An organisation cannot do anything of itself — but will do what the most powerful person or group of people want it to do. This top management group are therefore 'the organisation' for purposes of control and making the crucial decisions about the way in which the organisation should be structured.

In the earlier chapters methods have been described of preparing accounting information to help management. The analysis of costs in order that the products or services of the organisation can be costed is clearly of great importance. Similarly the extension from historic costs into future plans which is worked in budgeting and standard costing provides key information for control. However in these chapters most of the emphasis has been on the cost of activities, output or products, rather than the cost of an individual managers area of responsibility.

In a manufacturing business a cost centre is used for collecting costs related to the job or process. This focus of cost collection will often coincide with an area of management responsibility, although not always. In addition focusing on responsibility may be the only way of controlling non-manufacturing costs such as administration and marketing.

A responsibility centre is any part of an organisation for which a manager is responsible. It may be relatively small compared to the whole organisation for example a small department employing only two people on personnel work, but on the other hand a senior manager may be responsible for a major operating division of the organisation which is a major business in its own right. Like the organisation chart the responsibility at the lower levels will be limited and at the top level will cover the whole. Appropriate ways of collecting the information for areas of responsibility will have to be developed.

The following example illustrates the difference between analysis of costs by product and by responsibility center.

Green Company Ltd. manufactures two products X and Y in its small factory. Each product is manufactured in three process departments and in addition there is a packing and distribution department, a sales department and an accounting department.

The costs are analysed in the first instance every three months in terms of each product produced. For the first quarter of 19-1 the figures were: –

Product Costs	Product X	Product Y	Total
	£	£	£
Direct Material	8,000	15,000	23,000
Direct Labour	4,000	7,000	11,000
Factory Overheads	3,000	6,000	9,000
Packing & Distribution	2,000	4,000	6,000
Selling	2,000	3,000	5,000
Accounting	1,200	2,000	3,200
	20,200	37,000	57,200
Units Produced	4,000	12,000	
Unit Cost £	5.05	3.09	

However in order to determine responsibility for the costs they are also allocated to Departments which are responsibility centres.

Responsibility Centre Costs

	Process 1 Dept.	Process 2 Dept.	Process 3 Dept.	Packing & Distribution Dept.	Selling Dept.	Accounting Dept.	Total
	£	£	£	£	£	£	£
Direct Material	9,000	4,000	10,000				23,000
Direct Labour	4,000	3,000	4,000				11,000
Indirect Labour & Salaries	2,000	3,000	1,000	3,000	3,000	2,600	14,600
Sundry Supplies	1,000	1,500	500	2,000	500	600	6,100
Transport				1,000			1,000
Travelling					1,500		1,500
	16,000	11,500	15,500	6,000	5,000	3,200	57,200

At the lower levels of management very often it is only realistic to measure the expenses of a responsibility centre. To measure the output of many departments in monetary terms is not realistic. For example in the personnel department it is straightforward to measure the salary, wages and other costs of the department but the value of the work done in interviewing potential employees, maintaining staff record cards etc. can not be accurately assessed. Responsibility centres where only the costs can be measured are called Expense Centres.

Where the responsibility centre covers a broader section of the organisation it may be possible to measure revenues as well as expenses. Here we are usually talking about an activity which can be viewed as a smaller business within the overall organisation. If we can measure both revenues and expenses then we can prepare a Profit and Loss Account to measure performance. This type of responsibility centre is called a profit centre.

An extension of the Profit Centre is also very common in large organisations where the assets employed in the Profit Centre are exclusive to it. Here the responsibility centre has not only its Profit and Loss Account but its own Balance Sheet showing the resources invested in the centre. These are known as Investment Centres. Many of the largest companies in the world break down their activities into operating divisions which are Investment Centres.

Control of Profit and Investment Centres is similar to controlling a whole business and will not be further developed in this book. Control of expense centres is important and is relevant to topics covered earlier in the book on cost centres and budgeting.

For purposes of presenting the information to the responsible managers costs are collected for each responsibility centre and presented in a format resembling that in Exhibit 21.2.

Department Cost Report for Department B Period: January

	This Month £	Budget for Month £	Year to Date £	Budget Year to Date £	Budget Variance
Direct Materials	5,000	4,800	16,000	14,400	(1,600)
Direct Labour	3,000	3,500	8,500	10,500	2,000
Supervision Cost	1,000	1,200	3,500	3,600	100
Indirect Labour	800	790	2,700	2,370	(330)
Supplies	1,200	1,100	3,400	3,300	(100)
Other Costs	900	900	2,900	2,700	(200)
Total	11,900	12,290	37,000	36,870	130

Exhibit 21.2

The information included in Exhibit 21.2 may be extended to include columns for the previous years figures where this is judged to be useful.

The important thing to determine before a manager is judged on his departments performance is the extent to which he can genuinely influence the costs for that department. Some costs he may control entirely, others may be allocated to him and not be within his power to alter. Part of the solution has already been suggested by the use of flexible budgets described in Chapter 11 since the use of a flexible budget implies that careful thought has been given to varying the figures in line with actual levels of prevailing activity. However this will not entirely solve the problem of costs allocated from outside and care must be taken not to penalise people for things over which they do not have control. Just because a cost is variable does not mean it is automatically controllable. Detailed consideration will have to be given to the facts in each responsibility centre.

Assignment Exercises

Assignment exercises followed by a letter X do NOT have answers shown at the back of the book.

21.1x Explain what is meant by a cost centre and a responsibility centre.

21.2x What is the difference between expense centres, profit centres and investment centres?

21.3x What is the significance of 'controllable costs' for management control?

Chapter Twenty Two

Interpretation of Accounting Information

Accounting information is intended to be used in a number of ways. In this chapter some of the methods which are used to interpret accounts will be explained. The following profits are reported for a business:

	19-1	19-2
	£	£
Sales	10000	20000
Cost of Goods Sold	5000	12000
Gross Profit	5000	8000
Expenses	2000	5000
Net Profit	3000	3000

The profit has remained the same but the other figures comprised in the profit calculation have changed significantly. One convenient way of looking at this difference is by expressing the figures in the Profit and Loss Account as a percentage of the sales. The result would be in this example:-

	19-1	19-2
	%	%
Sales	100	100
Cost of Goods Sold	50	60
Gross Profit	50	40
Expenses	20	25
Net Profit	30	15

In the period under review the total sales have doubled but the gross margin percentage has reduced from 50% to 40% and expenses have increased from 20% to 25%. The Net Profit which reflects these changes has thus fallen from 30% to 15%.

How can these differences have arisen? If we examine the change in Gross Profit the differences can be the result of many different influences. For example it could be due to deliberate changes in management's policy in fixing prices. In 19-1 they may have added 100% to the cost price of a good to reach the selling price, whereas in 19-2 they may have decided to become more competitive and only add ⅔ or 66·7%. Thus an item which costs £12 in both 19-1 and 19-2 would be sold for £24 in 19-1 and £20 in 19-2. Provided that the volume of sales goes up the management might think this is worthwhile. In our example it might have been responsible for sales doubling and gross profit going up by £3000.

	19-1				19-2		
	£	%			£	%	
Cost	12.00	50		Cost	12.00	60	
Margin 100%				Margin			
on cost	12.00	50		⅔ (66.7%)	8.00	40	
				on cost			
Selling Price	24.00	100			20.00	100	

The same result as management changing its pricing policy might arise if the cost of the goods being sold rises, whilst the selling price remains the same. For example if the item costing £12 and sold for £24 in 19-1 increased in Cost to £14.40 with the selling price kept at £24, the profit on sales in 19-2 would have fallen from 50% to $\dfrac{9.60}{24.00} \times \dfrac{100}{1} = 40\%$.

	19-1				19-2		
	£	%			£	%	
Cost	12.00	50		Cost	14.40	60	
+ Margin 100%	12.00	50		Margin on			
				Cost			
				⅔			
				(66.7%)	9.60	40	
Selling Price	24.00	100			24.00	100	

There may be various other reasons for the change in gross margin in relation to sales. In particular in many businesses the calculation of the Cost of Goods Sold figure depends heavily on the calculation:- Opening Stock in Trade plus Purchases less Closing Stock in Trade equals Cost of Goods Sold. Frequently the exact counting of stock in trade is difficult and may not be accurate. Let us examine and example where the effect of stock undervaluation is shown.

Example
In 19-1 1200 units are bought @ £10
     500 units are sold   @ £20.

The stock at cost price should therefore be 700 units valued at £10 each = £7000.

The correct gross profit is thus

		19-1	
		£	%
Sales		10000	100
Purchases	12000		
less Stock in Trade	7000		
Cost of Goods Sold		5000	50
Gross Profit		5000	50

Suppose that 100 units of stock in trade were misplaced at the time of physical counting stock. The recorded closing stock is thus valued as only 600 units at £10 each = £6000.

The gross profit now will be shown as:-

	£	19-1 £	%
Sales		10000	100
Purchases	12000		
less Stock in Trade	6000		
Cost of Goods Sold		6000	60
Gross Profit		4000	40

The consequences for profits would have been exactly the same if 100 units of stock in trade had been destroyed or stolen. In all these cases the closing stock is at a lower value than it ought to be and gross profit is understated as a consequence. Exactly the reverse would be true if the stock value were overstated. i.e. profit would be too high. Overstatement is not going to arise from theft however!

If the example is now continued for another year it can be seen that the consequences of the error will effect the next year.

Example
In 19-2 the business buys a further 600 units @ £10 and sells 800 units @ £20. The stock in trade at the end of 19-2 should be 500 units at £10 = £5000. The position if all had been correct in 19-1 would be:-

		19-2 £	%
Sales		16000	100
Opening Stock	7000		
Purchases	6000		
	13000		
less Closing Stock	5000	8000	50
Gross Profit		8000	50

However if the profit is calculated with the incorrect figure of 19-1 stock but assuming that a correct physical count for 19-2 of 500 units was completed then the results would be (Opening Stock 700 units + Purchases 600 units — Sales 800 units = 500 units).

		19-2 £	%
Sales		16000	100.00
Opening Stock	6000		
Purchases	6000		
	12000		
less Closing Stock	5000	7000	43.75
Gross Profit		9000	56.25

The profits for 19-1 and 19-2 together add to the same total:-

	Correct Annual Profits	Incorrect Annual Profits
	£	£
19-1	5000	4000
19-2	8000	9000
	13000	13000

This would not be the case if the shortage of stock in 19-1 had been due to loss or theft since the subsequent calculation of 19-2 stock in trade would also have been short of the missing goods. Thus if the difference in stock in trade is due either to calculation errors or short counting the effect on one year will be corrected in the next, but the proper comparison of margins in both years will be impossible.

Another reason why the gross profit position can change over two periods is a change in the items which make up the sales. Most businesses sell more than one item and usually different items are sold at different profit margins. Thus if there is an increase in the proportion of units sold at a higher margin the total margin should increase.

Example
A business sells products X and Y

X costs £30 and the markup on cost is 50% thus selling for £45.

Y costs £15 and the markup on cost is 100% thus selling for £30.

In period 1.	sales are	1000 units of X
	and	500 units of Y
In period 2.	sales are	800 units of X
	and	800 units of Y

				£	%
Period 1.	Sales	X	£45000		
		Y	£15000	60000	100.0
	Cost of				
	Sales	X	£30000		
		Y	£7500	37500	62.5
	Gross Profit			22500	37.5
Period 2.	Sales	X	£36000		%
		Y	£24000	60000	100.0
	Cost of				
	Sales	X	£24000		
		Y	£12000	36000	60.0
				24000	40.0

Notice that the margin in Period 2 has improved because of more sales of Y. This is true despite the fact that there is an equal profit of £15 per unit on both X and Y.

The Management of a business in addition to wanting explanations for variations in the gross profit will also want to know in detail how the other expenses have changed between the gross profit and net profit levels. Again by breaking down the expenses as a percentage of sales it is possible to see from year to year which items are giving rise to variations. For example the Profit and Loss Account of B. Broughton is as follows for three years:-

	19-1		19-2		19-3	
	£	%	£	%	£	%
Sales	20,000	100.0	30,000	100.0	40,000	100.0
Cost of Goods Sold	10,000	50.0	15,000	50.0	20,000	50.0
Gross Profit	10,000	50.0	15,000	50.0	20,000	50.0
Salaries	3,000	15.0	4,000	13.3	8,000	20.0
Motor Expenses	2,000	10.0	3,000	10.0	4,000	10.0
Heating	1,000	5.0	1,500	5.0	2,000	5.0
Rent	3,000	15.0	3,000	10.0	3,000	7.5
Total Expenses	9,000	45.0	11,500	38.3	17,000	42.5
Net Profit	1,000	5.0	3,500	11.7	3,000	7.5
	10,000	50.0	15,000	50.0	20,000	50.0

The percentage figures show that Gross Profit Margins have been constant but that the expenses have varied. Two of the expenses Motor Expenses and Heating have remained a constant proportion of sales, but Salaries and Rent have varied. Salaries first reduced then increased in proportion to sales. Rent which has remained at a fixed money amount presumably under a lease has reduced as a percentage as sales increased.

Only someone with a detailed knowledge of the business can say whether the changes in these expenses are acceptable. The accountants job is to prepare the analysis which allows someone with the appropriate knowledge to judge whether the changes are satisfactory or not.

The Balance Sheet of a business contains Assets, Capital and Liabilities. The relationship between these component parts of the balance sheet is another area where comparisons are useful. Consider the following Balance Sheet for Juniper Company at 31st December 19-1:

Juniper Company
Balance Sheet at 31 December 19-1

	£		£
Fixed Assets	12,000	Capital	9,000
		Loan	7,000
Current Assets	8,000	Current liabilities	4,000
	20,000		20,000

Like the Profit and Loss Account the Balance Sheet can be expressed in percentage terms:-

Juniper Company
Balance Sheet at 31 December 19-1

	%		%
Fixed Assets	60	Capital	45
Current Assets	40	Loan	35
		Current Liabilities	20
	100		100

There are a number of ways in which this can be used. Firstly we might try to assess the company's ability to pay creditors. The creditors requiring payment in the immediate future are included in Current Liabilities. The company will pay its creditors from current assets which include bank and cash balances as well as from assets that will have changed into cash (e.g. by selling stock in trade for cash) by the time the creditors are due to be paid. Thus the relationship of Current Assets to Current Liabilities is a useful measure of the firms ability to meet its liabilities in time. For Juniper Company the ratio is:-

Current Assets £8000 : Current Liabilities £4000
= 2 : 1

or expressed from the percentages 40% : 20% = 2:1

From the creditors point of view he is interested in ensuring that Current Assets exceed Current Liabilities by a clear margin. A ratio of 2:1 is frequently thought of as appropriate but it is not really satisfactory to use rule of thumb figures like this without thought. In particular it is often necessary to look at the composition of Current Assets more closely. In one company the Current Assets may be 80% Stock in Trade in another 80% Cash. From a creditors point of view the Stock in Trade may represent a risk because it could be very hard to sell if trade for this business becomes bad. He may therefore prefer to see a high cash figure. However holding cash is not likely to be profitable in itself and the company will not wish to hold more cash than necessary. The level of stock in trade needs to be assessed in terms of its turnover and profitability as well as in terms of the Current Ratio.

If you refer back to the Balance Sheet for Juniper Limited note that the assets other than Current Assets are Fixed Assets which comprise 60% of the total Assets. This means that these Fixed Assets are part of the structure of the firm and unless the firm reduces in size by selling part of its structure this part will remain fixed over a number of years.

On the other side of the Balance Sheet it can be seen that Capital represents only 45% of the total. Notice that this is less than the percentage for Fixed Assets. The Loan represents 35% of the total and this with Capital amounts to 80%. The point which is important here is the terms of the loan with regard to repayment. If the lender is entitled to repayment in the near future the business may be in trouble. It will either have to raise a new loan or

Capital or the business will need to be sold off. The loan is being used to fund fixed assets which probably have a long life and may not be readily sold if the lender wants repayment.

The most important lesson is that the capital and loans of a business are matched to its investments in assets. In our example if the loan is for a longer period than the assets it is financing, the firm will have an opportunity to recover its cash in time to refund the loan, and all should be well. But if the firm borrows on a short term loan and invests these funds in long lived assets it may well get into difficulty, because the loans will need to be renewed before the assets life has ended, yet because of a Credit squeeze or some such reason new loans on capital may not be available when required.

Assignment Exercises

22.1 You are examining the accounts of the Super Sweet Company for three years and have been asked to report briefly to the management on the differences in the net profits.

Super Sweet Company

	19-1 £	19-2 £	19-3 £
Sales	200,000	250,000	300,000
Opening Stock in Trade	50,000	80,000	30,000
Purchases	130,000	100,000	140,000
	180,000	180,000	170,000
Less Closing Stock in Trade	80,000	30,000	50,000
Cost in Goods Sold	100,000	150,000	120,000
Gross Profit	100,000	100,000	180,000
Administration Expenses	20,000	25,000	30,000
Selling Expense	30,000	29,000	52,000
Net Profit	50,000	46,000	98,000
	100,000	100,000	180,000

In your report calculate the profit margins as a percentage of sales, and present the results in graphical form.

22.2x The Sales Manager of Juniper Limited has come to you for advice about the results which would arise from a change in the selling prices of the firm's products. At the present time all goods sold by Juniper Limited are priced at cost plus 50%. Currently, sales are as follows:

Product	Unit Selling Price £	Total Sales £
A	15	45,000
B	12	60,000
C	9	54,000
		159,000

What is the unit cost of products A, B and C?

What should the gross profit be on total sales of £159,000 in £ and percentage terms?

The Sales Manager wants to alter the pricing policy, giving you expected new sales figures as follows:

Product A	Cost + 30%	Expected sales 4,000 units
B	Cost + 60%	Expected sales 3,500 units
C	Cost + 40%	Expected sales 8,000 units

Assume Cost remains constant.

What would expected total sales be?

What should the gross profit be on the expected sales figures in £ and percentage terms?

22.3 The accounts of Aglow Torch Company Limited are in preparation and the first draft for 19-2 has been prepared and compared with the accounts for 19-1. These are as follows, at Gross Profit level:-

	19-1 £	%	19-2 £	%
Sales	500,000	100	600,000	100
Opening Stock in Trade	80,000		70,000	
Purchases	290,000		360,000	
	370,000		430,000	
Less Closing Stock in Trade	70,000		130,000	
Cost of Goods Sold	300,000	60	300,000	50
GROSS PROFIT	200,000	40	300,000	50

As the accountant responsible for preparing the accounts you are unhappy about the difference in gross margins, as your pricing policy and sales mix has remained the same. On checking the stock sheets for 19-1 you discover that there was an error in the calculations and the closing stock in trade should have been £120,000, not £70,000. In addition, you find that during 19-2, £5,000 of goods had been destroyed in a warehouse due to flooding. No entries to record this loss had been made.

Restate the accounts for 19-1 and 19-2 with the adjustments for these two items included.

22.4x Uranus Products Limited sells three types of gas heater for industrial use. In 19-1, the following information on sales and costs has been collected.

Type No.	Selling Price per unit	Cost Price per unit	Number of units sold	Total Costs	Total Sales
	£	£		£	£
1	50	25	10,000	250,000	500,000
2	40	30	20,000	600,000	800,000
3	80	48	4,000	192,000	320,000
				1,042,000	1,620,000

What is the gross profit margin on each type of product and in total?

In 19-2 it is expected that all costs will increase by 10%.

The mark-up on cost will be the same percentage as in 19-1.

The number of units expected to be sold will be:-

Type 1	9,000 units
2	21,000 units
3	5,000 units

What is the gross profit margin on each type of product and in total which you would expect in 19-2?

22.5 The Cranborn Corporation has been examining the results of its 'Sports and Recreation' facilities over the past three years. You have been asked to prepare a report for the committee responsible which is interested to know where, if possible, savings might be made in the contribution made by the Corporation.

	19-1	19-2	19-3
	£	£	£
Fees from hire of facilities	5,000	5,200	5,500
Fees from hire of equipment	600	900	1,300
Receipts from vending machines	400	450	460
	6,000	6,550	7,260
Salaries and Wages	8,000	8,800	10,200
Heating and Lighting	2,000	2,300	2,600
Repairs and Maintenance of Buildings	500	400	300
Repairs and Maintenance of Equipment	100	110	50
Goods used in vending machines	300	225	290
Telephone, Postage and Sundry Administration Costs	700	820	950
Advertising of facilities	300	100	50
	11,900	12,755	14,440
Contribution required from the Corporation	5,900	6,205	7,180

Chapter Twenty Three

Accounting Ratios

Accounting information summarises the economic performance and situation of a business. In order to make use of this information the user needs to analyse and interpret its meaning. When confronted with information it is useful to have a framework of analysis available to make an attempt to distil what is important from the mass of less important data.

A mechanic confronted with a car that is refusing to start has a set of routine checks which will by elimination help to identify the problem. Someone without the appropriate knowledge can feel helpless faced with the complex array of electrical and mechanical parts under the bonnet of a car.

A business is in many ways more complex than a motor car. In a car cause and effect can be traced through a mechanical sequence. A thorough check will show the fault and a repair can be made. If a business's sales decline however, the cause may be clearly identifiable on the other hand the problem may be due to a variety of causes, some of which are human problems and may not be so easily diagnosed. A business consists of people interacting amongst themselves as well as with the mechanical means of production at their disposal. The human behaviour element may not always lend itself to logical and systematic analysis.

Having said this however the first stage in analysis is the development of a systematic review of the accounting data. In this respect accounting ratios are relationships which bring together the results of activity which experience shows identify the key areas for success of the business.

The choice of ratios will be determined by the needs of the user of the information. In this chapter the ratios which are illustrated are divided into main groups which may be identified with the requirements of particular users. However this division whilst it is useful as an aid to our memory and in developing a logical approach should not be taken as a set of rigid rules. A supplier of goods on credit to a firm, will mainly be interested in his customers immediate ability to repay him, which will be measured by liquidity ratios, but he will also be interested in the overall future and prospects of the customer measured by the Profitability and other ratios.

The main parties interested in accounts include shareholders and potential shareholders, creditors, lenders, the Government for taxation and statistical purposes, potential take over bidders, employees particularly though their trade unions, as well as management. The interests of the various parties have been summarised in Exhibit 23.1 which divides the types of ratio into five main categories. In this book it is not possible to show all possibly useful ratios since these can run to many hundreds, rather generally useful common ratios are illustrated. In practice it is sensible to calculate as many ratios as appear useful for the required objective.

Exhibit 23.1

Examples of Parties with an immediate interest	*Type of Ratio*
Potential Suppliers of goods on credit; Lenders, e.g. Bank managers and debenture holders; Management.	*Liquidity (Credit Risk):* Ratios indicating how well equipped the business is to pay its way.
Shareholders (Actual and Potential); Potential take-over bidders; Lenders; Management; Competitive firms; Tax Authorities; Employees.	*Profitability:* How successfully is the business trading.
Shareholders (Actual and Potential); Potential take-over bidders; Management; Competitive Firms; Employees.	*Use of Assets:* How effectively are the assets of the firm utilised.
Shareholders (Actual and Potential); Potential take-over bidders; Management; Lenders and Creditors in assessing risk.	*Capital Structure:* How does the capital structure of the firm affect the cost of capital and the return to shareholders.
Shareholders (Actual and Potential); Potential take-over bidders; Management.	*Investment:* Show how the market prices for a share reflect a company's performance.

Exhibit 23.2 shows a set of accounts prepared for The Rational Company Ltd. The various types of ratio mentioned in Exhibit 23.1 will be illustrated using the data for The Rational Company Ltd.

Exhibit 23.2

The Rational Co. Ltd.
(Abridged) Balance Sheet at 31st December, 19-1

Share Capital		£	Fixed Assets			£
150,000 £1				Cost	Aggregate	
Ordinary Shares		150,000	Land		depreciation	*Net*
8% Preference Shares		30,000	& Buildings	500,000	150,000	350,000
		180,000	Plant	40,000	—	40,000
				540,000	150,000	390,000
Reserves						
Profit and Loss Account		120,000				
		300,000	*Current Assets*			
Mortgage Debentures 7%		210,000	Stock in Trade		90,000	
Current Liabilities			Debtors		105,000	
Trade Creditors	21,000		Cash at Bank		15,000	
Bank Overdraft	30,000					210,000
Current Taxation	39,000	90,000				
		600,000				600,000

(Abridged) Trading and Profit and Loss Account
for the year ending 31st December, 19-1

	£	£
Sales		900,000
Cost of goods sold		780,000
Gross Profit		120,000
General and Administrative Expenses	18,600	
Sales Expenses	8,400	
Depreciation	30,000	57,000
Net Operating Profit		63,000
Debenture Interest	14,700	
Bank Interest	1,000	15,700
		47,300
Income from Royalties		4,700
Profit for the year before taxation		52,000
Corporation Tax		22,000
Net Profit for the year after taxation		30,000
Dividends:		
Preference Shares (8 per cent)	2,400	
Ordinary Shares (10 per cent)	15,000	17,400
		12,600
Balance from previous years		107,400
		120,000

The Market Price of an Ordinary Share at 31st December, 19-1 was £3.

Liquidity Ratios

The analysis of credit risk was the historic starting point for formal ratio analysis. With widely scattered markets a firm is frequently asked to trade with companies it has little or no knowledge of. The risks of supplying goods on credit to a strange company are fairly obvious and in practice can be very hazardous. Many small businesses have themselves been forced to wind up because a large customer has failed to pay its debt. It is hardly surprising that firms specializing in giving advice on credit risks should have come into existence. These firms started the consistent use of ratios to analyze company balance sheets. Usually they are operating as outsiders and therefore have to rely on published information, in contrast to the management of a business who can obtain much more detailed information about that business. The following ratios are useful in the measurement of liquidity:-

The Current Ratio

The Current Ratio measures Current Assets: Current Liabilities. In general terms we are comparing assets which will become liquid in approximately twelve months with liabilities which will be due for payment in the same period. This ratio was described in the previous chapter.
Referring to Exhibit 23.2 the Current Ratio is 210,000:90,000 = 2.3:1.

This may also be conveniently expressed by $\dfrac{210,000}{90,000} = 2.3$ times.

The Acid Test Ratio

In order to refine the analysis of the Current Ratio another ratio is used which takes only those current assets which are cash or will convert very quickly into cash. This will normally mean Cash and Debtors or Current Assets less Stock in Trade. The Acid Test Ratio may, therefore, be stated as:-

Current Assets less Stock in Trade : Current Liabilities.

The ratio calculated from Exhibit 23.2 is:-

$$\frac{120,000}{90,000} = 1.3 \text{ times.}$$

This shows that provided Creditors and Debtors are paid at approximately the same time, the company has sufficient liquid resources to meet its current liabilities. If a large proportion of the Current Assets had been in the form of Stock in Trade the liquid position might have been dangerously low.

The ratios shown under Credit Risk have been concerned with liquidity. A useful supplement to this type of analysis is provided by Cash Flow Statements which have been dealt with in another chapter. From the point of view of management, the forecast cash flow statement is the most useful statement for control of credit. For those outside the firm, however, this information is not usually available and they must rely on the ratios.

Profitability Ratios

Profitability is the end product of the policies and decisions taken by a firm, and is its single most important measure of success.

Gross Profit/Sales

From Exhibit 23.2 the ratio for the Rational Company Ltd. is $\dfrac{120,000}{900,000}$

= .133 or as a percentage on sales = 13.3 per cent.

It is impossible to state a rule of thumb for this figure which will vary considerably from firm to firm and industry to industry.

Net Profit (after Tax)/Sales

The same comments apply to Net Profit/Sales as to Gross Profit/Sales. The difference between the two ratios will be explained by measuring the ratios of sales to the Expenses in the Profit and Loss Account. The ratio from Exhibit 23.2 in $\dfrac{30,000}{900,000}$ = .033 = 3.3 per cent. This percentage of 3.3 indicates by how much the profit margin can decline before the firm makes losses.

Return on Capital Employed

Great care must be exercised in measuring ratios of profit to Capital Employed. These are no standard definitions and thus for comparability it is necessary to ensure that the same method is used over time for the same firm or between different firms. Another problem is inherent in comparing profit which arises over a period of time, with Capital Employed which is taken from the Balance Sheet and is thus measured at one point of time. For a proper evaluation the Capital Employed needs to be an average figure for the accounting period in which the profit was calculated. As an external analyst the only data available is at the beginning and end of the accounting period. Since the year end is by no means likely to be representative of the average for a period any calculated figure must be taken with caution. If for examples an analyst knows that a major investment in fixed assets took place mid-way through the year he would tend to average the opening and closing figures. If little change has taken place then the year end figure may be used.

Net Profit (After Tax)/Total Assets

In this calculation of Return on Capital Employed the Total Assets are defined as all Fixed and other Non-Current Assets plus Working Capital. Working Capital is simply the figure reached by deducting Current Liabilities from Current Assets, (assuming that Current Assets exceed Current Liabilities). Using the data from Exhibit 23.2, the working capital is Current Assets £210,000 less Current Liabilities £90,000 = £120,000. The Total Assets are therefore Fixed Assets £390,000 + Working Capital £210,000 = £600,000 and the return is

$$\frac{\text{Net Profit (after tax)}}{\text{Total Assets}} = \frac{30,000}{600,000} = 5\%$$

One of the problems with using this approach to Return on Capital is that Net Profit after tax will already have had interest on debentures, loans and overdrafts charged against it and thus if this interest is significant the return on assets will be understated.

Similarly if the Assets of the business include items of an intangible nature such as Goodwill it is often felt that the return on assets is better related to tangible assets alone, since the accounting valuation of intangibles varies so much.

To answer these problems the following ratio is often used:-

Net Operating Profit/Operating Assets

The aim here is to take operating profit which is the outcome of operations before interest charges are made or any investment income is included. This profit will then be taken over Operating Assets which are the tangible assets used in the generation of the Operating Income. Operating Assets will not include intangibles nor investments in shares or other securities outside the firm, whether shown under a separate hearing or as Current Assets.

As with the previous calculation of Total Assets it is appropriate to take Working Capital as part of Operating Assets but in this definition it is frequently appropriate to exclude Bank Overdraft from Current Liabilities. Although from a legal point of view and from the Banks intention it is a Current Liability, since repayment can be demanded at short notice, in practice for a well run business the bank is usually happy to maintain an overdraft over extended periods of time. Unlike most of the other Current Liabilities interest is chargeable on overdrafts.

Thus this definition of Return on Capital Employed is Net Operating Profit: Tangible Operating Fixed Assets + (Working Capital + Overdraft). Referring to Exhibit 23.2 this is equal to £390,000 + £120,000 + £30,000 = £540,000. Which is equivalent to:-

Share Capital £180,000 + Reserves £120,000 + Debentures £210,000 + Bank overdraft £30,000 = £540,000

The Net Operating Profit which in Exhibit 23.2 = £63,000 is the profit obtained from the Capital Employed before paying interest or dividends to any of these sources of capital. This return on Capital Employed in the Rational Company Ltd. is therefore $\frac{63,000}{540,000}$ = 11.7 per cent.

Net Profit (After Taxes)/Owners Equity

In this case the net profit after tax (less Preference Dividends) is compared with Ordinary Shareholders stake in the business i.e. share capital plus reserves. From Exhibit 23.2 the ratio is

$$\frac{£27,600}{£270,000} = 10.2 \text{ per cent.}$$

In contrast to the previous ratio this one is not an overall measure of profitability but is specially concerned with the return an ordinary shareholder might expect.

Use of Assets Ratios

Although the way assets are utilized will effect profitability, these particular ratios deserve to be evaluated separately as they are of great importance. In effect they show how effectively management has been using the assets at their disposal.

A straightforward ratio between Assets and Sales can be used by the external analyst. For the Rational Co. Ltd we should show:—

Land and Buildings	: Sales	350,000 : 900,000 = 1 : 2.6
Plant	: Sales	40,000 : 900,000 = 1 : 22.5
Total Fixed Assets	: Sales	390,000 : 900,000 = 1 : 2.3
Stock in Trade	: Sales	90,000 : 900,000 = 1 : 10.0
Debtors	: Sales	105,000 : 900,000 = 1 : 8.6
Cash at Bank	: Sales	15,000 : 900,000 = 1 : 60.0
Total Current Assets	: Sales	210,000 : 900,000 = 1 : 4.3

It is often convenient to express these ratios in terms of 'per £1,000 of sales' to avoid too much "rounding off." For example Land and Buildings per £1,000 of sales would be £388.9 i.e. (350,000 ÷ 900).

A number of these activity ratios are sufficiently important to merit special mention and in some cases detailed development.

Sales/Fixed Assets

The ratio of Sales to Fixed Assets measures the utilisation a firm is obtaining from its investment in fixed plant. If the ratio is low it indicates that management may not be utilizing its plant very effectively. In the illustration from Exhibit 23.2, the ratio is = 2.3 times, or £433.3 per £1,000 of sales.

Stock Turnover

This important ratio is measured in the first instance by dividing Sales by Stock in Trade. Since Sales are at Selling Prices, the Stock should also be measured at selling price. Usually an easier way is to divide Sales at Cost Price (which is the Cost of Goods Sold total) by Stock in Trade at cost value. The stock figure used should be an average figure for the year. Whilst the true average will be known to management it will often not be available to outsiders. In this situation a very rough approximation is used by taking the average of the opening and closing stocks. if in the example in Exhibit 23.2, the stock at 1 January had been £50,000 and the stock at 31st December is £90,000 the average would be taken as

$$\frac{50,000 + 90,000}{2} = £70,000.$$

The Stock turnover therefore is

$$\frac{\text{Cost of Goods Sold}}{\text{Stock in Trade}} = \frac{780,000}{70,000} = 11.1 \text{ times.}$$

If the cost of Goods Sold is not know, it may be necessary to use the Sales figure instead. Although this is not a satisfactory basis, it may be better than nothing if like is compared with like. Notice that in this example Stock turnover = 12.9 times if the Sales figure is used.

Collection Period for Debtors

The resources tied up in debtors is an important ratio subject. We have already calculated the relationships of debtors to sales which in the example is 1:8.6. This means that for every £8.6 sold there is £1 of debtors outstanding.

This relationship is often translated into the length of time a debtor takes to pay. If we assume that the sales for Rational Ltd. are made over the whole of one year i.e. 365 days this means that on average a debt is outstanding for $365 \times \dfrac{1}{8.6} = 42.4$ days.

Notice that it is assumed sales take place evenly over the year, and we have ignored holidays. However it is useful to know that our customers take about 6 weeks to pay!

In recent years the interest in productivity measurement has raised interest in many ratios which combine information which is not essentially part of the accounts with accounting data. Published Account's for example are now required to show as supplementary information the average number of people employed by a limited Company. This information may be related to Sales to give an index of Sales per employee. For example if the average number employed by the Rational Company were 215 then sales per employee would be $\dfrac{900,000}{215} = £4,186$. This example is given as an illustration of the development of this type of measurement which may be a useful guide to assessment of a company's performance.

Capital Structure Ratios

The Capital Structure of a business is important because it has a significant influence on the risk to lenders, and on the return to shareholders.

In the first instance it is worthwhile to express the Balance Sheet in percentage terms. For the Rational Company using the main sub-totals it would be as follows:

Balance Sheet at 31 December 19-1

	%		%
Ordinary Shares	25.0	Fixed Assets	65.0
8% Preference Shares	5.0	Current Assets	35.0
Reserves	20.0		
	50.0		
Debenture	35.0		
Current Liabilities	15.0		
	100.0		100.0

Net Worth/Total Assets

From this can be seen immediately that Ordinary Shares and Preference Shares with the Reserves, which total is often called Net Worth is providing 50 per cent of the financing of Fixed and Current Assets. Thus the ratio Net Worth: Fixed Assets + Current Assets is an important measure of the shareholder stake in a business. (300,000: 390,000 + 210,000 = 1:2).

Fixed Assets/Net Worth

From the Balance Sheet it is also easy to see that a high proportion of the assets (65%) are Fixed Assets. A comparison of the Fixed Assets with Net Worth shows whether the longer term investment usually involved in Fixed Assets is provided by Shareholders. In our example the ratio is £390,000 : £300,000 (or 65%:50%) = 1:0.77. This ratio shows that shareholders are not providing all the investment required to finance the fixed assets quite apart from current assets. The remainder of the funding of assets is provided by borrowing. The important thing here is to ensure that the borrowing is sufficiently long term to match the investment in fixed assets. If the company has to repay borrowing whilst all its resources are locked into assets which cannot easily be converted into cash it can only make repayment by fresh borrowing or new capital issues which may cause problems.

Fixed Assets/Net Worth and Long Term Loan

Provided the Mortgage Debenture has a reasonably long life the Rational Company provides reasonable cover of its Fixed Assets since Fixed Assets: Net Worth + Long Term Loan are in the ratio 1:1.31.

Coverage of Fixed Charges

This relationship is obtained by dividing net profit by any fixed interest charges or rentals. Since these charges are allowable expenses for tax purposes, the profit before tax will be used. From Exhibit 23.2 the interest charges are £15,700 with no rental expense. The available profit before tax is £52,000 + £15,700 = £67,700. The Fixed Charges are, therefore, covered

$$\frac{\text{Profit before tax} + \text{Fixed Charges}}{\text{Fixed Charges}} \quad \frac{67,000}{15,700} = 4.3 \text{ times.}$$

This is low enough to indicate a company which is high geared.

High Geared means a company which has a high proportion of borrowing to net worth. A company with no gearing has all its funds provided by the ordinary shareholder. Gearing has also been measured indirectly in the ratio of Net Worth: Total Assets. The lower the proportion of funds provided from Net Worth, the higher the borrowing and hence gearing.

The coverage of fixed charges gives a very important measure of the extent to which the profit may decline before the company is not able to earn enough to cover the interest etc. it is legally obliged to pay. If charges are not paid legal steps will be taken against the company, which usually end in it being taken over or wound up.

Borrowing/Net Worth

This ratio is the most direct measure of gearing since it indicates the proportions in which all funds are provided for the business. Borrowing is taken as all the long term and current liabilities of the business and Net Worth as Share Capital and Reserves. In this definition Preference Shares are included in net worth. Although the return to Preference Shareholders is fixed like interest there is no legal obligation for the company to pay it, hence the inclusion with Net Worth. If you are however looking at the effect of gearing on the return to ordinary shareholders it may then be appropriate to treat Preference Share Dividends as a fixed charge.

The Ratio for Rational Co. Ltd. is thus £210,000 + £90,000 : 300,000 = 1:1.

Investment Ratios

These ratios are important for the investor and financial manager who is interested in the market prices of the shares of a company on the Stock Exchange.

Dividend Yield

This measures the real rate of return on an investment in shares, as distinct from the declared dividend rate which is based on the nominal value of a share. The Yield is calculated as follows, illustrated from Exhibit 23.2:

$$\frac{\text{The Dividend per Share}}{\text{Market Price per Share}} = \frac{£1 \times 10 \text{ per cent}}{£3} = 3.3 \text{ per cent.}$$

Dividend Cover for Ordinary Shares

This indicates the amount of profit for an ordinary dividend and indicates the amount of profit retained in the business. The cover is:

$$\frac{\text{Net Profit for the year after Tax} - \text{Preference Dividend}}{\text{Dividend on Ordinary Shares}}$$

$$= \frac{£30,000 - 2,400}{15,000} = 1.8 \text{ times.}$$

Earnings Per Ordinary Share

As is implied by the name this ratio is

$$\frac{\text{Net Profit for the year after tax} - \text{Preference Dividend}}{\text{Number of Ordinary Shares}}$$

$$= \frac{£30,000 - 2,400}{150,000} = £0.18 \text{ per share}$$

The calculation of this important ratio is now covered by the Statement of Standard Accounting Practice 3.

The Price Earnings Ratio

Finally the Price Earnings Ratio relates the earnings per share to the price the shares sell at in the market. From Exhibit 23.2 the ratio is:

$$\frac{\text{Market Price}}{\text{Earnings per Share}} = \frac{£3}{£.18} = 16.7$$

This relationship is an important indicator to investor and financial manager of the market's evaluation of a share, and is very important when a new issue of shares is due since it shows the earnings the market expects in relation to the current share prices.

Summary of Ratios

Type of Ratio	*Method of Calculation*
Liquidity	
Current Ratio	$\dfrac{\textit{Current Assets}}{\text{Current Liabilities}}$
Acid Test Ratio	$\dfrac{\textit{Current Assets less Stock in Trade}}{\text{Current Liabilities}}$
Profitability	
Gross Profit/Sales	$\dfrac{\textit{Gross Profit}}{\text{Sales}}$
Net Profit after Tax/Sales	$\dfrac{\textit{Net Profit after Tax}}{\text{Sales}}$
Return on Capital Employed	
Net Profit After Tax/Total Assets	$\dfrac{\textit{Net Profit After Tax}}{\text{Fixed and Other Assets} + \text{Working Capital}}$
Net Operating Profit/Operating Assets	$\dfrac{\textit{Net Operating Income}}{\text{Tangible Operating Fixed Assets} + \text{Working Capital and Overdraft}}$
Net Profit (after tax)/Owners Equity	$\dfrac{\textit{Net Profit after tax less Preference Dividend}}{\text{Ordinary Share Capital} + \text{Reserves}}$

Use of Assets

Asset/Sales

$$\frac{Individual\ Asset\ Totals}{Sales}$$

Fixed Assets/Sales

$$\frac{Fixed\ Assets}{Sales}$$

Stock Turnover

$$\frac{Cost\ of\ Goods\ Sold}{Average\ Stock\ in\ Trade}$$

Collection Period for Debtors

$$365 \times \frac{Debtors}{Sales}$$

Capital Structure

Net Worth/Total Assets

$$\frac{Ordinary\ Share\ Capital + Preference\ S.C. + Reserves}{Fixed\ Assets + Other\ Assets + Current\ Assets}$$

Fixed Assets/Net Worth

$$\frac{Fixed\ Assets}{Net\ Worth}$$

Fixed Assets/Net Worth and Long Term Loan

$$\frac{Fixed\ Assets}{Net\ Worth + Long\ Term\ Loan}$$

Coverage of Fixed Charges

$$\frac{Net\ Profit\ before\ tax\ and\ Fixed\ Charges}{Fixed\ Charges}$$

Borrowing/Net Worth

$$\frac{Long\ Term\ +\ Current\ Liabilities}{Net\ Worth}$$

Investment

Dividend Yield

$$\frac{Dividend\ per\ Share}{Market\ Price\ per\ Share}$$

Dividend Cover for Ordinary Shares

$$\frac{Net\ Profit\ after\ tax\ -\ Pref.\ Div.}{Ordinary\ Share\ Dividend}$$

Earnings per Ordinary share

$$\frac{Net\ Profit\ after\ tax\ -\ Pref.\ Div.}{Number\ of\ Ordinary\ Shares}$$

Price Earnings Ratio

$$\frac{Market\ Price\ per\ Share}{Earnings\ per\ Share}$$

Assignment Exercises

Assignment Exercises followed by the letter x do NOT have answers shown at the back of the book.

23.1x Describe the five main groups of ratios and indicate who may be interested in each type.

23.2 Explain what you think the following ratios indicate about a firm:
    (a)   Acid Test ratio.
    (b)   Net Operating Profit/Capital Employed.
    (c)   Collection Period for Debtors.

    (d)   Net Worth/Total Assets.

    (e)   Dividend Cover for Ordinary Shares.

23.3x Stock Turnover is sometimes calculated by dividing sales by the average of the opening and closing stock in trade figures. What is wrong with this method of computation?

23.4 For each of the following items select the lettered item(s) which indicate(s) its effect(s) on the company's accounts. More than one item may be effected.

    1.   Declaration and payment of a dividend on Preference Share Capital.

    2.   Declaration of a proposed dividend ordinary shares due for payment in one month.

    3.   Purchase of stock in trade for cash.

    4.   Payment of creditors.

    5.   Bad Debt written off against an existing provision for Bad and Doubtful Debts.

Effect

    A.   Reduces working capital.

    B.   Increases working capital.

    C.   Reduces current ratio.

    D.   Increases current ratio.

    E.   Reduces acid test ratio.

    F.   Increases acid test ratio.

23.5x Describe four ratios which might help you to assess the profitability of a company and explain their significance.

23.6 A limited company with 100,000 £1 Ordinary Shares as its Capital earns a profit after tax of £15,000. It pays a dividend of 10 per cent. The Market price of the shares is £1.50. What is the:

    (a)   Yield on Ordinary Shares?

    (b)   Earnings per share?

    (c)   Price/Earnings ratio?

23.7x What ratios might be of particular interest to a potential holder of debentures in a limited company?

23.8 The following is a Trading and Profit and Loss Account of a small limited company engaged in manufacturing for the year ending 31 December 19-2:

	£'000		£'000
Opening Stock	20	Sales (credit)	150
Purchases (credit)	120		
	140		
Less Closing Stock	40		
	100		
Direct Manufacturing Expenses	20		
Overhead Expenditure	10		
Net Profit	20		
	150		150

Balance Sheet at 31 December, 19-2

			£
Authorised and Issued Share Capital			100
Reserves			40
			140
5 per cent Debentures			60
			200

Fixed Assets:	Cost	Aggreg. depr.	
Freehold Property	100	–	100
Plant and Machinery	40	20	20
	140	20	120

Current Assets:			
Stocks at cost		40	
Debtors		50	
Quoted Investments at cost		60	
Bank		20	
		170	

Less Current Liabilities:			
Corporation Tax	10		
Bills Payable	20		
Tax Creditors	60	90	80
			200

Required

Select five major ratios and apply them to the above accounts and comment upon their relevance.

23.9x

Ironsides Limited
Balance Sheet as at 31 December, 19-8

	£		£	£
Authorised Share Capital		Fixed Assets at cost	7,200,000	
2,500,000 Ordinary £1	2,500,000	Depreciation	2,000,000	
				5,200,000
Issued and Fully paid Share Capital				
2,400,000 Shares of £1 each	2,400,000	*Current Assets*		
General Reserve	1,600,000	Stock	1,200,000	
		Debtors	800,000	
		Investments	600,000	
	4,000,000	Cash	200,000	2,800,000
6% Debenture	800,000			
5% Mortgage	2,000,000	2,800,000		
		6,800,000		
Bank Loan 8%		400,000		
Creditors	280,000			
Taxation	520,000	800,000		
		£8,000,000		£8,000,000

Condensed Profit and Loss Account for year ended 31 December, 19-9.

		£
Sales		12,000,000
Cost of Production		10,320,000
GROSS PROFIT		1,680,000
Other Expenses:		
Administration	120,000	
Selling	68,000	
Rent	112,000	
Depreciation	400,000	700,000
		980,000
Less Interest –		
Bank	32,000	
Mortgage	100,000	
Debenture	48,000	180,000
		800,000
Less Corporation Tax 45%		360,000
		440,000
Less Dividend		400,000
To General Reserve	£	40,000

You are required to calculate for Ironsides Ltd. ten significant ratios and comment on their meaning.

23.10 The annual accounts of the Wholesale Textile Company Limited have been summarized for 19-1 and 19-2 as follows:

	Year 19-1		Year 19-2	
Sales	£	£	£	£
Cash	60,000		64,000	
Credit	540,000	600,000	684,000	748,000
Cost of sales		472,000		596,000
Gross margin		128,000		152,000
Expenses				
Warehousing	26,000		28,000	
Transport	12,000		20,000	
Administration	38,000		38,000	
Selling	22,000		28,000	
Debenture interest	—		4,000	
		98,000		118,000
Net profit		30,000		34,000

	On 31 Dec. 19-1		On 31 Dec. 19-2	
	£	£	£	£
Fixed assets				
(*less* depreciation)		60,000		80,000
Current assets				
Stock	120,000		188,000	
Debtors	100,000		164,000	
Cash	20,000	240,000	14,000	366,000
Less Current liabilities				
Trade creditors		100,000		152,000
Net current assets		140,000		214,000
		200,000		294,000
Share Capital		150,000		150,000
Reserves and undistributed profit		50,000		84,000
Debenture loan		—		60,000
		200,000		294,000

You are informed that:—

1. All sales were from stocks in the company's warehouse.
2. The range of merchandise was not changed and buying prices remained steady throughout the two years.
3. Budgeted total sales for 19-2 were £780,000.
4. The debenture loan was received on 1 January, 19-2, and additional fixed assets were purchased on that date.

You are required to state the internal accounting ratios that you would use in this type of business to assist the management of the Company in measuring the efficiency of its operation, including its use of capital.

Your answer should name the ratios and give the figures (calculated to one decimal place) for 19-1 and 19-2, together with possible reasons for changes in the ratios for the two years. Ratios relating to capital employed should be based on the capital at the year end. Ignore taxation.

23.11x The following data relate to the financial results of the Gazco Ltd. for the years ended 31 December, 19-1, 19-2 and 19-3:—

Balance Sheets as at:—

Fixed Assets	31 Dec., 19-3 £(million)	31 Dec., 19-2 £(million)	31 Dec., 19-1 £(million)
Land	2	2	2
Buildings	24	22	19
Plant and Equipment	115	105	91
Mineral Deposits	1	1	1
Oil and Gas Properties—			
Producing	9	8	8
Oil and Gas Leaseholds—			
Undeveloped	1	1	1
Accumulated Depreciation	(71)	(60)	(51)
Accumulated Depletion	(3)	(3)	(3)
	78	76	68

202

Current Assets			
Inventories	19	17	15
Accounts Receivable	20	17	15
Marketable Securities	17	15	11
Cash	4	3	3
Development Expenses	3	2	2
	£141	£130	£114

	£(million)	£(million)	£(million)
Share Capital and Reserves			
Share Capital			
Authorised, Issued and Fully Paid in Ordinary Shares of £1 each	6	6	6
Capital Reserves			
Share Premium Account	40	36	32
Revenue Reserves			
Retained Earnings	32	30	27
	78	72	65
Long Term Liabilities			
Debentures	40	39	30
Bank Loans	3	2	2
Current Liabilities			
Accounts Payable and Accruals	12	12	11
Current Taxation	7	4	5
Bank Overdraft	1	1	1
	£141	£130	£114

Profit and Loss Accounts for the Year ended

	31 Dec., 19-3 £(million)	31 Dec., 19-2 £(million)	31 Dec., 19-1 £(million)
Income:			
Net sales	119	106	93
Other Income	1	1	1
	120	107	94
Deductions:			
Cost of Goods Sold	85	76	67
Selling and Administration	18	15	13
Interest on long-term liabilities	1	1	1
Other	1	1	1
Profit before Taxation	15	14	12
Provision for Taxation	7	6	5
Profit after Taxation	£8	£8	£7

(a) Prepare the following analyses of the company's liquidity at the end of 19-3 and 19-2:

    (i)   Amount of Working Capital;

    (ii) Current ratio;

    (iii) Acid test ratio.

(b) Prepare the following analyses of the company's operations: for 19-3 and 19-2:

    (i)   Rate of return after tax on capital employed at end of each year;

    (ii) Rate of return after tax on shareholders' equity; at end of each year;

    (iii) Turnover rate for fixed assets; at end of each year;

    (iv) Percentage of profit before tax to sales revenue;

    (v) Number of times fixed interest charge is covered.

    (vi) Earnings per share.

23.12 The Balance Sheet and Profit and Loss Account for Goodmark Ltd. are shown below:—

Balance Sheet at 31 December 19-1

		£	£
Fixed Assets:	Land & Buildings (net)		300
	Plant (net)		1,880
			2,180
Current Assets			
	Stock in Trade	710	
	Debtors	340	
	Cash	140	1,190
			3,370
Share Capital			
	£1 Ordinary Shares		520
	£1 10% Preference Shares		100
			620
Reserves			
	Retained Profits		1,000
			1,620
Debentures			1,270
Current Liabilities			
	Trade Creditors	450	
	Current Taxation	30	480
			£3,370

Profit and Loss Account for Year Ending 31 December 19-1

	£	£
Sales		3,640
Cost of Goods Sold		2,350
		1,290
Selling and Administration Expenses	810	
Depreciation	170	
Interest	60	
		1,040
Net Profit before Taxation		250
Taxation		100
Net Profit after Taxation		£150

Calculate

(a)   Acid Test Ratio.

(b)   Times Fixed Charges (i.e. Interest) Covered.

(c)   Profit after Tax on Owners Equity Ratio.

(d)   Collection period for Debtors.

(e)   Stock Turnover.

Chapter Twenty Four

Interpretation of Final Accounts

The Interpretation of Final Accounts through the use of ratios can conveniently be divided into two parts. Firstly there is analysis by those outside the firm who are seeking to understand more from the published accounting data. On the other side there is management wishing to interpret a much fuller range of internal information in a meaningful way. In both situations current information will be assessed in relation to past trends of the same business and with comparative information for similar firms.

Comparisons Over Time

One of the most helpful ways in which accounting ratios can be used is to compare them with previous periods ratios for the same organisation. Taking as an example Net Profit after Tax/Sales the results for the Rational Co. Ltd are as follows:—

	This year	1	2	3	4	5
			Years ago			
Net Profit after Tax/Sales	3.3	3.8	3.1	3.4	3.4	3.5

This years result acquires much more significance when compared to the previous five years. The appreciation of the trends is usually assisted by graphing the results as in Exhibit 24.1.

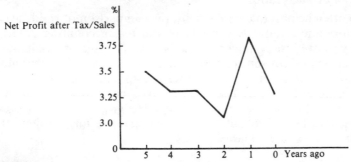

Exhibit 24.1

This graph very clearly illustrates how the net profit margin has fluctuated. In this type of case the ratio which is a comparative number is not expected to "grow" in the way that an expanding firm expects its Sales to grow. Thus for ratios an ordinary graph would normally be appropriate.

However when the ratio points have been plotted it can be helpful to insert a line of best fit to these points. Thus on the graph we drew of Net Profit After Tax/Sales a line of best fit gives a useful idea of the past trends of the ratio as an Exhibit 24.2.

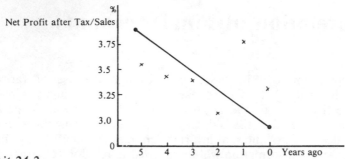

Exhibit 24.2

This can be drawn either by eye of better by using a statistical technique such as least squares.

It is very tempting to extend these trend lines into the future as a form of forecast. Past trends should not be used mechanically to predict the future. Only if you are sure that all conditions influencing a ratio are likely to remain constant next year should you extend the trend. Notice that in the graph we have just plotted the linear trend is relatively little influenced by the upturn in the current year. This improvement may in fact represent the start of an upward movement if we had sufficient information to explain it. Thus great care must be taken with predictions.

As with the interpretation of all ratios the best approach is to structure the analysis in an orderly fashion. The pyramid type of structuring explained later in the chapter is a useful model since it links together a set of ratios, in a way that helps to develop understanding — one ratio being explained by other more detailed ratios.

It is also often helpful to combine with the comparison of ratios over time, some information about the trends in the real accounting data. In the example we have just examined of the Net Profit after Tax/Sales ratio it is likely to be helpful for someone interpreting the accounts to have alongside his graphical analysis of the ratio other graphs showing the sales in £ and Net Profit after Tax in £. The ratio analysis must always be kept in the perspective of the real accounting results. The graphs of key figures from the Profit and Loss Account for example can usefully be developed on logarithmic scales to emphasise trends.

Comparisons with other firms

Comparisons over time are useful since they give a perspective on trends developing within a firm. However since firms operate in a competitive environment it is always necessary to have some basis of comparison with other organisations particularly those in the same type of business.

Whilst in principle inter-firm comparisons are very worthwhile there are considerable practical differences. Firstly in many cases organisations are not directly comparable with others in size or in the exact nature of business carried on. A large multinational company can be involved in a wide range of industries and countries of operation, as a whole therefore it is probably unique. Size can in itself have an important bearing on ratios. For example the Capital Structure Ratios of a large public company are not comparable with one which is small and privately owned. Secondly inter-company comparisons are frequently made misleading by differences in accounting methods and factors such as the age structure and location of assets.

Most of the difficulties mentioned can be overcome by a properly structured scheme of inter-firm comparison. Here firms agree to pool data and employ experts to ensure comparability of the data. However this type of scheme is only available internally for the management. For the external analyst relying on published data the development of accounting standards is helping to ensure a better basic source of information. The external analyst must by necessity look at the overall ratios for more general guidelines to a firm's performance.

External Analysis

The outsider is at some disadvantage in undertaking ratio analysis since he may have relatively little information about the underlying bases of accounting. He will, however, be able to obtain information which is now published, showing ratios by industry. These are calculated from the published accounts of public companies, and more limited information on accounts of private companies. This information would tend to be in a form similar to that shown in Exhibit 24.3, which is an abbreviated form of a broad schedule of ratios.

Using some information from Exhibit 23.2 in Chapter Twenty Three, let us set up the information we have available to assess the Rational Co. Ltd. which is a Building and Civil Engineering Firm.

The ratios shown are the median figures for the companies in the sample. In practice it would be common to show the two quartile figures as well.

Ratio	Rational Co. Ltd.		Industry Median for Building and Civil Engineering	
	19-0	19-1	19-0	19-1
Operating Profit/Capital Employed	13.2	11.7	14.5	14.8
Net Profit after Tax/Sales	3.8	3.3	3.9	4.6
Sales/Fixed Assets	3.1	2.3	7.7	7.0
Sales/Stock	13.5	12.9	10.1	7.3
Current Assets/Current Liabilities	2.2	2.3	1.32	1.36
Liquid Assets/Current Liabilities	1.1	1.3	.96	.93

Exhibit 24.3

Illustration of Published Ratios by Industry
Quoted Companies Year 19x0 and 19x1

Industry Classification	Year	Financial Performance				Credit Control	
		P/CE %	NP/S %	S/FA times	S/ST times	CA/CL times	LA/CL times
Building and Civil Engineering	19-0	14.5	3.9	7.7	10.1	1.32	.96
	19-1	14.8	4.6	7.0	7.3	1.36	.93
Specialist Construction Contractors	19-0	14.5	5.3	6.0	9.8	1.55	1.15
	19-1	17.8	6.0	6.3	12.1	1.66	1.08

Notes:

P.	= Net Operating Profit	S.T.	= Stock in Trade
N.P.	= Net Profit After Tax	C.A.	= Current Assets
C.E.	= Capital Employed	C.L.	= Current Liabilities
S.	= Sales	L.A.	= Liquid Assets or Current Assets
F.A.	= Fixed Assets		Less Stock

Whilst it must be appreciated that we are working with only a few ratios and that ideally we would look at least at five year's information we might draw some tentative conclusions:

Operating Profit/Capital Employed is lower than the median figure for the industry. Looking further we see that Sales/Fixed Asset Ratio is considerably below average. The two ratios are closely linked since Sales is an important contributor to Profit and Fixed Assets are part of Capital Employed. Net Profit after tax to Sales is also below average but the company is utilizing its stock above the average level. Both the liquidity ratios are above average, which may mean from the company's point of view that too much resources are tied up in non-productive cash or debtor balances, which would also contribute to a low return on capital employed.

In practice we could also look at the quartile figures in addition to the median. Our conclusions from the analysis can only be tentative but there is an impression which develops even from the limited information we have looked at that all is not right with the Rational Co. Ltd. Profitability is below average and the explanation seems to lie in a low net profit margin, and low utilization of fixed assets plus too many liquid assets. The trend of profitability figures cannot be assessed from two years, and it would have been useful to see information covering as many years back such as will give a reasonable guide. In preparing the graphs of trends over time for the ratios it is often very useful to show the Industry Data on the same graph as that for the firm. Using the example previously illustrated the graph for the Rational Co. Ltd. Profit after Tax/Sales would be improved by adding the Industry Median figures as in Exhibit 24.4

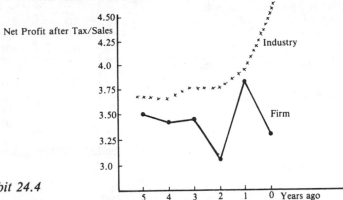

Exhibit 24.4

Internal Analysis

From a management point of view very useful information can be drawn from a detailed ratio analysis between companies using a full range of information not normally published. The Centre for Inter-firm Comparisons is a specialist organisation undertaking this work, maintaining secrecy as to the identity of participating firms, but ensuring that all firms taking parts prepare their information on a comparable basis. Several Trade Association and Professional Bodies run similar schemes for their members. The Centre for Inter-firm Comparison have developed what is known as the "pyramid" approach to ratios. This simply means that a key ratio at the top of the pyramid is explained by more detailed ratios which branch our below. One example is shown in Exhibit 24.5 developed from the key ratio Operating Profit/Operating Assets. Note that

$$\frac{\text{Operating Profit}}{\text{Operating Assets}} \text{ is the same as } \frac{\text{Sales}}{\text{Operating Assets}} \times \frac{\text{Operating Profit}}{\text{Sales}}$$

(cancelling out Sales in the multiplication).

In a working scheme very many detailed ratios would be developed from the framework illustrated in this chapter. The main benefit usually arises by the more general comparison, but the detail allows backup research if things are going wrong.

The ratios are as follows:-

Ratio	Last Year	This Year
Return on assets		
1. Operating profit/Operating assets (%)	8.2	11.1
Profit margin on sales and turnover of assets		
2. Operating profit/sales (%)	6.7	5.8
3. Sales/Operating assets (times per year)	2.5	1.7
Departmental costs (as a percentage of sales)		
4. Production	71.0	70.9
5. Distribution and marketing	16.3	18.2
6. Administration	6.0	5.1

Asset utilisation (£'s per £1,000 of sales)		
3a. Operating assets	703	653
10. Current assets	593	480
11. Fixed assets	102	101
Current asset utilisation (£'s per £1,000 of sales)		
12. Material stocks	142	141
13. Work in progress	156	152
14. Finished stocks	152	94
15. Debtors	143	103

The results of our firm can now be appraised alongside the other companies in the sample. Our firm is identified by "C".

THE INTERFIRM COMPARISON

Ratio	A	B	C	D	E
Return on assets					
1. Operating profit/Operating assets (%)	17.2	14.5	11.1	8.6	3.9
Profit margin on sales and turnover of assets					
2. Operating profit/sales (%)	14.0	14.3	5.8	7.9	2.0
3. Sales/Operating assets (times per year)	1.3	1.1	1.7	1.0	2.4
Departmental costs (as a percentage of sales)					
4. Production	74.0	70.5	70.9	71.7	77.0
5. Distribution and marketing	8.5	12.2	18.2	14.2	16.0
6. Administration	3.5	3.0	5.1	6.2	5.0
Asset utilisation (£'s per £1,000 of sales)					
3a. Operating assets	842	908	653	1030	500
10. Current assets	616	609	480	800	370
11. Fixed assets	250	320	101	241	160
Current asset utilisation (£'s per £1,000 of sales)					
12. Material stocks	131	120	141	172	84
13. Work in progress	148	120	132	175	140
14. Finished stocks	203	164	94	259	68
15. Debtors	134	205	123	194	78

Interpreting the Inter-firm Comparison we are able to see that our firm is below two other firms in return on operating assets. This can be traced to Operating Profit/Sales. Note that total departmental costs + operating profit as per cent sales = 100 per cent. The main factor in the profit being below firms A and B is high distribution and marketing costs. Action can be taken on these costs if appropriate.

Since firm C will have details of the general size and description of all the firms in the sample (although the names of firms are confidential) and knows that the Centre for Inter-firm Comparison makes sure that the figures used are comparable, very valuable information can be drawn for management.

When several periods data is available this type of information is much more readily appreciated in graphical form.

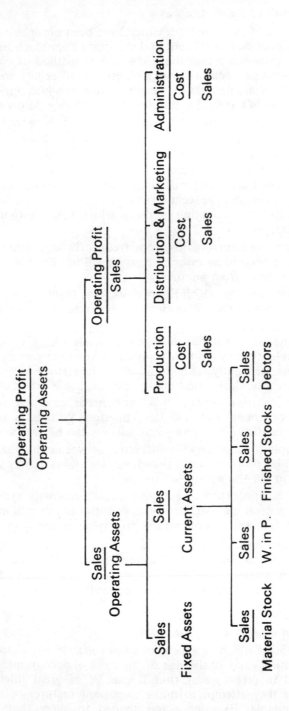

Exhibit 24.5

The Limitations of Ratio Analysis

The Advantages of ratio analyses which have been brought out in this text are that they provide a consistent and disciplined approach to the analysis of accounts. In addition they are a convenient method of comparing the performance of a particular firm with others and of seeing trends over time. Nonetheless there are dangers in accepting answers which appear to be put forward by ratio in too rigid a manner. The following points are relevant:-

1. Accounting Statements present a limited picture only of the business. The information included in accounts does not cover all aspects of the business.

2. The problem associated with differing bases of accounting are nowhere more important than in ratio analysis. In particular differences in valuing fixed assets, depreciation methods and in valuation of stock-in-trade can be mentioned. As you will appreciate from your study of accounting there is usually a variety of accounting methods which may be appropriate to a particular firm.

3. The accounts of large organisations frequently aggregate operations in different industries and an external analyst will not be able to split up the results of one sector from another.

4. Comparison of a firm which finances its fixed plant through rental, thus not showing it as an asset, with a firm which purchases its own assets will be difficult.

5. External analysis of balance sheets can be misleading because the picture at that particular time may not be representative of the year as a whole. For example firms frequently take stock when their stock levels are lowest. Average figures should be used but are not available externally.

6. Interpretation of a change in a ratio needs careful examination of changes in both numerator and denominator. Without a very full and detailed investigation some wrong conclusions can be drawn.

7. There is room for considerable difference between individual companies. It is wrong to lay down too rigid guidelines since what may be good for one successful firm may be wrong for another.

8. In general it is incorrect to compare small firms with very large firm. Many of the general industrial analyses of ratios are overall averages, and are, therefore, not strictly comparable to any particular firm.

The lesson is that whilst ratios are useful in indicating areas for investigation they cannot be relied upon to answer all the questions raised. Many of the limitations may, however, be reduced if a properly supervised scheme of inter-firm comparison is introduced.

Interpretation of Accounts for Employees

The interpretation which has been reviewed so far in this chapter has been for people with a good knowledge of the basis of accounting. Many firms have realised in recent years that it can be of great interest to their employees, if they attempt to make important features of the accounts generally available. Experience has tended to show that the average employee is very easily put off if too much detail is presented to him. Most firms attempt therefore to give a much more limited amount of information and to present it as imaginatively as possible in a special employee report. It is always far better to get over a limited amount of important information than to include so much detail that the message is obscured. Those who are interested can look for more detail in the main published accounts.

Firms have developed many different approaches in preparing their reports to employees. Many succeed by capturing interest through good graphics and design. Care must be taken however not to make these reports appear too trivial or condescending. Some examples of graphical illustrations which are also used in the main published accounts are shown below, however there is a very wide range of approach between different firms many of which include cartoons and 'comic-strip' types of presentation to capture interest. Space is not available here to do justice to this type of presentation. Try to find examples of company reports in libraries.

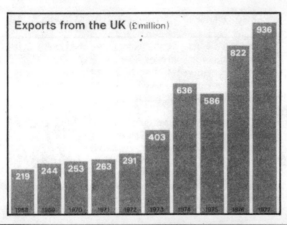

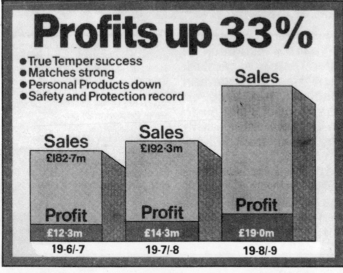

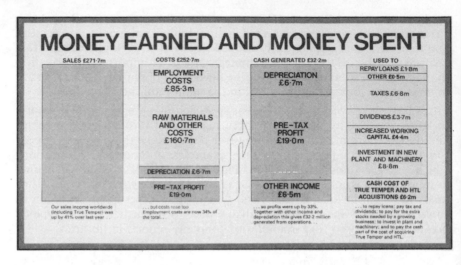

MONEY EARNED AND MONEY SPENT

SALES £271·7m	COSTS £252·7m	CASH GENERATED £32·2m	USED TO
	EMPLOYMENT COSTS £85·3m	DEPRECIATION £6·7m	REPAY LOANS £1·8m / OTHER £0·5m / TAXES £6·8m
	RAW MATERIALS AND OTHER COSTS £160·7m	PRE-TAX PROFIT £19·0m	DIVIDENDS £3·7m / INCREASED WORKING CAPITAL £4·4m / INVESTMENT IN NEW PLANT AND MACHINERY £8·8m
	DEPRECIATION £6·7m		
	PRE-TAX PROFIT £19·0m	OTHER INCOME £6·5m	CASH COST OF TRUE TEMPER AND HTL ACQUISTIONS £6·2m

Our sales income worldwide (including True Temper) was up by 41% over last year . . .

. . . but costs rose too. Employment costs are now 34% of the total . . .

. . . so profits were up by 33%. Together with other income and depreciation this gives £32·2 million generated from operations . . .

. . . to repay loans; pay tax and dividends; to pay for the extra stocks needed by a growing business; to invest in plant and machinery; and to pay the cash part of the cost of acquiring True Temper and HTL.

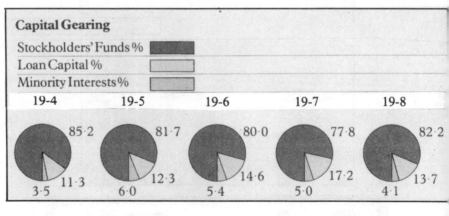

Capital Gearing

	19-4	19-5	19-6	19-7	19-8
Stockholders' Funds %	85·2	81·7	80·0	77·8	82·2
Loan Capital %	3·5	6·0	5·4	5·0	4·1
Minority Interests %	11·3	12·3	14·6	17·2	13·7

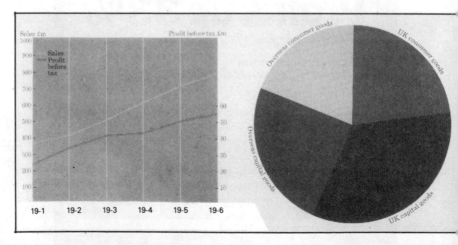

Sales £m
Profit before tax £m

Sales
Profit before tax

19-1 19-2 19-3 19-4 19-5 19-6

Overseas consumer goods
UK consumer goods
Overseas capital goods
UK capital goods

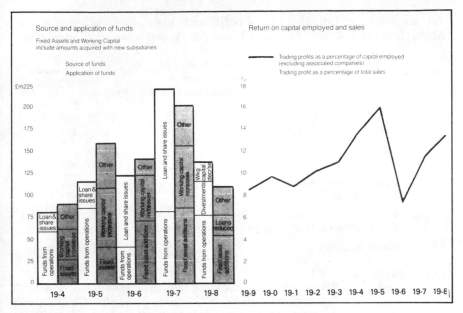

Value Added Statements

When presenting the results of a business organisation both for the employees and investors, particularly one which is involved in manufacturing, it has been proposed in recent years that the statement of Profit and Loss could be restated in terms of 'value added'. Value added is defined as Sales Income less materials and services purchased from outside the organisation. The total value added by the organisation is used to provide wages, dividends, interest, taxes and funds for new investment.

The basic Value-Added Statement will thus include the following information:

	£
Sales	xxx
less Bought in materials and services	xxx
Value Added	xxx
Applied as follows:-	
To pay employees:	
wages and pensions	xxx
To pay provider of capital:	
interest on loans	xxx
dividends on shares	xxx xxx
To pay government:	
corporation tax	xxx
To provide for maintenance and	
expansion of assets:	
depreciation	xxx
retained profits	xxx xxx
Value Added	

As an example the abridged Profit and Loss Account of Growth Manufacturers Ltd. will be restated in Value Added terms as shown below:

Growth Manufacturers Ltd.
Profit and Loss Account
for the year ended 31 December 19-1 (abridged)

	£
Sales	12,000,000
Costs (details as below)	8,400,000
Operating Profit	3,600,000
Interest	1,200,000
Profit before Taxation	2,400,000
Corporation Tax	1,100,000
Profit after Taxation	1,300,000
Dividend on Ordinary Shares	500,000
Profit Retained	800,000

Note: Costs include:

	£
Wages, pensions and other employee benefits	3,200,000
Depreciation	750,000
All other costs were bought in from outside.	4,450,000
	8,400,000

Growth Manufacturers Ltd.
Value Added Statement
for the year ended 31 December 19-1

	£
Sales	12,000,000
less Bought in materials and services	4,450,000
Value Added	7,550,000

Applied as follows:-

		£
To pay employees wages, pensions and other benefits		3,200,000
To pay providers of capital: interest	1,200,000	
dividends on shares	500,000	1,700,000
To pay government corporation tax		1,100,000
To provide for maintenance and expansion		
of assets: depreciation	750,000	
retained profit	800,000	1,550,000
Value Added		7,550,000

Assignment Exercises

Assignment Exercises followed by the letter x do NOT have answers shown at the back of the book.

24.1x Describe the sources from which an external investor might obtain financial information about a company in which he is interested.

24.2x In order to judge the performance of a business it may be necessary to set standards for comparison. How should such standards be established? Describe some of the standards which may be adopted.

24.3x Explain clearly the advantages and limitations of ratio analysis.

24.4 What is meant by the term a "pyramid" of ratios? What is the object of this kind of presentation?

24.5x What advantages might arise from using the services of the Centre for Inter-Firm Comparisons?

24.6x During 19-3 the comparative financial data for three companies in the same industrial sector were as follows:

	Z.A. Ltd. £	X.B. Ltd. £	C.L. Ltd. £
Issued Capital—			
6 per cent £1 Preference	10,000	40,000	—
£1 Ordinary Shares	70,000	60,000	120,000
Revenue Reserves	60,000	40,000	—
	140,000	140,000	120,000
Represented by—			
Fixed Assets (net)	52,000	76,000	54,000
Current Assets—			
Stock	48,000	40,000	64,000
Debtors	30,000	56,000	80,000
Cash	42,000	24,000	16,000
	172,000	196,000	214,000
Less Current Liabilities			
Creditors	(24,400)	(44,600)	(64,000)
Proposed Dividends	(7,600)	(11,400)	(30,000)
	140,000	140,000	120,000
Average Stock	50,000	72,000	60,000
Sales	250,000	240,000	800,000
Gross Profit	50,000	60,000	80,000
Net Profit	30,000	30,000	30,000

You are required:

(a) to write a report analysing and comparing the performance of the three companies;

(b) to advise a client with £5,000 to invest in shares of one of the three companies which company and which type of share to select.

24.7 Using the data which is attached to question 33.12 you are given the following data for the same company for the previous 4 years. Analyse the trends disclosed.

Years Ago:	4	3	2	1
Current Ratio	1.6	1.5	2.2	2.9
Acid Test Ratio	0.78	0.69	1.00	1.22
Times Interest Charges Covered	5.0	5.6	5.5	5.0
Net Profit after Tax/Owners Equity	21%	21%	16%	11%
Collection Period for Debtors (days)	29	30	39	35
Stock Turnover (times)	5.8	4.9	3.5	3.4

24.8x The Directors of Handbags Ltd. have asked you to assess the situation of their Company.

Preliminary investigations show the following results and median data from an Interfirm Association acting for the bag making industry of which Handbags Ltd. is a member.

	19-1 Interfirm % of Total	19-1 Handbags Ltd. £000's £	19-2 Interfirm % of Total	19-2 Handbags Ltd. £000's £	19-3 Interfirm % of Total	19-3 Handbags Ltd. £000's £
Land and Buildings at Current Valuation	20	300	25	300	30	240
Plant and Machinery at Current Valuation	20	60	25	54	40	45
Stocks at cost						
Materials	20	45	15	90	10	90
Finished Goods	20	45	25	90	10	135
Debtors	10	45	10	60	5	90
Cash	10	45	—	6	5	—
	100%	£540	100%	£600	100%	£600

REPRESENTED BY						
Share Capital	40	300	40	300	30	300
Capital Reserve	—	—	—	—	—	30
Reserves and P. & L.	10	90	20	60	30	—
10% Debentures	—	—	—	150	—	150
Creditors	50	150	40	90	40	120
	100%	£540	100%	£600	100%	£600

Note: Handbags Ltd. sold land (cost £60,000) for £90,000 in 19-3 to provide extra working capital.

PROFIT AND LOSS ACCOUNT DATA	19-1 Interfirm % of Sales	Handbags Ltd. £000's £	19-2 Interfirm % of Sales	Handbags Ltd. £000's £	19-3 Interfirm % of Sales	Handbags Ltd. £000's £
COST OF SALES						
Materials Consumed	20	180	20	165	15	150
Wages (Direct)	40	342	30	393	15	318
Depreciation of Plant and Machinery (charged by a machiner hour rate)	2	18	8	15	10	9
Power (fixed charge per unit consumed)	1	9	3	9	5	6
Other Variable Overheads (e.g. Salesmen's Commission)	2	18	4	15	5	12
Light, heat, salaries, rates, etc.	14	135	18	129	18	144
Depreciation of premises	1	9	2	9	2	6
OTHER DEBITS:						
Interest on Loan Capital	—	—	—	15	—	15
Taxation	8	84	6	—	12	—
Dividends	8	60	8	—	15	—
TOTAL DEBITS	96	855	99	750	97	660
SALES	100	900	100	720	100	600
DEFICIT for year	—	—	—	30	—	60
SURPLUS for year	4	45	1	—	3	—
BALANCES b/fwd	*	45	*	90	*	60
BALANCES cd./ fwd.	*	90	*	60	*	—
Bags sold	300,000		210,000		150,000	
Average price per bag	£3		£3		£2.15	

*Note it is not realistic to show interfirm balances as a per cent on sales.

Discuss the trends indicated and the preliminary conclusions you would draw from this data.

24.9 Read the following data, then attempt the questions shown at the end.

The Portroy Chemical Co. Ltd.

Balance Sheets

	30 June, 19-1		30 June, 19-2	
	£'000	%	£'000	%
Share Capital (£1 Shares)				
Ordinary	50,000	17.2	50,000	16.9
5% Preference	25,000	8.6	25,000	8.4
Reserves				
Profit and Loss	115,000	39.5	117,000	39.5
	190,000	65.3	192,000	64.8
8% Debentures	56,000	19.2	55,000	18.6
Current Liabilities				
Trade Creditors	35,000	12.0	36,000	12.2
Taxation	1,800	.6	2,500	.8
Bank overdrafts	8,200	2.9	10,500	3.6
Total Current Liabilities	45,000	15.5	49,000	16.6
	291,000	100.0	296,000	100.0

	£'000	%	£'000	%
Fixed Assets				
Land, Buildings, Plant and Equipment at cost	249,000	85.6	250,000	84.5
Aggregate depreciation	(126,000)	43.3	(128,000)	43.2
	123,000	42.3	122,000	41.3
Investments	14,000	4.8	15,500	5.2
Current Assets				
Stock in Trade	86,000	29.6	85,000	28.7
Debtors and Prepayments	58,000	19.9	58,000	19.6
Cash	10,000	3.4	15,500	5.2
Total Current Assets	154,000	52.9	158.500	53.5
	291,000	100.0	296,000	100.0

Portroy Chemical Co. Ltd.
Profit and Loss Accounts

	19-1 £'000	%	19-2 £'000	%
Sales	1,250,000	100.0	1,260,000	100.0
Cost of Goods Sold	1,150,000	92.0	1,149,120	91.2
Gross Profit	100,000	8.0	110,880	8.8
Operating Expenses				
Depreciation	11,250	0.9	10,080	0.8
Selling and Administration	68,750	5.5	70,560	5.6
General Expenses	15,000	1.2	12,600	1.0
Total Operating Expense	95,000	7.6	93,240	7.4
Operating Profit	5,000	0.4	17,640	1.4
Other Income	3,750	0.3	2,520	0.2
Total Income	8,750	0.7	20,160	1.6
Interest Charges	1,250	0.1	2,520	0.2
Net Profit before Taxation	7,500	0.6	17,640	1.4
Corporation Tax	2,500	0.2	6,300	0.5
Net Profit after Taxation	5,000	0.4	11,340	0.9

Additional information for the year ended 30 June, 19-2.
Stock Exchange Prices for Ordinary Shares ranged from £1.25 to £1.75.
Ordinary Dividend declared 5 per cent.

Inter Firm Comparisons
P represents the Portroy Company Ltd.
A, B and C are competitive firms of a similar size.

	19-0	19-1	19-2
Gross Profit per cent Sales			
A	10.2	9.7	10.4
B	6.3	5.9	6.1
C	8.4	9.6	9.3
P	9.3	8.0	—
Net Profit per cent Sales			
A	0.4	1.2	1.0
B	0.2	(0.2)	(0.1)
C	0.9	0.8	0.8
P	0.8	0.4	—
Current Ratio			
A	2.3	1.9	1.7
B	4.4	4.3	3.9
C	4.1	3.5	3.5
P	3.0	3.4	—

Acid Test Ratio

A	0.9	0.8	0.8
B	2.4	2.3	2.2
C	1.8	1.8	1.7
P	1.4	1.5	—

Debtors — Collection Period in Days

A	10.5	12.4	12.3
B	18.2	19.6	20.4
C	16.5	15.3	16.4
D	15.2	16.9	—

Stock Turnover (based on Cost of Goods Sold and assuming closing stock represents the average)

A	14.8	14.7	14.7
B	13.2	13.5	13.4
C	14.7	14.7	14.6
P	13.9	13.4	—

Net Worth as per cent of Total Assets

A	58.2	55.9	55.7
B	55.0	53.0	56.0
C	68.7	66.5	66.4
P	68.4	65.3	—

Number of Times Fixed Charges Earned

A	3.8	15.8	15.5
B	3.9	(2.0)	0.3
C	6.2	5.2	5.1
P	4.3	7.0	—

Operating Profit/Capital Employed

A	1.5	5.3	3.2
B	1.0	—	—
C	4.2	3.1	3.4
P	3.2	2.0	—

Earnings per Ordinary Share

A	£.06	0.32	0.29
B	£.02	(0.5)	(0.3)
C	£.33	0.26	0.26
P	£.15	0.08	—

Price Earnings Ratio (based on average of high and low price for the year)

A	75.0	14.2	0.29
B	45.0	—	—
C	12.0	19.2	17.0
P	17.6	19.8	—

Dividend Yield (based on average of high and low price for the year)

A	4.1	3.4	3.5
B	—	—	—
C	3.5	3.2	3.2
P	3.6	3.3	—

You are required to:
1. Calculate and fill in 19-2 ratios for the Portroy Co. Ltd.
2. What conclusions can be drawn from the data given?

24.10x From the following information for Growquick Ltd. prepare a Value Added Statement.

		£
Sales		30,000,000
Sundry costs:		
Wages, persons and benefits	5,000,000	
Depreciation	1,000,000	
Other items bought in from outside	8,000,000	14,000,000
Operating Profit		16,000,000
Interest charges		1,500,000
		14,500,000
Taxation — Corporation tax		7,000,000
Profit after Taxation		7,500,000
Dividend on Ordinary Shares		3,000,000
Retained Profit		4,500,000

Chapter Twenty Five

Working Capital and Flow of Funds

In the study of Business Ratios and Interpretation of Accounts the importance of Working Capital was emphasised. Defined as Current Assets less Current Liabilities the working capital can be thought of as the life-blood of an organisation. The fixed assets provide a body structure and the working capital provides one of the main means by which the structure is enabled to function. The following exhibit 25.1 illustrates how working capital flows within an organisation:-

WORKING CAPITAL FLOW
IN A MANUFACTURING FIRM

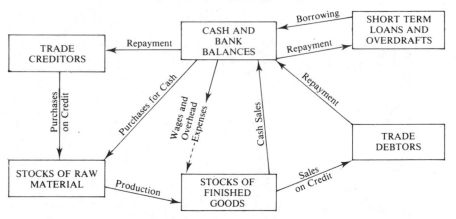

Note that part of the cost of wages and overheads will be added to the value of Stocks of finished goods. The other part will be charged against profit.

Exhibit 25.1

The important thing for management is to keep this cycle of transactions in balance. Perhaps the best way of doing this is through the development of budgets. For management the important thing is to anticipate the future. You have already studied budgets in this book and the development of the cash budget is a central element in the control of working capital. However because of the importance of working capital it is now standard accounting practice that a historic analysis of working capital change be included as an adjunct to the published accounts of larger organisations. This type of statement emphasises to users of accounts how management have controlled this important area during the past year.

In Exhibit 25.1 only working capital items were included. However in practice all the balance sheet items of Capital, Liabilities and Assets interact on Funds. Exhibit 25.2 illustrates the main headings of changes in funds in a Balance Sheet format.

Fixed Assets	Capital
Investments	Profits
	Loans
Current Assets less Current Liabilities	

Exhibit 25.2

Since we know from the accounting equation that Assets must equal Capital and Liabilities changes in any one of the items must be balanced elsewhere. For example if Fixed Assets increase in a period by £100 then either Capital or Profits or Loan must increase by £100 or Investments or Working Capital must be reduced by £100. Alternatively of course all these items might change in different combinations which amount to £100 net.

Exhibit 25.3 shows balance sheets for two dates a year apart for the Empton Company.

Empton Co.
Balance Sheets at 31 December

	19-1 £		19-2 £			19-1 £	19-2 £
Fixed Assets		500		600	Capital	300	500
Investments (long term)		450		400	Profits	360	400
Current Assets	300		400		Loans	440	300
less Current Liabilities	150	150	200	200			
		1100		1200		1100	1200

Exhibit 25.3

If we analyse the change between 19-1 and 19-2 in the Balance Sheets we get Exhibit 25.4.

Empton Co.
Changes in Year 19-2

	£			£
Fixed Assets	+ 100	Capital	+	200
Investments (long term)	− 50	Profits	+	40
Working Capital	+ 50	Loans	−	140
	+ 100		+	100

Exhibit 25.4

Exhibit 25.4 identified the major balance sheet changes over a year. On both sides of the balance sheet there are of course both positive changes (increases) and negative changes (reductions) in the items. There are potentially many ways in which these changes could be presented to users of accounts and there has therefore been a Statement of Standard Accounting Practice (Number Ten) prepared to suggest an appropriate format for most organisations to follow. In the Standard funds are taken to mean Working Capital. Thus the changes in all items other than working capital are expressed in relationship to working capital. Using Exhibit 25.4 as a guide we should analyse the data as follows in Exhibit 25.5:-

Empton Company
Fund Flow Statement for year ended 31 December 19-2

Sources of Funds		
Capital	200	
Profits	40	
Investments (sales of)	50	290
Application of Funds		
Fixed Assets	100	
Loans (repayment)	140	240
Increase in Working Capital		50

Exhibit 25.5

Note that Sources of Funds may include

(i)   Capital (increases)
(ii) Profits
(iii) Loans (increases)
as well as reductions in Fixed Assets and Investments through sale i.e.
(iv) Sales of Fixed Assets
(v) Sale of Long Term Investments.

Application of Funds may include

(i)   Increases in Fixed Assets
(ii) Increases in Long Term Investments
as well as
(iii) Losses
(iv) Repayment of Capital
(v) Repayment of Loan.

These are Summarised in Exhibit 25.6

	Effect on Working Capital	
	An increase in the following items changes working capital	A decrease in the following items changes working capital
Share Capital	+	−
Profit	+	−
Loans	+	−
Fixed Assets	−	+
Investments (long term)	−	+

Exhibit 25.6

When preparing a Fund Flow Statement for a detailed set of accounts it is useful to prepare a working analysis of the changes in a systematic fashion. One convenient way of doing this is to work out the differences between balance sheet figures according to the double entry rules. Increases in assets or reduction in capital or liabilities being debits and increases in capital and liabilities and reductions in assets being credits. In the following Exhibit 35.7 the differences are analyzed by these rules into debit or credit columns. These columns will then contain application of funds (debits) and sources of funds (credits) as well as balancing if our arithmetic is correct!

Bernardio Ltd.
Balance Sheets at 30 June

	19-1	19-2	Dr.	Cr.
Fixed Assets at Cost	8,000	9,000	1,000	
less Aggregate Depreciation	2,000	2,600		600
	6,000	6,400		
Investments at Cost	5,000	3,000		2,000
Current Assets				
Stock in Trade	6,000	8,000	2,000	
Trade Debtors	5,000	4,000		1,000
Cash at Bank	2,100	3,000	900	
	13,100	15,000		
Total Assets	24,100	24,400		
Share Capital				
Ordinary Shares of £1	10,000	12,000		2,000
Reserves				
Profit and Loss Account	5,000	7,500		2,500
	15,000	19,500		
Debenture Loan	4,000	—	4,000	
Current Liabilities				
Trade Creditors	5,100	4,900	200	
	24,100	24,400	8,100	8,100

Exhibit 25.7

Before preparing the final Fund Flow Statement a number of adjustments need to be made in order to give a clearer picture to the reader of the statement.

Any items in the accounts which do not have a direct impact on fund flow need to be adjusted. The main item under this heading is depreciation. Depreciation is charged in the accounts over the life of fixed assets, but it does not affect any element of working capital. The only time working capital is influenced is in the period the fixed asset is purchased, when for example cash is paid out. The adjustment made is in effect to reverse the original entry for depreciation. We add back the years depreciation to net profits and deduct the same figure from the aggregate provision for depreciation on the balance sheet. This leaves the change in Fixed Assets at cost price. This adjustment is usually shown as a separate line on the statement.

If Assets have been sold the balance sheet change will be at cost price. In Exhibit 25.7 for example Investments have reduced at cost price by £2000. If the cash received from selling these Investments had been £2,500, the profit over cost of £500 would have been included in the Profit and Loss Account figures. In this situation the profit on sales of investment would be taken out from Trading Profits and added back to the reduction of Investments at cost showing the figure of the cash received on sale £2,500 in the Statement.

Finally if a dividend of £800 has been paid out of the profits for the year, it would normally be added back to profit and shown as a separate application of funds.

Applying these adjustments to Exhibit 25.7 we would have a Fund Flow Statement as in Exhibit 25.8.

Bernardio Ltd.

Fund Flow Statement for Year ending 30 June 19-2

Sources of Funds		£
Sale of Investments (2000 + Profit 500)		2,500
Issue of Share Capital		2,000
Cash Contribution from Profits	2,800	
(£2,500 − Profit on Investment £500		
+ Dividend in Shares £800)		
add Depreciation for the year	600	3,400
		7,900
Application of Funds		
Purchase of Fixed Assets	1,000	
Payment of Dividend on Shares	800	
Repayment of Debentures	4,000	5,800
Increase in Working Capital		2,100

Exhibit 25.8

Note the Increase in Working Capital can be verified as follows: Working Capital in 19-1 is £8,000 (13,100 − 5,100) and in 19-2 £10,100 (15,000 − 4,900) i.e. an increase of £2,100.

The Fund Flow Statement would be completed by giving the details of the changes in items comprised in Working Capital as follows in Exhibit 25.9.

Increase in Working Capital	£
Increase in Stock in Trade	2,000
Increase in Cash at Bank	900
Reduction in Trade Creditors	200
	3,100
Reduction in Working Capital	
Reduction in Trade Debtors	1,000
Increase in Working Capital	2,100

Exhibit 25.9

Although a great many adjustments may be necessary in practice we have developed sufficient detail in the combinations of Exhibits 25.8 and 25.9 to show the basis of preparation of a Fund Flow Statement. The emphasis on the way in which the firm has raised funds and utilized them is a useful supplement to the standard form of Profit and Loss Account and Balance Sheet.

Cash Flow Statements

Some businesses prefer to emphasise cash change rather than working capital change. SSAP 10 emphasises working capital rather than cash because it tends to be easier for a business which wishes to manipulate the year end cash by for example not paying creditors for a longer than normal period or by extra efforts to collect cash from debtors. If however a business wishes to present the information in cash rather than working capital terms – the basic information is exactly the same. The working capital items other than cash are incorporated in the main statement leaving a single residual figure of cash change. This can be shown for Bernardio Ltd using the data in Exhibit 25.8 but restated as a cash flow statement.

Bernardio Ltd.
Cash Flow Statement for Year Ending 30 June 19-2

Sources of Cash

Sales of Investments	2,500	
Issue of Share Capital	2,000	
Cash Contribution from Profits	3,400	
Reduction in Trade Debtors	1,000	
		8,900

Applications of Cash

Purchase of Fixed Assets	1,000	
Payment of Dividends on Shares	800	
Repayment of Debentures	4,000	
Increase in Stock in Trade	2,000	
Reduction in Trade Creditors	200	
		8,000
Increase in Cash		900

Assignment Exercises

Assignment Exercises followed by the letter x do NOT have answers shown at the back of the book.

25.1x Describe with the use of a diagram the importance of working capital flows in a business.

25.2x Prepare a chart showing how changes in assets, capital and liabilities affect working capital.

25.3 The Balance Sheets of Jack Smith for two successive years are given below. You are require to prepare a fund flow statement for the year ending 31 December 19-5.

Balance Sheets at 31 December

	19-4 £'000	19-5 £'000		19-4 £'000	19-5 £'000
Capital Account					
1 January	8,400	9,400	Buildings at cost	5,200	5,500
Net Profit for the year	3,600	4,400	Plant (cost 4,000)	3,000	
	12,000	13,800	(cost 5,000)		3,500
Deduct Drawings	2,600	3,000	Current Assets:		
	9,400	10,800	Stock in Trade	1,320	1,260
Current Liabilities:			Trade Debtors	3,560	2,520
Trade Creditors	2,400	1,680	Cash at Bank	—	1,700
Bank overdrafts	1,280	—			
Loan	—	2,000			
	13,080	14,480		13,080	14,480

25.4x From the following information prepare a Fund Flow Statement.

Brentman Ltd.

Balance Sheets at 31 December	19-8 £	19-9 £
Fixed Assets at Cost	20,000	30,000
less Aggregate Depreciation	10,000	12,000
	10,000	18,000
Investments at Cost	6,000	3,000
Current Assets		
Stock in Trade	9,000	7,000
Trade Debtors	4,000	6,000
Cash at Bank	3,000	8,000
	32,000	42,000

	£	£
Share Capital		
Ordinary Shares of £1	12,000	15,000
Reserves		
Share Premium Account	–	3,000
Profit and Loss Account	11,000	14,000
Loan Stock	6,000	4,000
Current Liabilities		
Trade Creditors	3,000	6,000
	32,000	42,000

3,000 £1 Shares were issued during the year at a premium of £1 per share. The Profit and Loss Accounts in abbreviated form for the year ended 31 December 19-9 is:—

	£
Trading Profits	8,000
Depreciation	2,000
	6,000
Profit on Sales of Investments	1,000
	7,000
Corporation Tax	3,000
	4,000
Dividend on Ordinary Shares	1,000
	3,000
Retained Profit brought forward	11,000
Retained Profits carried forward	14,000

25.5 Using the data in 25.3 prepare a Cash Flow Statement for the year ending 31 December 19-5.

25.6x Express the solution to Brentman Ltd. in 25.4x as a cash flow rather than a working capital statement.

Chapter Twenty Six

Simple and Compound Interest Calculations

Most financial transactions involve interest calculations since interest is the charge for using money over time. If a business wishes to borrow money it will have to pay interest on the amount it borrows. The rate of interest will depend on the going market rates and the lender's assessment of the risk associated with lending to a particular type of customer. The higher the risk the higher the rate of interest.

Simple Interest

Simple interest applies where the period involved is not greater than a year. The amount of interest due is calculated from the formula:

Amount of interest (A) = Principal amount loaned (P) ×
Rate of Interest (r) × Unit of time (t)

Example: Interest has to be calculated on a loan from a Bank of £198,000 at a rate of 12% per annum for 59 days.

Rates of interest for loans will usually be expressed on an annual basis. The unit of time will therefore be the proportion of a year (365 days) for which the loan was obtained.

Thus

$$A = P r t$$

$$A = £198,000 \times .12 \times \frac{59}{365}$$

$$A = £3,840.66$$

Note in the formuli it is convenient to express r as a decimal rather than as a percentage i.e. .12 rather than 12%.

Another illustration where simple interest is common is where a business discounts a bill of exchange with a bank. The bill of exchange represents a promise to pay (by a third party usually a customer of the business) a specified sum of money at a fixed future date.

Example: A business holds a bill of exchange which promises to pay £20,000 in 90 days time. The business wants the cash now not in 90 days and the bank quotes a discount rate of interest of 15% on this type of transaction.

$$A = P r t$$

$$A = £20,000 \times .15 \times \frac{90}{365}$$

$$A = £739.73$$

The bank will thus pay to the business the Principal sum of £20,000 less the Amount of interest £739.73 which amounts to an immediate cash advance of £19,260.27.

Note that the interest rate which the business has really paid on this transaction is more than 15%. The business has in effect borrowed £19,260.27 for 90 days and paid interest of £739.73. This is equivalent to interest of 15.6% on the amount borrowed of £19,260.27. You can check this by using the interest formula:

$$A = P\,r\,t$$

$$r = \frac{A}{P\,t}$$

$$r = \frac{739.73}{9260.27 \times \dfrac{90}{365}} = 15.58\%$$

This represents the true rate of interest on the transaction as compared to the nominal rate of 15% used to work out the amount advanced on the bill of exchange.

In many borrowing situations it is important to note the difference between the nominal rate quoted by a lender and the real rate of interest being paid. Where a loan has to be repaid by instalments the real rate can be considerably higher than the nominal rate.

Example: John wants to borrow £1,000 for one year. The finance company quote interest of 10% but require £500 to be repaid after six months and the balance at the end of the year.

The interest to be paid is 10% of £1,000 =	£100
The amount borrowed will be 1,000 × ½ year =	500
500 × ½ year =	250
The equivalent amount borrowed for one year is	750

$$r = \frac{A}{P\,t} = \frac{100}{750 \times 1}$$

$$r = 13.33\%$$

The real rate of interest is thus 13.33% not 10%.

Compound Interest

Where a period of time greater than one year is involved the process of interest calculation becomes compound. This simply means that interest will become payable on the interest of the earlier period as well as the principal sum. If £100 is deposited in a bank for two years at 10% interest per annum, the interest earned is not twice the simple interest for one year which would be £20 (2 × £10). At the end of year one amount of simple interest of £10 would be added to the Principal and the total of £110 then reinvested for the second year at 10% which would earn £11 interest. The total interest earned over two years is thus £21.

If you compare the effect of compounding interest over a period of time with simple interest, for example where the interest earned is withdrawn at the end of each year, the difference is quite dramatic.

Example

Mr A invests £1,000 at 10% and allows the interest to be reinvested each year.

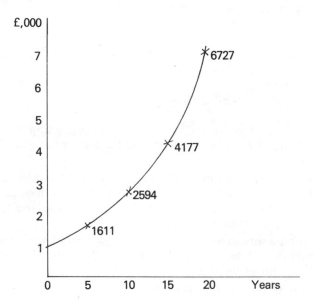

The graph shows the £1,000 increasing over 20 years to a sum of £6,727.

Compound Interest is calculated from the formula

Amount (A) = Principal (P) × (1 + rate of interest for the period (r)) to the power of the number of periods (n)

$$A = P(1 + r)^n$$

Example

What will £1,000 invested at 10% per annum compound accumulate to in 10 years?

$$
\begin{aligned}
A &= P(1 + r)^n \\
&= 1,000 (1 + .10)^{10} \\
&= 2,593.74
\end{aligned}
$$

The computations involved are not much problem if you have a calculator. It is also common to use tables which have been calculated for commonly used rates of interest. The tables are based on £1 invested at the rate of interest as shown in Exhibit 26.1.

Period of Compounding	£1 at compound interest at the end of the period Rate of interest per period			
	1%	2%	5%	10%
1	1.010	1.020	1.050	1.100
2	1.020	1.040	1.103	1.210
3	1.030	1.061	1.158	1.331
4	1.041	1.082	1.216	1.464
5	1.051	1.104	1.276	1.611
10	1.105	1.219	1.629	2.594
50	1.645	2.692	11.462	117.391

Example of a compound interest table

Exhibit 26.1

Example. You want to know what £500 will accumulate to over three years at 5% per annum interest.

The table shows that £1 invested for 3 periods at 5% will amount to £1.158. thus £500 will amount to £1.158 × 500 = £579.

If the compounding process is to take place more often than annually – the rate of interest must be changed to the rate for the compounding period rather than for a year.

Example. What will £500 accumulate to over three years at 5% per annum interest compounded on a quarterly basis?

The periods are now three months and therefore in total there are 12 periods in all. The rate of interest per period will be .05 ÷ 4 = .0125.

$$A = P (1+r)^n = 500 (1.0125)^{12}$$

$$A = 580.38$$

Notice that compounding quarterly as compared to annually, as in the previous example, makes a small difference of £1.38 to the accumulated amount. Because for most purposes the difference between annual and more frequent compounding is not material this text will normally use annual compounding.

It is sometimes useful to calculate the rate of return which an increase on an investment represents over a period of time.

Example. Jones bought a house for £10,000 on 1 January 19.1 and sold it for £12,100 on 31 December 19-2. What rate of return does this represent?

Using the tables requires the figures to be expressed in terms of £1. In this case 10,000:12,100 is equivalent to 1:1.210 for a two year period.

Looking across the table on the row for 2 periods compounding it can be seen that the return is equivalent to 10%.

Or Using the formula

$$A = P (1 + r)^n$$

$$r = \sqrt[n]{\frac{A}{P}} - 1 = \sqrt[2]{\frac{12,100}{10,000}} - 1$$

$$= .1 \text{ or } 10\%.$$

Assignment Exercises

Assignment Exercises followed by the letter X do NOT have answers shown at the back of the book.

26.1   (*a*)   What interest will be paid on a loan of £5,300 for 62 days at 17%?

         (*b*)   A bank offers to discount a bill of exchange for £9,000 with an outstanding period of 70 days at 19% interest. What will the bank pay for the bill of exchange.

26.2x   What is the real rate of interest involved in discounting the bill of exchange in 26.1?

26.3   Smith borrows £1,000 on 1 January 19-1 from a moneylender at an interest charge of £200. The repayment terms are £250 at the end of March, June, September and December 19-1. What real rate of interest is he paying?

26.4   How much interest is earned if £4,000 is held for 10 years at 10% p.a. interest compound?

26.5x   How much interest would have been earned if the compounding had been applied half-yearly?

26.6x   Jones bought some shares on 1 January 19-1 for £8,000 and sold them 4 years later on 31 December 19-4 for £9,728. What compound rate of interest does this increase represent?

Chapter Twenty Seven

Present Value

In the previous chapter we calculated that if £1,000 were invested at compound interest of 10% for 10 years it would accumulate to £2,594.

If we posed this question the other way round and asked what would be the value today of £2,594 if received 10 years into the future assuming interest at 10% the answer is a present value of £1,000.

Present value is simply the reciprocal of compound interest and is a useful approach to solving a number of investment problems.

The formula for compound interest is:

$$A = P (1 + r)^n$$

For the present value calculation we know the Amount (A) and wish to calculate the Principal (P). Divide both sides by $(I + r)^n$ gives

$$P = \frac{A}{(1+r)^n}$$

Example: You are promised a cash gift of £10,000 in two years time. The current rates of interest which you could obtain for this sum is 15%. What is its present value

$$P = \frac{A}{(1 + r)^n} = \frac{10,000}{(1.15)^2}$$

Present Value P = £7,561.4

As with compound interest the use of tables of present values is quite common. For example the value are shown here for the present value of £1 at a rate of interest of 10%. A full table is included in the appendix.

Periods	10%
1	.909
2	.826
3	.751
4	.683
5	.621

Example

If you are offered £1,000 at the end of each of the next five years in settlement of a debt of £4,000 should you accept? Assume interest at 10%.

			£
Year 1	£1,000 × .909 =		909
2	£1,000 × .826 =		826
3	£1,000 × .751 =		751
4	£1,000 × .683 =		683
5	£1,000 × .621 =		621
Present Value			3,790

The Present value of the five payments is £3,790 which is worth a little less than the debt of £4,000.

Sometimes in investment situations we happen to know in advance the Principal sum and the Amount and want to work out the rate of interest which completes the equation. This rate of interest is often called the internal rate of return.

Example

A friend offers to sell you the lease on some property which will entitle you to equal rent payments at the end of each of the next three years of £1,000.

He wants £2,550 for the lease and you want to calculate what interest rate is included in the deal.

This can be done by trial and error using the present value tables in the appendix. Firstly select a rate of interest as a guess − say 5%.

Year	£	Factor at 5%		£
1	1,000 ×	.952	=	952
2	1,000 ×	.907	=	907
3	1,000 ×	.864	=	864
				2,723

At five per cent interest the present value exceeds the amount asked for the lease of £2,500. A higher rate of interest will be required to reduce the amount closer to target. Try 8% and 9%: −

Year	£	Factor at 8%		£		9%		£
1	1,000 ×	.926	=	926	×	.917	=	917
2	1,000 ×	.857	=	857	×	.842	=	842
3	1,000 ×	.794	=	794	×	.772	=	772
				2,577				2,531

The rate of interest which will produce a present value of £2,550 lies between 8% and 9%. If we want to be more exact we can interpolate on an approximate basis as follows: –

$$\left.\begin{array}{l}8\% \text{ gives} \qquad 2,577 \\ \phantom{8\% \text{ gives} \qquad} \qquad \qquad -2,550 \\ 9\% \phantom{\text{ gives}} \qquad \underline{2,531} \\ \phantom{8\% \text{ gives} \qquad} \qquad \underline{46}\end{array}\right\} 19$$

2,550 is thus $\dfrac{19}{46}$ of 1% below 9%

i.e. $9 - .41 = 8.59\%$

Annuities

An annuity is a series, or one of a series, of equal payments at fixed intervals. For example, rent payable every month, quarter or year, is one form of annuity. The term annuity originated in the field of insurance where in exchange for a lump sum payment or a series of premiums a regular payment would be made to the annuitant during his life. Regular payments such as rents or purchase by instalments occur frequently in business and it is, therefore, useful to know something about the calculation of annuities.

In practice there are a number of different kinds of annuity varying mainly in the details of when the regular payments are made, for example at the beginning or end of the period. In this chapter attention is centred entirely on the Ordinary Annuity in which the equal periodic payments occur at the end of the period. In practice, with a little thought it will be possible to handle most situations with a knowledge of how to calculate an Ordinary Annuity.

Formula for the Amount of an Ordinary Annuity

The amount of an annuity of £1 per period for three periods at 5 per cent interest might be determined as follows:

The first rent payment of £1 accumulates at 5 per cent interest for two periods and grows to:

$$£1 (1 + 0.05)^2 = £1.1025$$

The second rent payment of £1 accumulates at 5 per cent
interest for one period and grows to: £1.05
The third rent is due at the end of the annuity period £1.00

These added up to £3.1525

To develop the formula for the annuity we need to examine the relationship between compound interest, and an annuity of the amount of interest. If £1 is invested for two periods at 5 per cent interest we have shown above that it will accumulate to £1.1025. Deducting the original investment from this amount we are left with the compound interest on £1 for two periods as

£0.1025. This amount is simply the amount of an annuity of 5 per cent of £1 for two periods at 5 per cent.

This can be set down as:

$$0.05 \times \text{Annuity} = 1 \, (1+0.05)^2 - 1$$

or $\qquad \text{Annuity} = 1 \dfrac{(1+0.05)^2 - 1}{0.05} = \dfrac{(1.05)^2 - 1}{0.05}$

Substituting generalized letters into the formula

$$\text{Annuity} = R\dfrac{(1+r)^n - 1}{r}$$

Where R = the annuity per period.

As in previous examples tables are available calculated on the basis of £1 to assist calculations; see the Appendix.

Example. A company plans to invest £1,000 at the end of the year for each of the next five years at an interest rate of 5 per cent per annum. How much will have accumulated at the end of the fifth year?

$$£1,000\dfrac{(1+0.05)^5 - 1}{.05} = £5,525.631$$

or using tables

$$£1,000 \times 5.526 = £5,526$$

It will frequently be useful to know the amount required by way of periodic rents to accumulate to a known future sum, for example when establishing a sinking fund.

It has already been established that where the amount of an annuity = *A*

$$A = R\dfrac{(1+r)^n - 1}{r}$$

$$R = \dfrac{Ar}{(1+r)^n - 1}$$

Example. A company wishes to set aside equal annual amounts at the end of each year of the next four years, to accumulate to a fund of £5,000 for the replacement of assets. The amounts set aside will be invested at 6 per cent per annum interest. What amounts should be set aside?

$$R = \dfrac{Ar}{(1+r)^n - 1} = \dfrac{5,000(0.06)}{(1.06)^4 - 1} = £1,142.9578$$

This figure can be proved correct by the table below worked (as would be normal) to the nearest £1.

	Deposit £	Interest £	Increase in fund £	Balance of fund £
End of year 1	1,143	–	1,143	1,143
End of year 2	1,143	69	1,212	2,355
End of year 3	1,143	141	1,284	3,639
End of year 4	1,143	218	1,361	5,000

Example. What amount invested annually at 5 per cent per annum will provide £1 in five years time?

$$R = \frac{Ar}{(1+r)^n - 1} = \frac{1(0.05)}{(1.05)^5 - 1} = £0.180975$$

The Present Value of Annuities

It will often be necessary to calculate the present value of an annuity to evaluate a business problem. The present value of an annuity is the amount which if it were invested now at compound interest would be just sufficient to allow for the withdrawal of equal amounts (rents) at the end of a fixed number of periods. For example, we may wish to know whether to pay £135 cash now for a television or five instalments of 30 over the next two-and-a-half years instead. By converting the five instalments to a present cash value we can make direct comparison with the £135 cash price. If the present value of the annuity is more than £135 we should choose to pay cash. If, however, it comes to less than £135 the instalment method is cheaper. The result obtained will depend on the rate of interest used in the calculation.

The present value of an annuity will be equal to the sum of the present values of every individual rent payment. This can be illustrated in the above example, assuming an 8 per cent rate of interest. The calculation shows it better at this rate of interest to pay by instalment.

Period	£		Present Value Multiplier from Tables		£
1	30	×	0.962	=	28.86
2	30	×	0.925	=	27.75
3	30	×	0.889	=	26.67
4	30	×	0.855	=	25.65
5	30	×	0.822	=	24.66
					133.59

(*Note:* when taking a half-yearly period the annual rate of interest is halved. The multiplier is therefore from the 4 per cent column of the Present Value tables.)

The formula for finding the present value of an ordinary annuity is developed as follows:

Compound discount (equivalent to compound interest) is the amount by which the total investment at compound interest will exceed the original capital. On the basis of £1:

$$\text{Discount} = 1 - \frac{1}{(1+r)^n}$$

By the same process of argument that was used when developing the formula for an ordinary annuity, it can be shown that the compound discount on £1 at 5 per cent is equal to 5 per cent of the present value of an annuity of £1. Thus

$$r \times \text{Present Value} = 1 - \frac{1}{(1+r)^n}$$

$$\text{Present Value} = \left[\frac{1 - \dfrac{1}{(1+r)^n}}{r}\right]$$

Tables are given in the Appendix to show the present values of an annuity of £1.

Example (details per previous example). The present value of five half-yearly payments of £30 at 8 per cent per annum would be: –

$$R = \left[\frac{1 - \dfrac{1}{(1+r)^n}}{r}\right] = 30\left[\frac{1 - \dfrac{1}{(1+0.04)^5}}{0.04}\right] = \text{£133.57}$$

or using the tables $30 \times 4.452 = \text{£133.56}$.

Finally, to prove that the present value of an annuity is the amount which if it were invested now at compound interest would be just sufficient to allow for the withdrawal of equal amounts at the end of a fixed number of periods, we can show that the present value of £133.57 just calculated would fulfil this condition for withdrawals of £30 over five half-yearly periods with interest at 8 per cent per annum.

		£	
Start		133.57	
Period 1	Interest	5.34	(133.57 at 8 per cent for 6 months)
	Payment	(30.00)	
Balance		108.91	
Period 2	Interest	4.35	
	Payment	(30.00)	
Balance		83.26	
Period 3	Interest	3.33	
	Payment	(30.00)	
Balance		56.59	
Period 4	Interest	2.26	
	Payment	(30.00)	
Balance		28.85	
Period 5	Interest	1.15	
	Payment	(30.00)	
Balance		00.00	

Assignment Exercises

Assignment Exercises followed by the letter X do NOT have answers shown at the back of the book.

27.1 A property developer offers to buy your rights under a lease to rents amounting to £5,000 p.a. for the next seven years. He offers you an immediate cash sum of £20,000. You can invest the money at 12% p.a. interest. Should the offer be accepted?

27.2x Using the information in question 27.1 what interest rate would exactly equate the developers' offer to the rental income?

27.3 A company obtains a loan of £100,000 for five years. One of the conditions of the loan is that the company will each year pay an equal amount into a sinking fund to accumulate over the five years to amount of the loan repayable. The sinking fund will earn interest at 10% p.a. How much must be paid into the sinking fund each year?

27.4x Using the data in 27.3 how much would the amount paid into the sinking fund be if the interest rate was changed to 15% p.a.?

Chapter Twenty Eight

Capital Budgeting

In the budgeting chapters earlier in the book attention was given to the application of budgets in the context of management control of operations. Operating budgets of this kind concentrate mainly on the control of activity within the next twelve months. Thus in this context it is not usual to include the specific interest cost of these activities since it could make the calculations over detailed and complex and would not make a significant difference to the decisions made.

When however the business is planning investment in fixed assets or things which involve a long term committment of the organisations resources then the budgeting process should include interest as an important cost element in the decision about whether to invest or not. This process is what is termed Capital Budgeting.

The process of evaluating investments taking into account interest requires that cash budgets are dealt with rather than the figures used in profit calculations. In profit calculation for example depreciation of fixed assets is included in the expenses. However since depreciation does not involve cash — it is not relevant for capital budgeting. Interest is only relevant to cash flows and it is these that Capital Budgeting concentrates on. The two aspects of cash flows on an investment are the cash outflows on the acquisition and setting up of the project and the cash inflows which are expected to be generated. It is the balance between outflow and inflow which determines whether the investment is worthwhile.

Investment Outlays

The cash outlay involved in an investment will include a variety of different items. If for example the investment is in plant and machinery the outlay will include not only the invoice cost of the equipment bought — but also the cost of installation, commissioning which means the costs of a period of adjustment until it operates at full efficiency, and possibly training of new personnel. In addition the introduction of new plant and machinery might involve extra funds for working capital tied up in the operation.

Example

Progress Ltd is planning to introduce new machines. The outlays anticipated on the acquisition are as follows: –

	Cash Flow – Outlay
	£
Invoice Cost of Machines	50,000
Carriage Inward	2,000
Installation – cost of wages of own employees	1,000
	53,000
Cost of materials and wages in commissioning machines	5,000
Training Cost – Wages of operatives	2,000
	60,000
Additional Working Capital	14,000
Cash Outlay	74,000

If the outlays in the Example for Progress Ltd had been on machinery designed to replace existing equipment – perhaps justified by claims of greater efficiency for the new machines – then the decision would be taken based on the incremental outlays compared to the incremental inflows – i.e. the net additional cash required to be invested on the new scheme compared to the additional cash earned or saved.

Thus in the example the additional outlay comparing with existing machines would not include working capital (assuming outputs are the same) since this is already required in the existing set-up. Also the buying of new equipment – implies that the old can be sold – thus the cash from sale should be deducted from the outlay

		£
i.e	Cost of Machines and installations etc.	60,000
	less Sale of old machines	10,000
	Net Cash Outlay	50,000

The net outlay of £50,000 will then be compared with the cash saved by using the new process.

This incremental approach is important for assessing improvements and where the equipment is for example part of a large factory where it will be impossible to identify all the cash flow implications of one small part of the total unit.

The Cash outflows on an investment in a large project may be spread over a number of periods. The development can spread over several years from its first inception. It may therefore be necessary to discount back the outlays to a present value at the start of the project.

Example: The cash outlays on a new factory development were estimated as follows: —

			£
Year 1.	Development and Buildings		100,000
2.	Installation of Equipment		50,000
3.	Commissioning		30,000
			180,000

The Present Value of these outflows if interest is assumed to be 10% would be: —

Period	£				£
1	100,000	×	.909	=	90,900
2	50,000	×	.826	=	41,300
3	30,000	×	.751	=	22,530
Present Value					£154,730

The Present Value of outlays at the start of the project — often called period 0 — is £154,730. This figure would be compared with the Present Value of Inflows.

An important aspect of investment cash flows is that they will give rise to tax implications. The purchase of Plant and Machinery for example will give rise to allowances which can be deducted from taxable income. Thus for a company which buys a new machine for £100,000 and pays Corporation Tax at 52% on its profits the cash flows will be firstly an outlay on purchase of £100,000 secondly its tax bill when due for payment will be reduced by 52% of £100,000 i.e. £52,000. The machine thus costs a net amount of £48,000 although since tax payments lag behind actual events the £52,000 saving of tax may be a year or more behind the original purchase date.

The actual calculation of tax payments can be complex and requires a detailed knowledge of the tax laws, which are beyond the scope of this book. However in principle all that needs to be taken into account are the cash outflows or inflows for tax which will arise from the investment decision. These may have to be calculated by a person competent in tax.

Cash Inflows

The other aspect of the Capital Budgeting process is to estimate the cash which will be generated by the new investment.

If the investment is in something new — then the estimates will be cash budgets of the sales and expenses expected to be generated by the new investment. The approach will be exactly the same as for the operating cash budgets prepared for management in planning its cash requirements — except that the requirement here is usually for the annual figures over the anticipated life of the investment, rather than on a month by month basis.

If the investment is in improvement or replacement of an existing process then the cash inflow will be the savings expected as compared to the existing situation.

As with the cash outflows the net inflows expected from an investment will be subject to tax. The tax consequences of the new business must be worked out and the cash payments for tax included in the calculation of net cash inflows.

Example. The expected results from buying a new machine for £6,000 have been estimated to produce sales of £6,000 per annum for four years and the production costs would be £2,500 for materials, labour and other cash outlays. Working Capital required will be £2,000 which will be recoverable at the end of the fourth year. Depreciation per annum would be £1,500 and the company pays Corporation tax nine months after its accounting year end at 52%.

The profit expected each year is thus:

		£
Sales		6,000
Material, Labour and		
other costs	2,500	
Depreciation	1,500	4,000
		2,000
Corporation Tax		1,040
Net Profit		960

But for Capital Budgeting the cash flow analysis would be: −

Investment Outlay	*Year 1*	*2*	*3*	*4*	*5*
Cost of Machine	(6,000)				
Working Capital	(2,000)			2,000	
Taxation Allowance on					
Capital Expenditure		3,220			
	(8,000)	3,220	−	2,000	−
Cash Flows					
Sales	6,000	6,000	6,000	6,000	
Costs of Material and Labour					
etc.	(2,500)	(2,500)	(2,500)	(2,500)	
Tax (52% × 3,500)		(1,820)	(1,820)	(1,820)	(1,820)
	3,500	1,680	1,680	1,680	(1,820)

Exhibit 28.1

The evaluation of the budgeted cash flows will be dealt with in the next chapter.

Assignment Exercises

Assignment Exercises followed by the letter X do NOT have answers shown at the back of the book.

28.1   The Raynor Company's project engineers have made the following estimates of costs on a new project: –

19-1

1 January	Rent paid for one year to 31 December 19-1 on premises for the plant	£5,000
31 January	Machinery purchased	£50,000
31 March	Installation costs paid for machinery	£10,000
31 December	Cost of Wages and material in commissioning plant	£15,000

19-2

1 January	Rent paid for year to 31 December 19-2	£5,000
31 March	Further commissioning costs	£8,000
30 June	Training costs for labour	£2,000
30 September	Working Capital provided for inventories and debtors (extra to that required in existing plant)	£10,000
31 December	Cash received from scrap value of old plant replaced by the project	£8,000

Ignoring taxation prepare a statement of the cash outlay on the project in 19-1 and 19-2. The plant is estimated to be in full use on 1 October 19-2.

28.2   Using the data in question 28.1 and assuming that the company is taxed at a rate of 50%, nine months after the end of its financial year on the 31 December, show the impact of tax on the cash flows. For tax purposes the company can obtain 100% allowance on the cost of machinery in its assessment based on 19-1. The scrap value cash in 19-2 will be fully taxable in that year.

28.3   Using the net of tax cash flows produced in question 28.2 and assuming an interest rate of 15%, what is the present value of the cash flows at the start of the project?

28.4x   The annual profit expected from a new project is calculated as follows: –

	£	£
Sales		50,000
Materials, Labour and Overheads	20,000	
Depreciation	5,000	
		25,000
Net Profit before tax		25,000
Corporation Tax at 50%		12,500
Net Profit after tax		12,500

The investment in machinery will take place on 1 July 19-1 amounting to £25,000 it will last five years with no residual value. Working Capital will also be required from 1 July 19-1 amounting to £10,000 and will be recovered at the end of the project. Tax allowances of 100% of the cost of machinery can be claimed in the first year. Tax at the rate of 50% of profits is payable 9 months after the accounting year end which is 30 June. Profits on the project will start immediately the machinery is installed.

Prepare a budget of the cash flows arising from the project.

28.5x What is the Present Value of the Net Cash flows in question 28.4x if the interest rate is 10% p.a.

28.6x The installed and commissioned cost of a new machine is estimated to be £100,000. Corporation Tax payable will be reduced by 52% of the cost of machinery in the year following its purchase. The new machinery is estimated to have a five year life with nil residual value and will be depreciated straight line. The new machine replaces an old piece of equipment which would be depreciated over the next five years at £3,000 per year, if not replaced, and would then have a nil book value. The new equipment is estimated to save material costs each year of £30,000. The old equipment could be sold (in the first year) for £6,000, but tax at 52% would payable next year. All profits are taxed at 52% payable a year after the accounting date.

Prepare the cash flow statement necessary to evaluate the project.

How will the reported profits change in the financial accounts?

Chapter Twenty Nine

Capital Expenditure Evaluation I

There are several ways of working out whether or not a capital expenditure is worthwhile. The simplest systems do not include interest in the evaluation and are therefore deficient in this important respect. They are however frequently used and may be a worthwhile addition to the more complete evaluations which include interest.

Payback

This measures the time taken to recover the cash outlay on the project. If we use the data on cash flows from Exhibit 28.1 the cash figures are as follows: –

Year	Investment Outlay £	Cash Inflow £	Net Cash Flow £	Cumulative Cash Flow £
1	(8,000)	3,500	(4,500)	(4,500)
2	3,220	1,680	4,900	400
3	–	1,680	1,680	2,080
4	2,000	1,680	3,680	5,760
5	–	(1,820)	(1,820)	3,940

The net cash flow is negative in the first year but becomes positive in the second year. To work out the time when the cash outlay is recovered assuming the cash flows evenly during the year we calculate $\dfrac{4,500}{4,900} \times 365$ days = 335 days. Thus the payback on this project occurs after 1 year 335 days or approximately 1.92 years.

Firms using payback as a method of evaluation would normally have a period fixed as a cut off point. For example if the cut off time were 3 years then all projects which had a payback of more than 3 years would be rejected.

The advantage of the payback method is that it emphasises the early return of cash which may be of utmost importance to a firm with liquidity problems. The disadvantage it has is that it ignores the results after payback has been achieved. For example if we had a project which showed a cumulative cash flow of: – year 1 £(4,500) and year 2 £400 and no further cash flows then the payback would still be 1.92 years and no regard is given to subsequent years. It would therefore be given the same evaluation as the previous example where cash flows conformed with the future. Whilst in this case the difference between the two would be clear – in a more complicated case it may not be easy to discriminate between alternatives.

Accounting Rate of Return

This is defined as: $\dfrac{\text{Average annual net profit after tax}}{\text{Average investment}}$

If again we use the information from Exhibit 28.1 in the previous chapter we know that the expected profit after tax in each of the four years is expected to be £960. The investment in machinery is £6,000 at the start and nil at the end assuming it is being depreciated straight line. The average investment would normally be calculated at $\frac{1}{2}$ the opening value + closing value i.e. $\frac{1}{2}(6,000+0) = £3,000$. The working capital remains constant at £2,000 – the calculation for working capital is the same $\frac{1}{2}(2,000+2,000) = £2,000$. Thus the total average investment would be £3,000 + £2,000 = £5,000. The tax relief on the capital expenditure is included with the corporation tax assessed on profits.

The return is therefore $\dfrac{960}{5,000} = 19.2\%$.

This accounting rate of return relates to the results shown in the annual accounts. However as an average it should not be forgotten that there will be significant differences between the start and end of the projects life. In the example given the figures each year would be: –

Net Profit	Year 1	Year 2	Year 3	Year 4
Net Book Value of Machine + Working Capital at mid-year	$\dfrac{960}{7,250} = 13.2\%$	$\dfrac{960}{5,720} = 16.7\%$	$\dfrac{960}{4,250} = 22.6\%$	$\dfrac{960}{2,750} = 34.9\%$

With a depreciating asset the rate of return appears to increase as the net book value declines, even though profits are constant.

Present Value and Internal Rate of Return

So far the methods employed to evaluate capital expenditure have ignored interest which means that only in certain circumstances would these methods approximate to the correct evaluation employing compound interest. Taking the facts again from the previous example in Exhibit 28.1 we can calculate the return assuming a required rate of interest of 15%.

	Investment Outlay	Cash Inflow	Net Cash Flow
1	(8,000)	3,500	(4,500)
2	3,220	1,680	4,900
3		1,680	1,680
4	2,000	1,680	3,680
5		(1,820)	1,820

	Investment Outlay			Cash Inflow			Net Cash Flow	
1	(8,000) × .870 =	(6,960)	3,500 × .870 =	3,045		(4,500) × .870 =	(3,915)	
2	3,220 × .756 =	2,434	1,680 × .756 =	1,270		4,900 × .756 =	3,704	
3	–	–	1,680 × .658 =	1,105		1,680 × .658 =	1,105	
4	2,000 × .572 =	1,144	1,680 × .572 =	961		3,680 × .572 =	2,105	
5	–	–	(1,820) × .497 =	(904)		(1,820) × .497 =	(904)	
		(3,382)		5,477			2,095	

The Net Present Value of this project using an interest rate of 15% is £2,095, which indicates that the discounted value of the inflows exceeds the discounted value of the investment outlay by this net amount. The project is therefore worthwhile provided the funds of the business do not cost more than 15%.

The Internal Rate of Return is the rate of interest which will when applied to the cash flows equate Investment Outlay and Cash Inflow or in other words discount the Net Cash Flow to zero.

As was previously illustrated this is done by trial and error. Using the rates from the tables at 50% and 60% we get

Year	Net Cash Flow	r = 50% factor		r = 60% factor	
1	(4,500)	.667	(3,001)	.625	(2,812)
2	4,900	.444	2,176	.391	1,916
3	1,680	.296	497	.244	410
4	3,680	.198	729	.153	563
5	(1,820)	.132	(240)	.095	(173)
Net Present Value			161		(96)

Interpolating between the two one can estimate that the rate producing a Net Present Value of zero will fall $\frac{96}{257}$ × 10% below 60% i.e. at approximately 56% which is the Internal Rate of Return on the Project. The actual return in this project is therefore well above the cost of capital to the company – assuming that this is 15%.

Exercises Exercises

Assignment Exercises followed by the letter X do NOT have answers shown at the back of the book.

29.1 A project to install new equipment has the following estimated cash flows: −

Year	Investment Outlay	Cash Inflow	Net Cash Flow
1	20,000	(11,000)	9,000
2	–	(6,000)	(6,000)
3	–	(3,000)	(3,000)
4	(2,000)	–	(2,000)
	18,000	(20,000)	(2,000)

(figures in brackets represent cash inflows)
What is the payback period for the project?

29.2 Using the data in 29.1 calculate the Net Present Value of the project with a discount rate of 10%.

29.3 Using the data in 29.1 calculate the Internal Rate of Return generated by the project.

29.4x Project Delta involves the outlay of £400,000 at the start of the project with net cash inflow of £200,000 at the end of year 1 and £100,000 at the end of year 2 and £300,000 at the end of year 3.

Calculate − payback period, internal rate of return and net present value with interest at 15%.

29.4x The Rathbone Company buys a machine for £100,000 which will be depreciated straight line over five years to a residual value of £5,000. The Profits estimated on the project will be as follows (for each of the five years)

		£
Sales		60,000
Operating Costs	30,000	
Depreciation	19,000	
		49,000
Net Profit		11,000

Ignoring taxation − what is the accounting rate of return?

29.6x Using the data in 29.5x calculate the internal rate of return. Assume cash arises in the same year as sales − and no working capital is required.

Chapter Thirty

Capital Expenditure Evaluation II

In the majority of cases both the Present Value method and the Internal Rate of Return method will give the same result. In certain circumstances there can be conflict and it is necessary therefore to know which method is yielding the right result.

The circumstances in which the conflict arises is where projects are mutually exclusive − that is where only one can be chosen − and where there are differences in the timing of cash flows or in the size of cash flows on the projects.

Example. The Cash Investment in each of two projects is £10,000 Project A has a cash inflow in year 2 of £13,000 whilst Project B for a cash inflow in year 5 of £17,620.

Assuming that the rate of interest used by the company is 10% then the Present Value of the projects is

	Cash Outlay Year 0	Cash Inflow Year 2	Cash Inflow Year 5	Present Value Factor at 10%	P.V. of Inflow	Net Present Value
Project A	10,000	13,000		.826	10,739	738
Project B	10,000		17,620	.621	10,942	942

Exhibit 30.1
i.e. Project B would be selected.

The Internal Rate of Return on these cash flows is: −
Project A approximately 14% (13,000 × .769 = 9,997)
and Project B approximately 12% (17,620 × .567 = 9,991)
i.e. Project A would be selected.

The conflict in the two measures arises because of the difference in the timing of cash flows between the two alternative investments. Project A produces its cash inflow in year 2 whereas Project B is delayed until year 5. To determine which method is the best selector − the opportunity value of the cash funds generated has to be considered i.e. what rate of return can be earned on the funds elsewhere. It Project A's inflow can be reinvested at 14% then it is the best choice. However if only 10% can be generated then B is better.

This problem could be looked at rather like a bank deposit problem. Up until the end of year 2 both A & B are overdrawn by £10,000. At the end of year 2 project A receives £13,000 and thus goes into credit for year 3, 4 and

5. if interest is less than 14%, whereas project B stays overdrawn until the end of year 5. Numerically the accounts would be as follows if 10% and 14% interest were charged and earned in the account.

	Project A		Project B	
	using 10%	using 14%	using 10%	using 14%
Year 0	(10,000)	(10,000)	(10,000)	(10,000)
Year 1 interest	(1,000)	(1,400)	(1,000)	(1,400)
	(11,000)	(11,400)	(11,000)	(11,400)
Year 2 interest	(1,100)	(1,596)	(1,100)	(1,596)
cash	13,000	13,000	(12,100)	(12,990)
	900	Say 0		
Year 3 interest	90		(1,210)	(1,819)
	990		(13,310)	(14,815)
Year 4 interest	99		(1,331)	(2,074)
	1,089		(14,641)	(16,889)
Year 5 interest	109		(1,464)	(2,365)
cash	–		17,620	17,620
	1,198	0	1,515	(1,634)

As we showed using the present value approach project B has accumulated a bigger value at the end of the project using 10%. Notice that these end values in year 5 can be discounted back to the Net Present Value at the start i.e. $1,198 \times .621 = 744$ and $1,515 \times .621 = 941$ (small differences are due to rounding errors). Using 14% interest Project A just breaks even whilst Project B loses − remaining in overdraft!

Thus the assumption about what the finds generated will earn elsewhere can be crucial in this type of choice where it is a question of deciding between alternatives which are mutually exclusive. As a rule of thumb many firms choose the Net Present Value since the assumption about the rate of interest earned is likely to be realistic − but this is by no means always so.

The problem just considered also raises the difficulty in general of comparing projects which have different life cycles. For example one project may involve buying equipment which requires replacement every two years whilst another requires replacement every five years. In comparing the alternatives it may be helpful to work out the annualised cost of each based on a period of time which is the lowest common multiple of the two or more choices. For example a 10 year cycle would be taken for projects with 2 and 5 year lives.

The way to calculate the annualised figure of cash flow is to firstly calculate the net present value of the alternatives. If for example using data in Exhibit 30.1 the N.P.V. of a project with a two year life were £738 and assuming that a 10% rate of interest were appropriate then the annualised figure is the amount of the annuity for two years with a present value of £738. Referring to the tables we can see that the present value of £1 per period for two years at 10% is £1.736. It x is the annualised amount then

$$1.736x = 738$$
$$\therefore x = 425$$

Diagrammatically what we have done is convert cash flows as follows: –

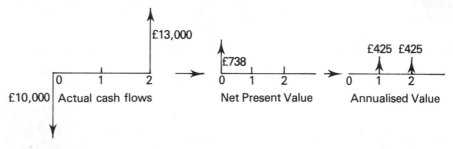

Exhibit 30.2

Using the data from Exhibit 30.1 for Machine B which has a five year life the accumulated net cash flow figure would be calculated using the N.P.V. of £942 and the figure from the tables for the present value of an annuity for five years at 10% which equals 3.791 then

$$3.791 \ x = 942$$
$$x = 248$$

We can then compare annualised net cash flow for machine B of £248 with that for machine A of £425. Selecting the alternative with the highest net cash flow on an annualised basis would give project A.

This technique can be used to compare projects on the basis of costs rather than net cash flows – when the alternative with the lowest annualised cost would be selected.

Assignment Exercises

Assignment Exercises followed by the letter X do NOT have answers shown at the back of the book.

30.1   A company is considering a project which has two possible alternative solutions A or B. The estimated data is shown below – calculate Internal Rate of Return and N.P.V. using 12% interest. Which should be selective?

Project	Net Cash Outlay Year 0 £	Net Cash Benefit Year 4 £
A	16,000	(28,984)
B	44,000	(74,324)

30.2x A company is considering two mutually exclusive projects X and Y. Calculate the internal rate of return and N.P.V. at a 10% discount rate. Which alternative should be chosen.

	Net Cash Outlay	*Net Cash Benefits*	
	Year 0	*Year 2*	*Year 6*
Project	£	£	£
X	30,000	(39,012)	–
Y	30,000	–	(59,172)

30.3 A machine is estimated to generate the following cash flows: –

Year	*Net Cash Flows*
0	8,000
1	(4,000)
2	(2,000)
3	(6,000)

(Cash inflow shown in brackets)

(1) Calculate the N.P.V. using 12% interest.

(2) What is the annualised amount of the net benefits from this project.

30.4 An alternative to the machine in question 30.3 is equipment with an expected life of 6 years. The N.P.V. of the unequal net cash flows from this equipment amounts to £2,624 using 12% interest rate. What is the annualised equivalent of the £2,624 N.P.V.? Would you choose the machine from 30.3 or this equipment – based on annualised benefits?

30.5x The Repair Co. is considering alternative investments in machines. Machine X costing £2,000 will last for 3 years only and cost £1,000 p.a. to operate. Machine Y costs £5,000 but will last for 6 years. It will cost £100 p.a. for the first three years and £600 p.a. for the last three years of its life to operate. Calculate the annualised cost of Machine X and Y over a six year period, assuming that the replacement cost for Machine X at the end of year 3 is £1,800 and interest rate of 10%. Which machine would you choose based on this data?

Chapter Thirty One

Leasing

Leasing is an important method for many organisations to acquire assets. Things as diverse as motor vehicles, televisions, computers, machinery and buildings are commonly leased rather than bought. In a lease the lessor owns the object and leases it to the user, the lessee. The agreement which is legally binding and non-cancellable usually covers the major part of the economic life of the asset. The lessee in exchange for the use of the asset agrees to pay a rental, keep the item in good condition, insure it and properly service it. The rental payments and other costs are fully chargeable against the taxable profits of the lessee. The lessor as owner of the assets can claim all Capital Allowances for tax purposes against his taxable profits.

Leasing is possible because of the different costs of capital and tax situations between lessors and lessees. For example a company wishing to obtain a computer costing £100,000 may find it attractive to lease because the financial institution funding the operating can borrow at much lower rates than the company and its marginal tax rates against which the capital allowances on the computer can be set are significantly higher for the financial institution than the company.

The problem facing an organisation therefore is to compare the relative attractiveness of obtaining the use of an asset by buying it outright funding from normal sources of capital or whether to lease it.

The Interest Rate Implied in a Lease

In the type of decision which has to be made the purchase price of an asset is known, as are the rental terms. From this an interest rate can be derived: —

A computer costing £100,000 has an expected life of 5 years with no scrap value. It can be leased for £27,740 per annum. The interest rate is that at which: —

The Cost of the Item = Present Value of the annual rental payments

$100,000 = 27,740 \times x$ (where x is the factor for the present value of an annuity of £1 for 5 years)

$$\therefore x = \frac{100,000}{27,740} = 3.605$$

By looking across the tables for the present value of an annuity on the five year period it will be seen that 3.605 corresponds to a rate of interest of 12%.

If scrap values are involved the calculation would have to be made as in the trial and error method of calculating internal rate of return.

This calculation has ignored the impact of taxation which may be crucial in the ultimate choice between leasing or buying. In the example we have just examined the rental payments would be deducted from taxable income and the net of tax cost would therefore be reduced by the tax borne by the company on its profits. If the tax rate were 42% of profits then the net of tax cost of the lease could be 58% of £27,740 = £16,089 and the corresponding interest rate would be 58% × 12% = 6.96%. (This ignores possible time lags in obtaining tax relief).

This net of tax rate of interest can be compared with the organisations net of tax cost of capital.

Using annualised cost

In the previous chapter the method of converting cash flows into annualised amounts is one method of comparing the buying decision with the alternative of leasing. The cost of buying the computer we know is £100,000. Capital Allowances for tax purposes of 100% of costs would be obtained in year 1 at the tax rate of 42%. There is a nil residual value at the end of 5 years. The Company's net of tax cost of capital is 10%.

Cash Flows

Year 0   (100,000)
1   42,000   (assuming tax bill reduced by 42% × 100,000)
2   –
3   –
4   –
5   –
$$\text{N.P.V.} = (100,000) - (42,000 \times .909) = (61,822)$$

The annualised figure is thus: –
$$61,822 = 3.791 \times x$$
$$x = 16,307$$

The annualised cost of buying the asset is £16,307 and should be compared with the net of tax cost of leasing which amounted to £16,089. Since these figures are so close − the organisation would consider all the other factors surrounding the decision before making its choice.

It would also have been possible to compare the N.P.V. of the lease payments with the N.P.V. for buying.

For leasing the N.P.V. net of tax =
Rental × Present Value of an annuity of £1 for 5 years at 10% =
$$16,089 \times 3.791 = £60,993.$$

The N.P.V. of leasing is an outlay of £60,993 compared to buying of £61,822. Notice that the organisations costs of capital of 10% has been used to discount the rental payments to a N.P.V. rather than the interest rate implied in the lease of 6.96%. It is normal to use the average cost of capital rather than the marginal rate implicit in the particular transaction.

Notice that the benefits of the investment in the equipment have not been considered. We have simply compared alternative costs of buying or leasing the same equipment. The overall investment decision could be taken by comparing these costs with the benefits accruing from the investment.

The Financial Implications of Leasing

Signing a lease creates a legal obligation to continue paying the rental. The amount of the obligation to the lessor and the benefits obtainable by the organisation under the lease do not normally appear on the face of the organisation's Balance Sheet in conventional accounting. In considering the organisations financial structure however – a lease represents the equivalent of a loan (as a clear alternative to a direct loan to acquire an asset).

The equivalent loan would be the N.P.V. of the outstanding lease payments discounted by the rate of interest for borrowing. For example the N.P.V. of a five year lease with rental of £27,740 and a rate of interest of 14% (before tax) would be $27,740 × 3.605 = £100,000.

Assignment Exercises

Assignment Exercises followed by the letter X do NOT have answers shown at the back of the book.

31.1 Some Plant can be leased for five years at a rent of £13,190 per annum. The cash price is £50,000. What is the implied interest rate?

31.2x A company is considering buying or leasing a computer which has a four year life. The rental would be £8,000 per annum and the cash price £23,000. The company pays corporation tax one year after its accounting year end at a rate of 52%. 100% of the cost of the computer would be allowed against taxable profit reducing tax paid in year 2. If a net of tax cost of capital is 10%, calculate the net present value of the lease and of the purchase after tax.

31.3x The net of tax annual cost of renting the computer if timing of tax relief is ignored would be 8,000 $(1 - \cdot 52)$ = £3,840 p.a. Using the data in question 31.2x what is the real annualised cost of the leasing transaction using 10% interest?

31.4 A company which could buy an asset for £80,000 with a four year life and nil residual value is offered a lease with rental of £26,338 p.a. for four years. The tax rate is 40% – assuming tax relief is obtained in the same year as payments – what is the implicit interest in the lease?

31.5 A company enters into a lease which requires rental payments of £5,000 per annum over 10 years. The rate of interest payable on borrowing for this type of funding is 14%. What is the capital value of the lease?

Chapter Thirty Two

Capital Expenditure Evaluation and Uncertainty

In the previous chapters the budgets of capital expenditures were based on an assumption of average certainty. In reality however different types of project have widely different levels of uncertainty attached to their outcomes. The outcome of replacement of machinery on an existing product line is likely to be much easier to estimate than the result of investment in a totally new product line of an innovatory kind. Methods need to be developed to deal with uncertainty in this type of situation. Some of the most common methods of allowing for uncertainty are described below.

Scaling down benefits and scaling up uncertain costs

Perhaps the commonest method of allowing for uncertainty is to adopt a very conservative approach to the estimated data used in capital budgets. This may simply mean reducing estimates of revenues by a fixed percentage and increasing estimates of costs likewise. Perhaps a more useful approach is to obtain from the estimates a range of likely outcomes which might range over

"Best Likely Outcome",	"Most Likely Outcome",	"Worst Likely Outcome".

Continual vigilance is necessary in preparing estimates for capital budgets since people become highly committed to projects and tend to produce figures to prove their case, rather than objective estimates.

Adjusting the cut-off rate

Another common method of allowing for uncertainty is to increase the rate of return required from a project. Most businesses find that the actual rate of return earned by the business as a whole falls short of the returns promised by individual projects. It is always hard after the event to effectively trace what happens — although post-auditing of capital budgets is very desirable in principle. In practice therefore businesses tend to fix cut off rates some way higher than the estimated cost of capital to allow for shortfalls from the budget. Different cut-off rates are also often applied to projects in different classes of uncertainty. Replacement of existing plant will require a lower cut-off than investment in a new and untried development.

Estimates using subjective probabilities

Some organisations have used estimating techniques which require the estimators to consider the range of likely outcomes and relate to them a subjective assessment of the probability of occurence. For example instead of a single estimate of sales the likely range is associated with its probability.

1 *Sale Estimates* £	*2* *Probability of Outcome*	*3 = 1 × 2* *Expected Sales*
1,000	0.1	100
2,000	0.3	600
3,000	0.4	1,200
4,000	0.2	800
	1.0	2,700

The probability of the outcome in the second column is assigned by the estimator to the range of sales estimates in column one. The probabilities add to one as they cover the full range of likely outcomes. The expected sales from this estimate amount to £2,700.

This type of approach is only likely to prove better than other methods if there is reasonable basis for assigning the probability of outcome — based on analysis of previous experience for example.

Sensitivity Analysis

When the data to be analysed has been assembled — particularly if it is to be analysed on a computer — it may be helpful to run the calculation through a number of times — each time varying an item of input to the budget. For example on the first run using the best estimate figures — the present value may be positive. On the second run the sales estimates may be reduced by 10% and the new result compared with the first run. If the second outcome shows a negative present value it is clear that the result is sensitive to the estimates of sales. In this way all the items crucial to the success of the project can be identified and special additional scrutiny given to their validity.

Assignment Exercises

Assignment Exercises followed by the letter X do NOT have answers shown at the back of the book.

32.1   What are the main ways in which organisations allow for uncertainty in evaluating investment decisions?

32.2 The marketing managers have been asked to estimate the likely sales of a new product by applying their subjective judgement to the probability of achieving a range of estimates of sales. The probabilities they apply as a percentage must add to 100% since it is certain than some level of sales will be achieved. Their estimates are totalled and summarised as follows:

Estimated Sales in Units	Probability of achievement %
100,000	5
200,000	20
250,000	30
300,000	40
350,000	5
	100

What is the expected level of sales in units?

32.3x The following estimates of cash flows are made in respect of a new project: –

Period	Capital Investment outlay	Sales	Expenses	Net Cash Flow
0	45,000	–	–	45,000
1		(40,000)	22,000	(18,000)
2		(40,000)	22,000	(18,000)
3	(2,000)	(40,000)	22,000	(20,000)

(Figures in brackets are cash inflows)

Show the effect of the following events happening separately

(a) Capital Investment increasing + 10%

(b) Sales reducing – 10%

(c) Expenses increasing + 5%.

Start from the original estimates calculating the N.P.V. at an interest rate of 10%.

Chapter Thirty Three

Risk and Accounting Structure

In Chapters 17 and 18 the ideas of Break Even Analysis were introduced. The Break Even Chart shows clearly how risk emanates from variations in sales in relation to costs. Risk is usually defined in terms of the variability in profits and of course ultimately in the likelihood of failure, implied in bankruptcy or liquidations. A Business with a high proportion of fixed cost will show a much higher rate of increase in profit as sales rise above break-even compared to one with a high proportion of variable cost. Correspondingly the high fixed cost company will show a much more dramatic decline into loss as sales reduce.

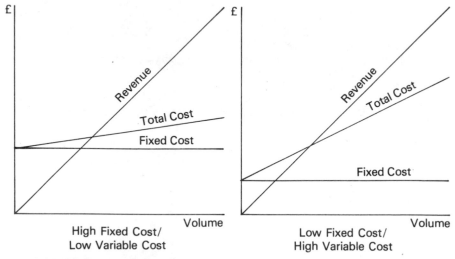

High Fixed Cost/
Low Variable Cost

Low Fixed Cost/
High Variable Cost

Exhibit 33.1

In numerical terms this can be illustrated as follows: –

Fixed Costs are £200 and Variable Costs are 60% of Sales. The Break Even Point is therefore at Sales of £500. The Break Even is worked out from the fact that we know Fixed Cost is £200 and that the contribution is: Sales – 60% Sales = 40% Sales. Thus every £1 sold will make a contribution of 40p. The point of break even is where contribution equals fixed costs i.e.

$$\frac{200}{.4} = £500 \text{ sales.}$$

	£	£	£	£	£	£
Sales	400	500	600	700	800	900
Variable Cost	240	300	360	420	480	540
Contribution	160	200	240	280	320	360
Fixed Cost	200	200	200	200	200	200
Profit/Loss Before Interest and Tax	−40	0	40	80	120	160

Exhibit 33.2

The impact of changes in sales level can be seen to have a more than proportional impact on profit −

Sales Increase   from £600 to £700 = + 16.7%
Profit Increase   £40 to £80 = +100.0%
Sales Increase   from £600 to £800 = + 33.3%
Profit Increase   £40 to £120 = +200.0%

The effect of the level of fixed cost on the returns of a business is called gearing. A highly geared company is one with a high proportion of fixed cost.

A business often has to think carefully about investment in new plant because of its impact on gearing. Using the data in Exhibit 33.2 as a starting point we can see the effect on its profitability if the business invests in some new plant the impact will be to increase fixed cost from £200 to £300 and reduce variable cost to 50% of sales. The Break Even Point will this move up to sales of £600.

	£	£	£	£	£	£
Sales	400	500	600	700	800	900
Variable Cost	200	250	300	350	400	450
Contribution	200	250	300	350	400	450
Fixed Cost	300	300	300	300	300	300
Profit/Loss before Interest or Tax	−100	−50	−	50	100	150

The impact of the new investment has been to increase the Break Even Sales from £500 to £600 in exchange for which the rate of profitability has increased. This can best be seen on the graph Exhibit 33.1 where a higher geared situation shows the widest angle between the Revenue and Total Cost Line.

In numerical terms increasing sales from £700 to £800 i.e. 14.3% increases profits from £50 to £100 i.e. 100%.

The analysis we have examined which relates to the change in gearing from operating factors does not in itself indicate whether the investment is a good one or not. It does however show that new investment can have a significant impact on the operational risk of the business. The decision will have to be taken as to whether the increased profitability justifies the increase in break even position. If sales are hard to come by, this may not be justified.

Financial Gearing

The impact of a firm borrowing money and paying interest on it, rather than funding itself entirely from its equity capital is very similar in effect to operational gearing. The interest on borrowing is the same in its impact as a fixed cost.

To illustrate this the data from Exhibit 33.2 will be taken.

	£	£	£	£	£	£
Sales	400	500	600	700	800	900
Profit/Loss before Interest and Tax	− 40	0	40	80	120	160

If the business is funded entirely from Ordinary Share Capital amounting to £1,000, then if we ignore tax the rates of return would be

	£	£	£	£	£	£
Sales	400	500	600	700	800	900
Return = $\frac{\text{Profit/Loss}}{\text{Share Capital of £1,000}}$	− 4%	0	4%	8%	12%	16%

If instead of funding entirely from ordinary shares. If the business raised its £1,000 funds − £600 from Ordinary Shares and £400 from a 10% Loan then the returns amend be as follows: −

	£	£	£	£	£	£
Sales	400	500	600	700	800	900
Profit/Loss before Interest and Tax	− 40	0	40	80	120	160
Interest	− 40	− 40	− 40	− 40	− 40	− 40
Net Profit before tax	− 80	− 40	0	40	80	120
Return = $\frac{\text{Profit/Loss}}{\text{Share Capital of £600}}$	− 13.3%	− 6.7%	0	6.7%	13.3%	20%

The impact of borrowing money on the return to the Ordinary Shareholders is to increase the return to him beyond the point where operating profits exceed a return of 10% on the capital i.e. Sales of £750. After this point the returns to the ordinary shareholder accelerate. Notice however the significant increase in Break Even Point from £500 to £600 and that sales must in fact exceed £750 before the shareholder is better off.

Quite apart from the increased risk from gearing the introduction of borrowing brings a legal risk that the lender may − if for example interest is not paid on time − take a legal charge over the company's assets.

The net cost of borrowing is reduced if tax is taken into account, since the interest charge is deductible from profit subject to tax. If we assumed a 50% tax rate the figures would be as follows: —

100% Share Capital

	£	£	£	£	£	£
Sales	400	500	600	700	800	900
Net of Tax Profit/Loss	− 20	0	20	40	60	80
Return	− 2%	0	2%	4%	6%	8%

60% Share Capital

	£	£	£	£	£	£
Net of Tax Profit	− 40%	− 20	0	20	40	60
Return	− 6.7%	− 3.3%	0	3.3%	6.7%	10%

The Measurement of Gearing is also cover in Chapter 23 on Ratio Analysis. The ratios give an indication of the level of gearing in a company both measured from the Balance Sheet and the Profit and Loss Account. In this chapter we have examined the impact of the gearing on risk.

Assignment Exercises

Assignment Exercises followed by the letter x do NOT have answers shown at the back of the book.

33.1 Plant A has fixed costs of £30,000 p.a. and its variable costs are 50% of Sales.
Plant B has fixed costs of £20,000 p.a and its variable costs are 60% of Sales.
Both plants produce the same product. Compare the returns from the two plants and say which appears to be most risky.

33.2x Using the data for plant A show the return on Ordinary Shares by assuming that the plant is owned by
(a) a Company whose capital consists of £100,000 Ordinary Shares.
(b) a Company whose capital consists of £60,000 Ordinary Shares and £40,000 10% Loan Stock.
What other differences does the introduction of borrowed capital introduce?

33.3x The Exmoor Company produces a single product which it sells at £10, per unit and which has a variable cost of £4 per unit. The fixed costs per annum are £42,000 and its current levels of operation are funded from share capital and reserves amounting to £70,000. It currently sells 10,000 units a year at full capacity but could expand this to 15,000 by investing £10,000 which it would have to borrow at 15% interest. Fixed Cost would increased by £2,000 p.a. but variable cost would stay the same. Show the impact of the increase on break even and return on share capital.

Chapter Thirty Four

Cost of Capital I

The Cost of Capital to an organisation is the rate of return which must be earned if it is to meet its obligations to lenders and the expectations of investors who are thinking of buying shares or other securities in the organisation. If it is to increase the wealth of its owners it will need to earn more profit than the cost of its capital.

The Cost of Capital covers the whole range of its Ordinary Shares, Preference Shares, Debentures and Loan Stock as well as Overdrafts and other Creditors. The whole range will be combined to give an average cost for the whole organisations capital. Before this is done however the cost to the organisation of the individual sources of capital will be discussed.

Short Term Borrowing

Short terms loans come mainly in the form of loans and overdrafts from banks and other financial institutions. The interest rates charged on these accounts are normally based on the daily balance of the account, in which case the interest charged is a 'real' rate. If some other basis of charging interest is used the equivalent real rate must now by law be quoted.

The rates of interest charged on overdrafts fluctuate with the central bank base lending rate. How much more than the base rate a bank charges is based on the creditworthiness and size of the borrower. This type of lending is only normally made in 'low-geared' situations where the bank feels it has adequate security for the loan.

Short term funds may also be obtained by issuing Bills of Exchange – which are promises to pay a fixed sum at a specified future date. The Bill of Exchange can, provided the signatory is creditworthy, be discounted for immediate cash. As was illustrated in chapter 26 the real rate of interest is different from the nominal rate – in this type of transaction.

Since interest charged will be deductible from taxable profit the net cost of interest will be reduced by the rate of tax paid by the company. If the tax rate is 42% the net cost will be 58% of the gross amount i.e. £100 gross interest would only cost £58 after taking the tax into account. In more formal terms the net cost of the loan is: The gross interest $\times$ (1 – tax rate). Example if the gross interest is 10% and tax rate 42%, the net cost is 10% $\times$ (1 – .42) = 5.8%.

Intermediate Term Loans

Banks and other Financial Institutions offer term loans usually for specific developments or projects over periods from 5 to 10 years. The arrangements for making the loan usually require repayment by instalments in the later years of the loan period. Interest is again based on a predetermined formula — often calculated at the amount owing at the start of each year — the real rate of interest has therefore to be calculated.

Trade Creditors and accruals

Trade creditors and accruals do not normally involve interest payments and are often described as costless forms of finance. In considering the overall cost of capital it is convenient to treat these current liabilities as a deduction from current assets. This is in line with the calculation of return on capital employed described in Chapter 22, where current liabilities excluding overdrafts are deducted from current assets. If this method is used the cost of capital is directly comparable with the return on capital employed.

Debentures and Long Term Loan Stock

A company may be fortunate enough to have sold debentures at a time in the past when interest rates were low. The actual rate of interest paid may thus be well below the current market rates. For example if a company issued debentures ten years ago carrying interest of 5% — the current rate of interest today required being 10% — what will happen to the market price of the debenture? Taking a £100 unit of Debenture the interest paid will be £5 per annum. An investor now expects a yield of 10% — therefore he will only pay such a price for the debenture as will yield him 10%. Let x = the market price of the debenture. Then

$$\frac{£5}{x} \times \frac{100}{1} = 10\%$$

$$\text{Then } x = £50$$

The investor will thus only pay £50 for £100 face or par value of debentures. It is the yield on this market value which represents the real cost of the debentures. In this example the cost of debentures would be 10% less the tax rate adjustment.

If the company pays tax at 52% on profits the net cost of the borrowing is $10\% \times (1 - .52) = 4.8\%$.

Preference Share Capital

The difference between Preference Share Capital and Debentures is in two main respects. Firstly a dividend does not have to be declared if the directors consider it inadvisable or there are insufficient profits, and there are no legal remedies for the preference shareholder when dividends are not paid. If debenture interest is not paid then the company is defaulting on its debt and the debenture holder can obtain legal redress. In every other respect however the payment of a fixed preference dividend has the same impact on gearing as the payment of interest — taking a fixed amount of the profit each year it is paid. In a normally successful business — preference dividends are paid as a matter of course since no dividend on other shares can be paid until they have received their dues.

The other difference between preference dividend and interest is that for tax purposes the dividend is paid out of taxed profit and is not allowable as a deduction for tax purposes. The cost of a preference share is therefore the yield of its dividend over the market price without adjustment for tax.

Example: A company has £1 Preference Shares which pay a fixed dividend of 10p per share. The market value of the shares is 80p. The cost of this capital is therefore $\dfrac{10p}{80p} = 12.5\%$.

Some Financing Decisions

When issuing shares, debentures or loans, a company will have to decide on the precise terms of the issue. It can choose whether they should be issued at par, at a premium or at a discount. It can in the case of redeemable preference shares, debentures or loans decide both on the rate of interest to be paid, and a date for redemption. While all the factors involved are complex and cannot be considered here, by applying interest calculations a proper decision can be made on the basis of financial costs.

Example. A company needs £500,000 cash for a ten-year period. The company's financial advisers have made the following offers:

14 per cent Ten-year debentures at 110
12 per cent Ten-year debentures at 100
10 per cent Ten-year debentures at 90

Repayment at par will be made at the end of ten years.

Which offer should be accepted on cost considerations alone?

In order to consider the cost of the various issues, each will have to be converted to its present value at the date of issue. In order to do this a rate of interest will have to be used in the calculations. For this example since 12 per cent is the rate when debentures are issued at par this will be assumed to be the Market rate of interest. The present value of the issues will comprise:

1. The present value of the interest payments to be made over ten years.

2. The present value of the capital repayment at the date of redemption ten years hence.

The nominal value of debentures issued will vary according to the terms of issue:

(*a*) 14 per cent Debentures at 110

$$\frac{£500,000}{1} \times \frac{100}{110} = £454,545 \quad \left(\begin{array}{c} £ \\ \textit{Check } 454,545 \\ \textit{Add } 10 \textit{ per cent} \quad 45,455 \\ \hline 500,000 \end{array} \right)$$

(*b*) 12 per cent Debentures at 100

$$\frac{£500,000}{1} \times \frac{100}{100} = £500,000$$

(*c*) 10 per cent Debentures at 90

$$\frac{£500,000}{1} \times \frac{100}{90} = £555,556 \quad \left(\begin{array}{r} £ \\ \textit{Check } 555,556 \\ \textit{Less } 10 \text{ per cent } \underline{55,556} \\ \underline{500,000} \end{array}\right)$$

The interest payments on the bonds sold will be:

		£
(*a*) Nominal Value £454,545 at 14 per cent =		63,636
(*b*) Nominal Value £500,000 at 12 per cent =		60,000
(*c*) Nominal Value £555,556 at 10 per cent =		55,556

Calculation of the Present Value of the Capital Sum and Interest:

(*a*) 14 per cent Debentures

		£
Capital Sum £454,545 at 12 per cent = £454,545 × 0.322	=	146,363
Interest of 63,636 at 12 per cent = 63,636 × 5.650	=	359,543
		505,906

Appendix Present Value of £1 table = 0.322
Appendix Present Value of an Annuity of £1 table = 5.650

(*b*) 12 per cent Debenture

		£
Capital Sum £500,000 at 12 per cent = £500,000 × 0.322	=	161,000
Interest of £60,00 at 12 per cent = £60,000 × 5.650	=	339,000
		500,000

(*c*) 10 per cent Debenture

		£
Capital Sum £555,556 at 12 per cent = £555,556 × 0.322	=	178,889
Interest of £55,556 at 12 per cent = £55,556 × 5.650	=	313,891
		492,780

In this example, therefore, the 10 per cent debenture is the cheapest.

Assignment Exercises

Assignment exercises followed by the letter X do NOT have answers shown at the back of the book.

34.1 A Bill of Exchange for 90 days with a face value of £100,000 is discounted at the prime market rate of 12%. What is the real rate of interest?

34.2x What would the real rate of interest have been if the Bill of Exchange had been for six months?

34.3   A company has some non redeemable debentures which pay 5% interest on each £100 unit of stock. The debentures currently sell on the market for £40 a unit. What is the market yield on these debentures?

34.4   If the company pays corporation tax at 52% on its profits, what is the net of tax market rate for the debentures in question 34.3?

34.5x   A Company has issued £1 6% Preference Shares. The Market price for these shares is currently £0.35. What is the cost of this Preference Share Capital?

34.6x   If the company pays corporation tax at 52% on its profits, what is the net of tax market rate for its preference shares as detailed in question 34.5x?

34.7x   A company is seeking to raise £200,000. It has been offered the choice of issuing debentures with a ten year life either at

(a)   15% interest and issued at 105 redeemable at par

(b)   13% interest and issued at 97.5 redeemable at par

The current market rate for debentures is 14% which option should the company choose?

Chapter Thirty Five

Cost of Capital II — Ordinary Shares

The cost of capital for borrowing is relatively easy to establish because there is a fixed rate of interest determined for each security. If we establish the price for the security then the yield is established. With ordinary share capital there is no established rate for dividends — other than the hope of investors that the company will continue to prosper.

When an investor buys an ordinary share he anticipates a return based not only on the dividends he receives but also on capital gains he hopes to make when he sells the share, i.e. that the value of the share will rise.

For example Mr. X buys a share in Y Ltd. for £2. He expects a dividend of 50p at the end of a year, at which time he also expects to sell the share for £2.50. The return is therefore:

Value at the end of year 50p + £2.50 =		£3.00
Cost		2.00
Gain		1.00

$$\text{Return} = \frac{\text{Gain}}{\text{Cost of Investment}} = \frac{£1}{£2} = 50\%.$$

If the dividend and capital gain were not to be received until the end of the second year the rate of return would be reduced to 22%.

$$\frac{A}{(1+r)^n} = P$$

$$\frac{3.00}{(1+r)^2} = 2$$

$$r = \sqrt{\frac{3}{2}} - 1$$

$$r = .22 \text{ or } 22\%.$$

To develop this line of approach to the valuation of a share we will refer back to the methods of Present Value used in Chapter 27 where the basic formula $P = \dfrac{A}{(1+r)^n}$ was stated where P is the Principal or present value and A the future amount.

If we want to value a share at its present value P then we need to estimate the future amounts we expect to receive from it and the rate of return expected from a share of this type. The value P will equal the future Dividend and the future Sale Price, discounted at the market rate. Using the data in the earlier example the value of a share where the dividend in the first year is expected to be 50p and the value at the end £2.50 with a required rate of return of 50% then

$$P_0 = \frac{D_1}{(1+r)^1} + \frac{P_1}{(1+r)^1}$$

Where P_0 is the share price now
D_1 is the dividend in year 1
P_1 is the share price in year 1

$$P_0 = \frac{0.5}{1+0.5} + \frac{2.50}{1+0.5}$$

$$P_0 = .333 + 1.667 = £2.00.$$

If the dividend in year 1 is nil but expected to be 50p at the end of year 2 and a sale price of £2.50 at the end of year 2 then: --

$$P_0 = \frac{D_1}{(1+r)^1} + \frac{D_2}{(1+r)^2} + \frac{P_2}{(1+r)^2}$$

$$= \frac{0}{(1+0.5)^1} + \frac{0.5}{(1+0.5)^2} + \frac{2.50}{(1+.05)^2}$$

$$= 0 + 0.22 + 1.11$$

$$= £1.33$$

(Note the price would be £2 if the required return was 22%).

If we start with the one year horizon of

$$P_0 = \frac{D_1}{(1+r)^1} + \frac{P_1}{(1+r)^1}$$

and then consider that

$$P_1 = \frac{D_2}{(1+r)^2} + \frac{P_2}{(1+r)^2} \text{ and } P_2 = \frac{D_3}{(1+r)^3} + \frac{P_3}{(1+r)^3} \text{ and so on}$$

then in place of the P_1 and P_2 etc. we can substitute dividend flows with only a terminal Price at the end of the series: --

$$P_0 = \frac{D_1}{(1+r)^1} + \frac{D_2}{(1+r)^2} + \frac{D_3}{(1+r)^3} + \frac{D_4}{(1+r)^4} + \ldots\ldots + \frac{D_n}{(1+r)^n} + \frac{P_n}{(1+r)^n}$$

where n is a large number. At this point the impact of discounting with large numbers will reduce the value of P_n to something very small and insignificant — which for practical purposes may be ignored. Thus the present price may be considered to represent the discounted value of future dividends.

In anticipating future dividends it is common in an established and stable business to estimate the rate of growth after the first year as a percentage rather than estimate each dividend separately. If the dividend is expected to grow at 5% per annum then in year 2 the dividend will be $D_1 \times (1+.05)$ and in year 3 the dividend will be $D_1 \times (1+.05)(1+.05)$ or $D_1(1+.05)^2$. If we use g as the growth rate rather than 5% then we can express the general formula to value a share as follows: –

$$P_0 = \frac{D_1}{(1+r)^1} + \frac{D_1(1+g)}{(1+r)^2} + \frac{D_1(1+g)^2}{(1+r)^3} + \frac{D_1(1+g)^3}{(1+r)^4} + \cdots\cdots + \frac{D_1(1+g)^{n-1}}{(1+r)^n}$$

If we make the assumption from that the growth rate will continue constantly to infinity then the above expression can be reduced mathematically to

$$P_0 = \frac{D}{r-g} \text{ provided that } r > g.$$

If g is higher than r then the full formula must be used. Example: The current dividend on a share is 50p. The rate of return expected on similar shares is 8% and the growth rate of dividends is expected to be 3% per annum.

$$P_0 = \frac{50}{.08 - .03} = \frac{50}{.05} = 1000p.$$

The current price expected would be £10 per share.

Note that if there were no growth rate expected – as for instance would be the case for fixed interest securities the formula can still be used e.g. facts as before but nil growth.

$$P_0 = \frac{50}{.08 - 0} = \frac{50}{.08} = 625p.$$

The current price is reduced to £6.25 with no growth. Since in this chapter we are concerned with the cost of capital the formula just developed can be expressed in terms of a rate of interest

$$P = \frac{D}{r-g} \text{ is equivalent to}$$

$$r = \frac{D}{p} + g$$

Expressing this in words we have earlier in the book in Chapter 22 defined $\frac{D}{p}$ as the Dividend Yield. Thus the rate of return is the Dividend Yield plus growth rate.

Some analysts prefer to consider share prices from the profits basis rather than dividends. The commonest way of expressing this is through the Price Earnings ratio which was introduced in the Chapter on ratio analysis. The Price Earnings ratio represents the capitalisation factor that the market applies to a firms profits to a price at the Share Price. Thus if a firm has a P/E ratio of 9 and Earnings per share of £3 then the Market Price of the share will be £27. The capitalisation factor will be related both to the particular firms rating for risk and performance and also the general market rates of return. In order to use the P/E ratio for predicting prices it is therefore necessary to predict both the future pattern of the ratio as well as the future pattern of earnings.

Example

The data for Alpa Ltd. relating to EPS and P/E ratio was as follows: –

	EPS	P/E ratio
19-1	20p	8.1
19-2	22p	8.4
19-3	25p	8.3
19-4	28p	8.5

The analyst expects earnings for 19-5 to increase by 10% and the P/E ratio to remain constant. The expected market price for 19-5 will therefore be

$$\text{EPS } 28 + 2.8 \times \text{P/E } 8.5 = 261.8p.$$

This type of prediction of share price is most likely to be useful for short term prediction of less than one year, since there is no adequate way of forecasting the longer term factors when market conditions are unstable.

Relating the Price Earnings ratio to the Dividend approach developed earlier in this chapter is possible if the proposition of earnings distributed as dividends is expected to remain constant so that

$$D = a E \text{ where} \quad \begin{aligned} D &= \text{Dividends} \\ E &= \text{Earnings} \\ a &= \text{The proportion of earnings paid out as dividends.} \end{aligned}$$

The rate of return formula expressed earlier was: –

$$r = \frac{D}{P} + g$$

if we replace D by a E in this formula then

$$r = \frac{a E}{P} + g$$

$$\frac{a E}{P} \text{ is the same as } \frac{a}{\dfrac{P}{E}} = \frac{a}{\text{P/E ratio}}$$

$$\therefore r = \frac{a}{\text{P/E ratio}} + g$$

$$\text{or P/E ratio} = \frac{a}{(r - g)}$$

The P/E ratio is thus dependent on the proportion of profit paid out as dividend, the expected rate of return on the investment and the growth rate.

Example if a company pays out 50% of its profit as dividends, the expected rate of return is 10% and the growth rate of dividends is expected to be 5% p.a. then

$$P/E = \frac{0.5}{(.1 - .05)} = 10 \text{ times}$$

The methods of valuing shares discussed in this chapter will only be helpful in periods of stability. Where markets are fluctuating it becomes very difficult to predict the future and hence the simple models based on established trends are no longer helpful.

Assignment Exercises

Assignment exercises followed by the letter x do NOT have answers shown at the back of the book.

35.1 An analyst estimates that the return on a share will be £1.00 in year 1, £2.00 in year 2 and it can be sold at the end of year 2 for £5.00. What is the share worth now if the market rate of interest is 12%?

35.2x What would the price have been for the share in 35.1 if the market rate of interest were 15%?

35.3 A share in Company X currently pays a dividend of £0.60 per annum. The dividends paid have grown at a rate of 5% p.a. for many years and are expected to continue at the same rate in future. The market rates of return for such shares are 10%. What price should a share in company X be?

35.4 If no growth rate were expected in dividends on the shares of Company C in question 35.2 what would the price be?

35.5x A share priced at £5 pays a dividend of £0.60 per annum. The growth rate expected to coninue on dividends is 2% p.a. What rate of return is implied?

35.6 The expected earnings per share in a security is £0.13 in the coming year. The Price Earnings ratio is expected to remain at current level of 9.2. What is the expected price?

35.7x If a company pays out 60% of its profit as dividends and the rate of return on its shares is expected to be 15% with a growth rate in dividends of 4% what would you expect its P/E ratio to be?

Chapter Thirty Six

Cost of Capital III –
Weighted Average Cost of Capital

Chapters 34 and 35 considered different elements in the Capital Structure of a Company. In order to arrive at an overall cost of capital for the firm these different parts – share capital and loans need to be combined. Ideally a company should be seeking to create a capital structure that produces the lowest overall cost of capital that it can achieve. There is however no simple way of achieving this nor is it possible to provide any correct method of measuring the actual cost of capital. This is because of the dynamic nature of the markets within which companies operate. Only if we could predict the future with certainty could we say for sure what the risks and returns were and therefore the associated costs.

Nonetheless it is very important for a firm to estimate its cost of capital since this provides a minimum level below which capital project returns may not be allowed to fall. Many firms as we have already indicated set a cut-off rate somewhat higher than estimated cost of capital. Nonetheless it is useful to know what the base is – rather than plucking a figure from pure guesswork.

In combining the various elements of capital structure some weighting of the different components has to be used. The most easily obtained weighting is the book value from the Balance Sheet of the different items.

Example:

	Balance Sheet Book Value £	Weights
Share Capital	100,000	.67
Debentures	50,000	.33
	150,000	1.00

The Weights obtained would then be applied to the cost of capital rates.

Example

	Cost of Capital %	Weight	Weighted Average %
Share Capital	9.8	.67	6.57
Debentures	6.5	.33	2.15
			8.72

The calculated weighted average cost of capital at 8.72% would give an approximate idea of the basis for capital budgeting decisions.

Rather than use the book value of the capital there is a strong argument for using the market values of the capital sources in the Balance Sheet. For example for Ordinary Shares if the company has 100,000 Ordinary Shares outstanding and the market price per share is £2.30 then the weighting for Ordinary Shares and the Reserves would be 100,000 × £2.30 = £230,000.

In calculating the weighted average cost of capital it is convenient to combine together various components where a company has a whole variety of different sources. The following headings are normal: –

Equity: Ordinary Share Capital and all Reserves

Preference Share Capital.

Debt: All debentures and loans both short and long term.

If a company has debentures or other securities which may at some future time be converted to ordinary shares, they should be included in Equity.

Exhibit 36.1

Combine the following balance sheet items to calculate weights based on book value: –

Share Capital 100,000 £1 shares			100,000
Reserves			
Retained Profits		75,000	
Share Premium Account		25,000	
			100,000
Preference Shares 50,000 10% £1 shares			50,000
8% Debenture Stock			70,000
Short Term Loans			20,000

			Weight %
Equity 100,000 + 100,000 =		200,000	58.8
Preference		50,000	14.7
Debt 70,000 + 20,000		90,000	26.5
		340,000	100.0

Using the information in Exhibit 36.1 with Market Values it would change the weightings. If the market price for

Ordinary Shares	. £2.50
Preference Shares	£0.90
Debenture Stock	95
Short Term Loan	par

			Weight %
Then	Equity (100,000 × 2.50)	250,000	65.5
	Preference (50,000 × 0.90)	45,000	11.8
	Debt (66,500 + 20,000)	86,500	22.7
		381,500	100.0

Exhibit 36.2

If the market rate for Equity is 10% for Preference Share 14% and Debt 12% calculate the weighted average cost of capital using book values as in Exhibit 36.1 and Market Values from Exhibit 36.2.

	Book Value Weight %	Market Value Weight %	Cost of Capital	Book Value WACC	Market Value WACC
Equity	58.8	65.5	.10	5.88	6.55
Preference	14.7	11.8	.14	2.06	1.65
Debt	26.5	22.7	.12	3.18	2.72
	100.0	100.0		11.12%	10.92%

When considering the rate of interest to use as a cut off on projects it is important to remember that the items comprising the total sources of funds are interdependent. A company can only borrow funds if it has an adequate equity base. The lenders of funds will only tolerate certain levels of gearing which depend on the riskiness of the business in which it operates. Thus it is for most purposes appropriate to use the average cost of capital in assessing projects. However the marginal cost of raising funds is always important and any major investment which will require large scale fund raising should also be assessed against the specific cost of those funds raised.

Assignment Exercises

Assignment exercises followed by the letter X do NOT have answers shown at the back of the book.

36.1   Glory Company Ltd has the following sources of capital as extracted from the balance sheet: –

		£
500,000 £1 Ordinary Shares		500,000
250,000 £1 6% Preference Shares		250,000
Reserves		
Retained Profit	170,000	
Revaluation Reserve	50,000	
Share Premium Account	60,000	
		280,000
Long Term Loan Stock (12%)		100,000
Short Term Loan (15%)		50,000
		1,180,000

Calculate the weighting factors to establish the weighted average cost of capital based on book values.

36.2   The market value of sources capital for Glory Co. Ltd. in 36.1 is as follows: –

Ordinary Shares	£2.50
Preference Shares	£0.50
Long Term Loan	95
Short Term Loan	par.

What are the weighting factors using the market values?

36.3   Using the weighting factors based on values calculated in 36.1 and 36.2 establish what the WACC is based on book value weighting and market value weighting using the following rates: –

Equity	12%
Preference	15%
Debt	14%

36.4x   Emperor Glass Fittings Ltd has the following extract from its balance sheet sources of capital: –

	£
1,000,000 £0.50 Ordinary Shares	500,000
100,000 £2 7% Preference Shares	200,000
Reserves	
Profit and Loss Account	400,000
	1,100,000
Debentures – 10%	600,000
Short Term Loan 12%	100,000
	1,800,000

The Quoted Price of its Ordinary Shares which yield 10% is £3 per share. The Preference Shares are quoted at £1 per share. Debentures are quoted at 80 and Short Term Loan at par.

The company is taxed at 40%.

What is its weighted average cost of capital.

Chapter Thirty Seven

Valuing a Business

In order to value a business with a view to buying or selling it there are two main parts to be evaluated. Firstly there are the tangible assets which the business owns such as buildings, machinery or stock in trade. Secondly there is the particular ability which this business has to earn profits. This second part arises from a variety of reasons such as good employees, patents and so forth which give it special advantages. It is the combination of the two values for assets and profitability which creates the total worth of a business.

In the position where a business has been unsuccessful and trading at a loss the second element may be worthless. The value of the assets is then no more than they can be sold for in the market. Assets can be auctioned item by item in a public sale. If the assets are of good quality in general demand they may reach prices which are comparable with the market replacement price for similar items. Often however specialized items such as machinery may only reach scrap values to dealers. Ideally the seller of assets would like to sell to an eager buyer who will pay the equivalent of the market price which a buyer setting up a new business would pay for replacing all the assets. The knockdown price for assets sold piecemeal at an auction is usually the last resort. It is impossible to be much more specific about the value that such assets will be worth since they differ to much in kind.

In current cost accounting assets are valued in terms of their 'value to the business'. This means the value of assets in their current use expressed in terms of the best alternative means of supplying that use.

For example a Widgit Machine Mark A which originally cost £10,000 has been owned for six years and is to be valued in current cost terms. It is depreciated at £1000 per annum over 10 years. The firm would decide on the facts surrounding the particular asset. If the machine were to be destroyed what would happen in the following circumstances: –

(a) Because the machine is in current use it would be replaced by an exactly comparable machine which is the best available equipment. The current value is thus the current market replacement value of the machine now £15,000 less allowance for depreciation based on six years wear and tear, $15,000 \times {}^6/_{10} = £9,000$ depreciation. the net value is thus £6,000.

(b) Because the machine is obsolete and it is not in current use, its replacement value is not relevant. Its only value to the firm is its realisation value – what it can be sold for, in this case £500.

(c) The machine is in current use, but is no longer the best equipment for the job. However it is not considered economic to replace the existing equipment. The value of the existing equipment will be based on the new equipment values. If the new equipment is superior because it is cheaper to buy, now only £8,000, but does the same job — then the value of the old equipment will simply be reduced to the new lower replacement price less depreciation for the six years use i.e. £8,000 less $^6/_{10}$ = £3,200.

(d) Using the circumstances as in (c) but assuming that the new equipment is superior because it produces the goods at a lower cost for materials — then the value will have to be adjusted. The starting point would be the value of the new machine since this is the best current choice, this would cost £16,000. The existing equipment however costs £1,000 per annum more to run — which disadvantage will reduce its value. By working out the present value of the extra costs, the amount to be deducted from the new equipment replacement value can be worked out. Assuming the existing equipment will last for five years and a 10% cost of capital the present value of the extra cost disadvantage would be £1,000 × 3.791 = £3,791. The net value to the business of the existing machine would be: —

$$£16,000 - ^6/_{10} = 9,600 \text{ less } £3,791 = £5,809$$

A business may own assets like leaseholds whose value can be readily ascertained in the market. If for example a lease is owned which entitles the business to receive rentals of £5,000 per year for 15 years then the value is the present value of this set of cash flows. If the market interest rate is 12% then £5,000 × 6.811 = £34,055 for the value of the lease.

In summary therefore the value of assets to a business may be either: —

Replacement: where the business is a successful going concern and the asset if lost would be replaced.

Realisation: where the business is unsuccessful and assets will have to be sold off or if the assets are no longer useful

Present Value: particularly where there is a clear right to future cash flows from an asset such as a lease.

The ability of a firm to earn profits which are better than its competitors will entitle it to a price in excess of its asset value if it is sold. The term *Goodwill* is frequently used for the amount paid for this benefit of what are often called super profits.

Example

XYZ Company is expected to earn the following profits for the next five years in comparison to standard profits for the industry: —

Year	1	2	3	4	5
XYZ profit	500,000	550,000	600,000	660,000	700,000
Standard profit	200,000	250,000	300,000	400,000	600,000
Extra Profit of XYZ	+ 300,000	+ 300,000	+ 300,000	+ 260,000	+ 100,000

After five years the special patents which give XYZ its advantage expire. What is the current value now of its advantage?

The extra profits can be discounted back to a present value at the market rate of return expected from companies like XYZ — say 15%. The Goodwill is therefore worth: –

Year	Extra Profit £	P.V. factor at 15%	Net Present Value £
1	300,000	.870	261,000
2	300,000	.756	226,800
3	300,000	.658	197,400
4	260,000	.572	148,720
5	100,000	.497	49,700
			£883,620

The business will therefore be valued at Goodwill £883,620 plus the market value to the business of its assets, evaluated in much the same terms as for current cost accounting.

Another approach to the valuation of a business is to consider it in much the same way that was used with regard to ordinary shares in Chapter 35. The approach so far as a share was concerned was to estimate future returns from the investment in the form of dividends and sales proceeds.

$$P_0 \quad \frac{D_1}{(1+r)} + \frac{D_2}{(1+r)^r} + \cdots + \frac{D_n}{(1+r)^n} + \frac{P_n}{(1+r)^n}$$

If the whole company is bought then cash generated from the company replace dividends and the terminal price the amount the business will eventually he sold off for.

Example: A take over bidder estimates that if he buys X Ltd he will hold it for three years and in each year withdraw cash of £50,000. At the end of the three years he will sell it off to £100,000. The market rate for this type of venture is 25%. What is X Ltd worth?

$$P_0 = \frac{50,000}{1.25} + \frac{50,000}{(1.25)^2} + \frac{50,000}{(1.25)^3} + \frac{100,000}{(1.25)^3} = £148,000$$

In practice the price actually paid will depend a great deal on the competition in the market to buy the company. The methods described of using asset value and goodwill or valuing on cash returns expected do provide some basis from which to judge a reasonable price. Where these two methods produce different answers as they inevitably do working from different bases some businessmen work from an average of the two although this is purely expedient.

Many takeover situations develop into an auction and the price offered to buy a business, or control a majority of its shares may escalate more in response to the competetiveness of the bidders than any rational evaluation of the business's worth. The reverse situation also exists where a company in financial difficulty may find very few bidders and a buyer may acquire it at well below its current operating values for assets.

The price quoted on the Stock Exchange for a share does not represent the price of obtaining a majority of the shares in that company, it is a price only for buying a small holding at current conditions of supply and demand. A sudden increase in demand will change the situation considerably. In addition the Stock Exchange operates a special code of conduct for take-over bidders to protect the interest of small shareholders who may be tempted to sell before they know of a bid.

For small businesses, not quoted on the market there are frequently customary methods which are applied to establish the value of a business. For example the price is quoted as: − 'stock in trade and other assets at valuation plus two years purchase of the net profits'. This type of valuation may be satisfactory if the business concerned is of a very standard kind. However it is only a short cut to the more detailed evaluation of value previously discussed and the short cut may produce a seriously incorrect solution.

Assignment Exercises

Assignment exercises followed by the letter x do NOT have answers at the back of the book.

37.1 What factors are likely to contribute to a business being able to earn super-profits?

37.2 A company owns a machine which cost £50,000 and is now written down by 50%. A new but identical machine which would have to be bought if the current machine were destroyed would cost £80,000. What is the current value to the business of the existing machine?

37.3x A machine which cost £90,000 and has been depreciated by £60,000 and has a remaining life of 3 years it would be replaced if lost by a new machine which costs £100,000. The new machine produces labour savings of £2,000 p.a. compared to the old machine. What is the current value to the business of the existing machine if cost of capital is 10%?

37.4 A company owns a licence which will entitle it to royalties of £60,000 for the next 5 years. If cost of capital is 10% what it the licence worth?

37.5x Logo Company is expected to earn a profit of £600,000 p.a. for the next ten years which is twice the profit rate for other firms in the industry. Using a cost of capital rate of 16% what are the super profits worth?

37.6x The Cash generated by Long Ltd. is estimated currently to be £50,000 p.a., and growing into the foreseeable future at 5% per annum. If the rate of return required is 12% what is Long Ltd. worth?

Chapter Thirty Eight

Inflation

The impact of inflation on budgeting whether capital or operational may be quite significant depending on the time horizon within which estimates are made and the prevailing rates of inflation in the economy. In capital budgeting inflation is likely to have an impact on estimates of revenues and expenses as well as on market rates of interest on capital.

Many firms prepare their capital budget revenue and expense estimates in terms of current prices, and because they know that sales prices will be increased to cover future cost increases they do not make any specific further allowances for inflation expecting the impact in future to be cancelled out. If however there is reason to believe that for example selling prices will be fixed by law when prices rise, then the budgets should allow quite specifically for the future escallation of costs.

Inflation has an important impact on the cost of capital. If a debenture holder lends £100 to a company at the start of a year in which there is 5% inflation of prices then be would expect his debt to increase to £105 simply to remain as well off as he was at the start of the year. However there is no provision in law to allow this increase in entitlement − he remains only entitled to £100. The inflation loss must therefore be made up from his interest. If the debentures pays 8% then he is only obtaining a real 3% interest return. From the investors point of view the matter is made worse since he is taxed on the 8% interest as income. Long term lenders with obligations fixed in historic terms clearly lose out badly in inflationary periods since they lose both on capital and interest. New lenders tend to limit the duration of loans and try to obtain a high interest rate to compensate for inflation.

Shareholders are in a similar situation in that £100 invested in a company's ordinary shares will need to increase to £105 (with 5% inflation) before there is any gain to the shareholder in real terms. Share Prices should however increase to reflect the rise in value of its real assets as well as from increasing retained profits. However yields required generally will increase, as does interest, to allow for inflation.

Solutions

1.2 Raw Materials 210,000 + Direct Labour 120,000 = PRIME COST 330,000 + Factory Overhead: Factory Indirect Labour 110,000, Other Factory Indirect Expenses 66,000, Firms Canteen Expenses ¾ 6,000, Depreciation Machinery in Factory 6,000 = PRODUCTION COST 518,000 + Selling & Distribution Expenses: Wages, lorry drivers 2,500, Salaries: Salesmen 7,000 Commission on Sales 1,200, Depreciation: Delivery Vehicles 1,500, Showroom Equipment 100, Administration Expenses: Salaries, Employees in Admin Block 80,000, Firms Canteen Expenses ¼ 2,000, Depreciation, Accounting Machinery 500, Finance Expenses: Interest on loans 2,000 = TOTAL COST 614,800.

1.4 (i) f, h (ii) m (iii) a, c, e, g, j, 4/5ths of n.t.v. ¾ of w, x. (iv) b.d.i. 1/5th of n, p, q, part of ¼ of w (v) l, r, s, z, part of ¼ of w (vi) o, k, u, y.

1.6 Raw Mats 120,000 + 400,000 − 160,000 = 360,000 + Haulage Costs 4,000, Direct Labour (70% × 220,000) 154,000, Royalties 1,600 = (a) PRIME COST £519,600: Factory Overhead: Factory Indirect Labour 66,000, Other Factory Indirect Exps 58,000, Travelling Expenses 100, Depreciation Factory Machinery 38,000, Firm's canteen expenses 4,000 = (b) PRODUCTION COST 685,700: Administration Expenses: Salaries 72,000, Travelling Expenses 200, Firms Canteen Expenses 2,000, Depreciation Accounting & Office Mac'nery 2,000 + Cars of Admin Staff 1,600, Other Admin Expenses 42,000, Selling & Distribution Expenses: Salaries 8,000, Commission 1,400, Travelling Expenses 2,900, Depreciation Equipment 300 + Salesmen's Cars 3,800, Other Selling Expenses 65,000, Carraige Costs on Sales 7,800: Finance Costs 3,800 (c) TOTAL COST 898,500.

1.7 (i) c, e (ii) d, q, w, (iii) i, m, t, v, z, x (iv) a, g, k, n, u, y (v) b, f, j, l, o, s, (vi) h, p, r.

2.1 Manufacturing A/c: Dr Opening Stock Raw Materials 18,450, + Purchases 64,300 + Carriage Inwards 1,605 − Closing Stock Raw Materials 20,210 = Cost of Raw Materials Consumed 64,145 + Direct Labour 65,810 = Prime Cost 129,955, Factory Overhead Expenses: Fuel & Power 5,920, Rent & Rates ⅔rds 1,800, Depreciation; Machinery 8,300, + Work in Progress 1.1.19-7, 23,600, − Work in Progress 31.12.19-7, 17.390 = Production Cost of Goods Completed c/d 152,185. Trading A/c: Opening Stock Finished Goods 17,470 + Production Cost of Goods Completed 152,185, less Closing Stock Finished Goods 21,485 = Cost of Goods Sold 148,170; Gross Profit 52,430; Cr. side: Sales 200,600. Profit & Loss: Dr. Office Salaries 16,920, Rent & Rates ⅓ 900, Lighting & Heating 5,760, Depreciation: Office Equipment 1,950, Net Profit 26,900.

2.3 Manufacturing A/c: Dr. Opening Stock Raw Materials 8,565, + Purchases 39,054 less Closing Stock Raw Materials 9,050 = Cost of Raw Materials Consumed 38,569, Manufacturing Wages 45,775 = PRIME COST 84,344, Factory Overhead Expenses: Rates 4,800, General Expenses 5,640, Light & Heat 2,859, Depreciation 2,000 = Cr: Production Cost of Goods Completed c/d 99,643. Trading: Dr. Opening Stock Finished Goods 29,480. + Production Cost of Goods Completed b/d 99,643 — Closing Stock Finished Goods 31,200 = Cost of Goods Sold 97,923, Gross Profit c/d, 38,577, Cr. Sales 136,500. Profit & Loss: Dr. Admininistration Expenses: Office Salaries 6,285, Light & Heat 1,110, General Expenses 1,950, Rates 2,200, Depreciation: Office Equipment 1,500 = 13,045, Selling & Distribution Expenses: Advertising 1,758, Salesmens Commission 7,860, Delivery Van Expenses 2,500 = 12,118, Net Profit 13,414. Cr. Gross Profit b/d 38,577. Balance Sheet: Capital 137,456 + Net Profit 13,414 − Drawings 8,560 = 142,310, Current Liabilities: Creditors 19,450, Accrued Expenses 305 = 19,755. Totals 162,065. Fixed Assets: Premises 40,000, Machinery 50,000 less depreciation 19,500 = 30,500, Office Equipment 15,000 less depreciation 5,500 = 9,500. Current Assets: Stocks, Raw Materials 9,050, Finished Goods 31,200, Debtors 28,370, Prepayments 108, Bank 13,337.

3.1 C. Dean: Trading: Dr Purchases 100,000 − Closing Stock (800 units) 16,000 = Cost of Goods Sold 84,000, Gross Profit 126,000, Cr. Sales 210,000. Profit & Loss: Dr Wages & Salaries 50,000, Rent & Rates 9,000. Other Expenses 40,000, Finance Expenses 1,000, Net Profit 26,000, Cr. Gross Profit b/d 126,000.

D. Warren: Trading: Dr. Cost of Raw Materials 100,000, Direct Wages 28,000 = Prime Cost 128,000, Factory Indirect Expenses 38,000, Indirect Factory Labour 8,000, Cr: Factory Cost Goods Completed c/d 174,000. Profit & Loss, Dr: Factory Cost Goods Completed 174,000, less Closing Stock Finished Goods (800/5,000 × 174,000) 27,840 = Cost of Goods Sold 146,160, Gross Profit 63,840, Cr: Sales 210,000. Profit & Loss: Dr. Salaries Admin 10,000, Salaries Salesmen 4,000, Other Selling & Admin. 11,000. Finance Expenses 1,000, Net Profit 37,840. Cr. Gross Profit 63,840.

3.3 C. Dean: Trading: Dr: Opening Stock 16,000, Add Purchases 120,000, less Closing Stock (1,200 units) 24,000 = Cost of Goods Sold 112,000, Gross Profit c/d 168,000, Cr. Sales 280,000. Profit & Loss: Dr. Wages 53,000, Rent & Rates 9,000, Other Expenses 42,000, Finance Expenses 2,000, Net Profit 62,000, Cr: Gross Profit b/d 168,000.

D. Warren: Manufacturing A/c: Dr: Raw Materials 120,000, Direct Wages 30,000 = Prime Cost 150,000, Factory Indirect 39,000, Factory Indirect Labour 9,000. Cr: Factory Cost Goods Completed c/d 198,000.

Trading A/c: Dr: Opening Stock Finished Goods 27,840, Add Factory Cost of Goods Completed 198,000, less Closing Stock Finished Goods (1,200/6,000 × 198,000) 39,600, Cost of Goods Sold 186,240, Gross Profit c/d 93,760. Cr: Sales 280,000, Profit & Loss: Dr. Salaries, Administration 10,000, Salaries, Salesmen 4,000, Other Selling 8,000, Other Admin. Expenses 4,000, Finance Expenses 2,000, Net Profit 65,760. Cr: Gross Profit b/d 93,760.

4.1 (i) FIFO Stock 800 (ii) LIFO Stock 688 (iii) AVCO Stock 740.

4.2 In each case Sales 1,040, Purchases 1,440, Gross Profit: FIFO 400, LIFO 288, AVCO 340.

4.5 None at all. There can be one but there doesn't have to be one.

4.7 (a) (i) FIFO 6 units at £13 each = £78, (ii) LIFO 6 units at £10 each = £60, (iii) AVCO 6 units at £12.50 each = £75. (b) Sales in each case 1,092, Purchases in each case 830, less different amounts for stock so that Gross Profits become (i) FIFO 340, (ii) LIFO 322, (iii) AVCO 337.

5.1 FIFO Stocks: end Year (1) 280, Year (2) 180, Year (3) 336.

5.2 LIFO Stocks: end Year (1) 240, Year (2) 120, Year (3) 234.

5.3 AVCO Stocks: end Year (1) 260, Year (2) 170, Year (3) 320.

5.4 Trading Accounts each method: Sales: Year (1) 660, Year (2) 1120, Year (3) 1324. Purchases: Year (1) 780, Year (2) 700, (3) 1200.
(i) FIFO Gross profits Year (1) 160, (2) 320, (3) 280.
(ii) LIFO Gross Profits Year (1) 120, (2) 300, (3) 238.
(iii) AVCO Gross Profits Year (1) 140, (2) 330, (3) 274.

5.5 The answer would be exactly the same as in 5.1. It makes no difference as to whether the perpetual or the periodic method is in use.

5.6 Year (1) 20 × £12 = £240, (2) 10 × £12 = £120, (3) 10 × £12 + 6 × £19 = £234.

5.7 Year (1) Average cost is £780 ÷ 60 = £13. Closing Stock is 20 × £13 = £260. Year (2) Average cost is £960 ÷ 60 = £16. Closing Stock is 10 × £16 = £160. Year (3) Average cost is £1360 ÷ 70 = £19.43. Closing Stock is 16 × £19.43 = £310.88.

5.8 The Trading Accounts for FIFO and LIFO would have been exactly the same as in 5.4. The AVCO figures would give gross profits of Year (1) 140, (2) 320, (3) 252.

5.22 Gross Operating Profits, Year 1 £150   Year 2 £220   Year 3 £271.

5.23 Gross Operating Profits, Year 1 £330   Year 2 £196   Year 3 £347.

6.1 (A) Marginal cost per unit: Direct Labour 3 + Direct Materials 3.5 + Variable 2.25 = 8.75. Price offered is £9. It will therefore increase the profit of the firm to accept the order. Could give proof showing total costs if order not accepted 20,000, Sales 22,000 = Net Profit 2,000 compared with if order accepted, total costs 20,875, Sales 22,900 = Net Profit 2,025.

(B) Marginal cost per unit: Direct Labour 3 + Direct Materials 3.5 + Variable costs 2.25 + Depreciation extra machine £3,000 ÷ 150 units = £2 + Running costs extra machine £600 p.a. ÷ 150 = £4. Total 14.75.

Variable costs more than selling price, therefore do not accept order. Proof would show total costs if order not accepted 20,000, Sales 22,000 = Net Profit 2,000. If order accepted total costs 22,212, Sales 23,500, = Net Profit 1,288.

6.5   Marginal cost per unit under normal production, Direct Labour £4 + Direct Materials £5.25 + Factory Indirect Expenses (£9,000 × ⅔ ÷ 4,000) £1.50 = £10.75. Under normal production therefore (all things being equal) extra sales at a figure above £10.75 will bring in extra profit.

(a) Special case — not normal production. Marginal cost per unit as above £10.75 + Extra machine costs: Running cost (£1,800 ÷ 200) £9 + Depreciation (£3,000 − £200 = £2,800 ÷ 800) £3.50 = total £23.25. Selling price £25 is above marginal cost, therefore (all being equal) ACCEPT. (b) Selling price £13 is above marginal cost on normal production therefore ACCEPT. Advice qualified under (a) and (b) − depends on effect on sales to other customers, existing sales to customer under (b) etc. Price-cutting wars with other producers etc. etc.

6.6   With both methods the figures of sales per year and of Direct Labour, Materials, Variable overhead and Fixed Overhead will reamin the same. What will vary will be the calculation of the figures for stocks, and thus profits. Year 1, Sales 144,000, Direct Labour 40,000, Direct Materials 30,000, Variable Overhead 50,000, Fixed Overhead 16,000. Marginal method, closing stock (£120,000 × 1,000/10,000) 12,000, Gross Profit 20,000. Absorption method, closing stock (£136,000 × 1,000/10,000) 13,600, Gross Profit 21,600. Year 2, Sales 160,000, Direct Labour 48,000, Materials 36,000, Variable Overhead 60,000, Fixed Overhead 16,000. Marginal method Opening stock b/fwd 12,000, Closing stock (£144,000 × 3,000/12,000) 36,000, Gross Profit £24,000. Absorption method Opening stock b/fwd 13,600. Closing stock £160,000 × 3,000/12,000) 40,000. Gross Profit 26,400. Year 3, Sales 240,000, Direct Labour 64,000. Materials 48,000, Variable Overhead 80,000, Fixed Overhead 16,000. Marginal method, Opening stock b/fwd 36,000, Closing stock (£192,000 × 4,000/16,000) 48,000, Gross Profit 44,000. Absorption method, Opening stock b/fwd 40,000, Closing stock (£208,000 × 4,000/16,000) 52,000, Gross Profit 44,000.

7.1

	Materials	Direct Labour	Factory Overhead	Total
Job 1001	118	60 × £0.9 = 54	60 × £1.3 = 78	250
Job 1002	206	50 × £0.9 = 45	50 × £1.3 = 65	316
Job 1003	310	71 × £1.0 = 71	71 × £1.4 = 99.4	480.4
Job 1004	205	80 × £1.1 = 88	80 × £2.3 = 184	477
Job 1005	98	60 × £1.2 = 72	50 × £2.8 = 140	310
Job 1006	306	110 × £0.9 = 99	80 × £1.5 = 120	525
Job 1007	401	130 × £1.0 = 130	130 × £4 = 520	1051
Job 1008 Dept. E	180	70 × £0.9 = 63	60 × £1.5 = 90	
Dept. A	44	40 × £0.9 = 36	40 × £1.3 = 52	465
Job 1009 Dept. C	388	50 × £1.1 = 55	50 × £2.3 = 115	
Dept. A	—	40 × £0.9 = 36	40 × £1.3 = 52	
Dept. F	68	70 × £1.0 = 70	59 × £4 = 236	1,020

7.3

	Production Departments				Service Departments		
	A	B	C	D	K	L	M
Indirect Labour	4,000	6,000	8,000	2,000	1,500	3,000	4,100
Other Expenses	2,700	3,100	3,600	1,500	4,500	2,000	2,000
	6,700	9,100	11,600	3,500	6,000	5,000	6,100
Apportionment of costs:							
Dept. K	1,500	1,800	1,200	600	(6,000)		900
Dept. L	3,000		1,500	500		(5,000)	
							7,000
Dept. M		2,100	3,500	1,400			(7,000)
	£11,200	13,000	17,800	6,000	—	—	—

(a) Overhead rates per direct labour hour

Department A $\dfrac{£11,200}{2,000} = £5.6$

Department C $\dfrac{£17,800}{4,450} = £4.0$

(b) Overhead rates per machine hour

Department B $\dfrac{£13,000}{2,600} = £5.0$

Department D $\dfrac{£6,000}{24,000} = £2.5$

8.4

	Jan.	Feb.	Mar.	Apl.	May	Jun.
Opening Stock	740	690	780	1,100	1,400	1,160
Add production	750	1,010	1,410	1,620	1,240	800
	1,490	1,700	2,190	2,720	2,640	1,960
Less sales	800	920	1,090	1,320	1,480	1,020
Closing stock	690	780	1,100	1,400	1,160	940

8.5 (a) Opening Stock 140, Add Production (figure to be deduced) less Sales of 1,550 = Closing Stock 150. By deduction, given the figures already known the only figure which could be inserted for production so that the equation worked out is 1,560. An even production flow of 1,560 ÷ 12 = 130 units. This has been tested to ensure that stock never becomes a negative figure.

(b) Starting with above figures the closing stock at the end of each month would be Jan 160, F 110, M 70, Apr 50, May 60, Jn 90, Jy 150, Aug 250, S 210, Oct 230, N 210, D 150. Lowest closing figure for stock is April 50. if stock is not to fall below 80 units an extra 30 units (80 − 50) will have to be produced in January making production for that month of 160 units.

8.6 Opening stock? (to be deduced) add Production 1,500, less Sales 1,230 = Closing stock 430. By arithmetical deduction the only figure that could be inserted to make the equation agree is 160 units.

9.4   Jan Capital 1,000 + Debtors 3,900 = 4,900 less Payments 5,800 = Overdraft c/f 900, Feb b/f − 900 Add Debtors 5,900, less Payments 7,500 = Overdraft c/f 2,500, March B/f − 2,500, Add Debtors 6,000, Loan 700, Less Payments 10,000, Overdraft c/f 5,800, April B/f − 5,800, Add Debtors 7,100, less Payments 10,800, Overdraft c/f 9,500, May B/f − 9,500, Add Debtors 8,400, Less Payments 9,900, Overdraft c/f 11,000, June B/f − 11,000, Debtors 9,500, Less Payments 8,000, Overdraft c/f 9,500. As permission for overdraft only 10,000 some action will have to be taken to keep overdraft below 11,000 in May.

9.5   Payments Schedules: July, Materials (320 × £4 + 300 × £1) 1,580, D Labour 320 × £8 + 2,560, Variable (300 × £1 + 320 × £1) 620, Fixed Expenses 400, Drawings 300, Total 5,460. August, Materials (350 × £4 + 320 × £1) 1,720, D Labour 350 × £8 = 2,800, Variable (320 × £1 + 350 × £1) 670, Fixed 400, Drawings 300, total 5,890. September: Materials (370 × £4 + 350 × £1) 1,830, D Labour 370 × £8 = 2,960, Variable (350 × £1 + 370 × £1) 720, Fixed 400, Drawings 300, Total 6,210. October, Materials (380 × £4 + 370 × £1) 1,890, D Labour 380 × £8 = 3,040, Variable (370 × £1 + 380 × £1) 750, Fixed 400, Machinery 2,000, Drawings 300, Total, 8,380. November, Materials (340 × £4 + 380 × £1) £1,740, Labour 340 × £8 = 2,720, Variable (380 × £1 + 340 × £1) 720, Fixed 400, Drawings 300, Total, 5,880. December, Materials (310 × £4 + 340 × £1) 1,580, Labour 310 × £8 = 2,480, Variable (340 × £1 + 310 × £1) 690, Fixed 400, Drawings 300, Total 5,410.

Cash Budget Jul, Bal b/f 1,200 + Debtors 4,000, less Payments 5,460, O/d c/f 260, Aug O/d b/f 260, Debtors 6,400, less Payments 5,890, Bal c/f 250, Sept Bal b/f 250, Debtors 5,800, less Payments 6,210, O/d c/f 160, Oct O/d b/f 160, Debtors 8,000, less Payments 8,380, O/d c/f 540, Nov O/d b/f 540, Debtors 6,000, less Payments 5,880, O/d c/f 420, Dec O/d b/f 420, debtors 7,000, Legacy 2,500, less Payments 5,410, Bal c/f 3,670.

10.5   Payments Schedule: Jan, Wages 800, Directors 1,200, Total 2,000. Feb, Purchases 48,000, Wages 800, Directors 1,200, Premises 30,000, Other 600, Total 80,600. March, Purchases 16,000, Wages 800, Directors 1,200, Equipment 6,000, Other 600, Total 24,600. April, Purchases 18,000, Wages 800, Directors 1,200, Other 600, Total 20,600. May, Purchases 20,000, Wages 800, Directors 1,200, Other 600, Total 22,600. June, Purchases 14,000, Wages 800, Directors 1,200, Equipment 6,000, Other 600, Total 22,600. Receipts Schedule: Jan, Capital 60,000, Sales: April 12,000, May 16,000, June 28,000 + and − Balances end of each month: Jan + 58,000, Feb − 22,600, March − 47,200, April − 55,800, May − 62,400, June − 57,000.

Trading A/c: Dr Purchases 126,000, less Closing stock 21,800, Gross Profit 23,800, Totals 128,000. Cr Sales 128,000. Profit & Loss: Dr Salaries 4,800, Other 3,840, Debenture Interest 280, Depreciation 1,200, Directors 7,200, Net Profit 6,480, Totals 23,800. Cr Gross Profit b/d 23,800. Balance Sheets, Fixed Assets, Premises 30,000. Equipment 12,000 less depreciation 1,200 = 10,800, Current Assets, Stock 21,800, Debtors 72,000, Totals 134,600. Ordinary Share Capital 52,000, Profit & Loss 6,480, Debenture 8,000, Current Liabilities, Bank Overdraft 57,000, Creditors 10,000, Other Expenses 840, Debenture Interest owing 280.

10.6 Trading Account: Dr Opening Stock 11,000, Add Purchases (this figure is found by inserting all the other figures in the Trading Account, leaving this as the missing figure to make it balance) 99,000, less Closing Stock 20,000, Gross profit 18,000 (this is 16⅔% of sales), Totals 108,000. Cr Sales 108,000. Profit & Loss, Dr Wages 6,600, Administration 4,320, Depreciation 450, Net Profit 6,630, Totals 18,000. Cr Gross Profit b/d 18,000. Balance Sheet, Fixed Assets 9,000 less Depreciation 450, Current Assets: Stock 20,000, Debtors 36,000, Totals 64,550. Ordinary Shares 15,000. Share Premium 1,250, Profit & Loss 21,700, Current Liabilities: Creditors 16,500, Bank Overdraft 9,380, Administration Expenses owing 720. Bank: June, Bal b/f 5,400. Debtors 9,600, less Wages 1,100, Admin 600, Purchases 9,330, Bal c/f 3,970. Jul, Bal b/f 3,970, less Wages 1,100, Admin 720, Purchases 16,500, O/d c/f 14,350. Aug, O/d b/f 14,350, Debtors 18,000, less Wages 1,100, Admin 720, Purchases 16,500, O/d c/f 14,670. Sept, O/d b/f 14,670, Ordinary Shares 6,250, Debtors 18,000, less Wages 1,100, Admin 720, Purchases 16,500, O/d c/f 8,740. Oct, O/d b/f 8,740, Debtors 18,000, less Wages 1,100, Admin 720, Purchases 16,500, O/d c/f 9,060. Nov, O/d b/f 9,060, Debtors 18,000, less Wages 1,100, Admin 720, Purchases 16,500, O/d c/f 9,380.

13.5 (i) Price Variance (F) 68, Usage (A) 54, Net (F) 14, (ii) Usage (F) 68, Price (A) 92, Net (A) 24, (iii) Price (A) 36, Usage (A) 36, Total (A) 72, (iv) Price (F) 81, Usage (F) 74, Total (F) 155. (v) Price (A) 154, Material (A) 63, Total (A) 217, (vi) Price $9,850 \times £3 = 29,550$ (F), Usage $150 \times £22 = 3,300$ (F) Total (F) 32,850.

13.7 (i) Price Variance (F) 964, Usage (F) 306, Total (F) 1,270. (ii) Price (A) 100, Usage (A) 150, Total (A) 250. (iii) Actual cost 2,292, Standard cost 2,160 = (A) 132. (iv) Price (A) 214, Usage (A) 112, Total (A) 326. (v) Actual cost 19,800, Standard cost 21,000 = (F) 1,200. (vi) Usage (F) 2,000, Price (A) 594 = Net (F) 1,406.

14.5 (i) Efficiency variance (F) 16, Wage (A) 28.4 = Net (A) 12.4. (ii) Rate (F) 44, Efficiency (A) 23.8, Net (F) 20.2. (iii) Rate (F) 4.8, Efficiency (F) 3.8, = Total (F) 8.6. (iv) Rate (A) 35.2, Efficiency (A) 12.0 = Total (A) 47.2. (v) Rate (F) 42, Efficiency (A) 16.2 = Net (F) 25.8. (vi) Efficiency (F) 11.2, Rate (A) 105.2 = Net (A) 94.

14.9 Standard cost $136 \times £3.6 = 489.60$, Actual cost $136 \times £3 = 408.00$. Fav. wage rate variance 81.60, (ii) Standard cost $200 \times £3.8 = 760.00$, Actual cost $200 \times £4 = 800.00$. Adv wage rate variance 40.00. (iii) Standard cost $140 \times £1.6 = 224.00$, Actual cost $154 \times £1.6 = 246.40$. Adv. labour efficiency variance 22.40. (iv) Standard cost $180 \times £2.2 = 396.00$, Actual cost $164 \times £2.2 = 360.80$. Fav. labour efficiency variance 35.20. (v) Fav. wage rate variance $£0.2 \times 70 = 14.00$, Fav. labour efficiency $£2 \times 5 = 10.00$, Total £24.00. Compares with standard cost $75 \times £2 = 150.00$, Actual cost $70 \times £1.8 = 126.00$, Variance 24.00. (vi) Fav. labour efficiency variance $14 \times £1.60 = 22.40$. Adv. wage rate variance $526 \times £0.40 = 210.40$. Net Adv. labour variance 188.00. (vii) Fav. wage rate variance $468 \times £0.20 = £93.60$. Adv. labour efficiency variance $28 \times £1.80 = 50.40$. Net fav. labour variance 43.20. (viii) Adv. wage rate variance $74 \times £0.10 = 7.40$. Adv. labour efficiency variance $4 \times £2.0 = £8.00$. Total adv. labour variance 15.40. (ix) Adv. wage rate variance $214 \times £0.10 = 21.40$. Adv. labour efficiency variance $34 \times £2.0 = 68.00$. Total Adv. labour variance 89.40.

14.10   A   Bonus £20 Salary £80; B   Bonus £26 Salary £86; C   Bonus − Salary £60.

14.12   X Bonus £80; Y Bonus £53.3; Z Bonus £36.

15.1   (a)   Actual overhead   5,840
                  Overhead applied to production × £6   6,000

                  Favourable budget (or spending) variance   £   160

      (b)   Actual overhead   21,230
                  Overhead applied to production 5,000 × £4   20,000

                  Adverse budget (or spending) variance   £ 1,230

      (c)   Actual Fixed Overhead   11,770
                  Budgeted Fixed Overhead   12,000

                  Favourable Fixed Overhead Spending Variance   £   230

      (d)   Actual Fixed Overhead   41,390
                  Budgeted Fixed Overhead   40,000

                  Adverse Fixed Overhead Spending Variance   £ 1,390

      (e)   Actual hours × standard rate (7,940 × £3)   23,820
                  Budgeted hours × standard rate (8,000 × £3)   24,000

                  Favourable efficiency variance   £   180

      (f)   Actual hours × standard rate (15,000 × £4)   60,000
                  Budgeted hours (4,860 × 3) × standard rate (14,580 × £4)   58,320

                  Adverse efficiency variance   £ 1,680

15.2   (a)   Actual Fixed Overhead   36,420
                  Budgeted Fixed Overhead   37,000

                  Favourable Fixed Overhead Spending Variance   £   580

      (b)   Actual hours × standard rate (242 × £6)   1,452
                  Budgeted hours × standard rate (250 × £6)   1,500

                  Favourable efficiency variance   £   48

      (c)   Actual overhead   18,000
                  Overhead applied to production (8,820 × £)   17,640

                  Budget (or spending) variance   £   360

      (d)   Actual overhead   8,790
                  Overhead applied to production (3,000 × £3)   9,000

                  Favourable budget (or spending) variance   £   210

      (e)   Actual Fixed Overhead   129,470
                  Budgeted Fixed Overhead   120,000

                  Adverse Fixed Overhead Spending Variances   £ 9,470

      (f)   Actual hours × standard rate (30,000 × £8)   240,000
                  Budgeted hours (9,880 × 3) × standard rate £8   237,120

                  Adverse efficiency variance   2,880

15.3 (a) Actual hours × standard rate 10,320 × £3   30,960
Budgeted hours × standard rate 10,000 × £3   30,000

Favourable volume variance   £   960

(b) Actual Fixed Overhead   39,640
Budgeted Fixed Overhead   40,000

Favourable Fixed Overhead Spending Variance   £   360

(c) Actual hours × standard rate 9,600 × £0.5   4,800
Budgeted hours × standard rate 10,000 × £0.5   5,000

Adverse volume variance   £   200

(d) Actual Fixed Overhead   62,390
Budgeted Fixed Overhead   60,000

Adverse Fixed Overhead Spending Variance   £ 2,390

16.1 Adverse Price Varance £18,750   Favourable Volume Variance £25,000.

16.3 Price Variance – nil – Adverse Volume Variance £520 Favourable Mix Variance £56.

17.11 (a) (i) £44,000, (ii) £60,000, (iii) £76,000, (b) (i) Loss £4,000, (ii) Profit £4,000, (iii) Profit £16,000, (iv) Profit £10,000, (c) 5,000 units.

17.12 (a) (i) £450,000, (ii) £590,000, (iii) £1,030,000, (b) (i) Loss £30,000, (ii) Profit £24,000, (iii) Profit £78,000, (iv) Profit £138,000, (c) 25,000 units.

18.8 $$\frac{16,000}{9-6.5} = \frac{16,000}{2.5} = 6,400 \text{ units}$$

18.9 $$\frac{13,000}{9-7} = \frac{13,000}{2} = 6,500 \text{ units}$$

18.10 £8,000.

18.11 (b) 350 units, (c) (i) 280, (ii) 700, (iii) 500, (iv) 300, (v) 700, (vi) 280.

19.3 (a) Selling prices A 33: B 44: C 77: D 77: E 44.

(b) Discontinue C.

(c) (i) Followed your advice. Sales A 3,200 + B 4,900 + D 6,600 + E 4,800 = 19,500. Less Costs: Direct Materials & Labour (16 + 19 + 44 + 23) × 100 = 10,200: Variable Costs (11 + 17 + 14 + 9) × 100 = 5,100: Fixed Costs 3,600. Total Costs 18,900. Net Profit 600.
(ii) Produced all items. Sales A 3,200 + B 4,900 + C 5,600 × D 6,600 + E 4,800 = 25,100. Less Costs: Direct Materials and Labour (16 + 19 + 38 + 44 + 23) × 100 = 14,000: Variable Costs (11 + 17 + 23 + 14 + 9) × 100 = 7,400: Fixed Costs 3,600. Total Costs 25,000. Net Profit 100.

(d) Discontinue A and E.

(e) (i) Followed your advice. Sales B 3,800 + C 6,800 + D 6,400 = 17,000. Less Costs: Direct Materials & Labour (19 + 38 + 44) × 100 = 10,100: Variable Costs (17 + 23 + 14) × 100 = 5,400; Fixed Costs 3,600. Total Costs 19,100. Net Loss 2,100.

(ii) Produced all items. Sales S 2,400 + B 3,800 + C 6,800 + D 6,400 + E 2,900 = 22,300. Less Costs: Direct Labour and Material (16 + 19 + 38 + 44 + 23) × 100 = 14,000: Variable Costs (11 + 17 + 23 + 14 + 9) × 100 = 7,400: Fixed Costs 3,600 = Total Costs 25,000. Net Loss 2,700.

19.4 (a) Cork: Labour & Materials 14, Variable o/h 22, Marginal cost 36, Fixed Costs 4, Full Cost 40 + Profit 10% 4 = Selling Price 44. Plastic: Labour & Materials 5, Variable o/h 13, Marginal Cost 18, Fixed Costs 2, Full cost 20, Add Profit 10% 2 = Selling Price 22. Screwtop: Labour & Materials 37, Variable o/h 9, Marginal Cost 46, Fixed Costs 14, Full cost 60, Add Profit 10% 6 = Selling Price 66. Wedge: Labour & Materials 23, Variance o/h 17, Marginal Cost 40, Fixed Costs 10, Full Cost 50, Add Profit 10% 5 = Selling Price 55. (b) Discontinue only those products which are selling at less than marginal cost, i.e. Plastic. (c) Sales: Cork 100 × £43 = £4,300, Screwtop 100 × £58 = £5,800, Wedge 100 × £59 = £5,900, Total Sales 16,000. Less: Direct Labour Cork 1,400, Screwtop 3,700, Wedge 2,300, Total 7,400, Variable o/h Cork 2,200, Screwtop 900, Wedge 1,700, Total 4,800, Fixed Costs 3,000, Profit 800. (d) Discontinue Wedge. (e) (i) Sales: Cork 4,900, Plastic 2,000, Screwtop 5,500, Total 12,400, Less: Direct Labour & Materials, Cork 1,400, Plastic 500, Screwtop 3,700, Total 5,600, Variable o/h Cork 2,200, Plastic 1,300, Screwtop 900, Total 4,400, Fixed Costs 3,000, Loss 600. (e) (ii) Sales, Cork 4,900, Plastic 2,000, Screwtop 5,500, Wedge 3,700, Total 16,100. Less: Direct Labour & Materials, Cork 1,400, Plastic 500, Screwtop 3,700, Wedge 2,300, Total 7,900, Variable o/h, Cork 2,200, Plastic 1,300, Screwtop 900, Wedge 1,700, Total 6,100, Fixed Costs 3,000, Loss 900.

20.1 To manufacture 1,500 parts would cost: –

	£
Direct Material (+ 50%)	150,000
Direct Labour (+ 50% + 10%)	99,000
Variable Overhead (+ 50%)	82,500
Fixed Overhead	95,000
	426,500

To buy in the 1500 parts would cost: –

	£
1,500 × £240	360,000
Unabsorbed Fixed Overhead	55,000
	415,000

The company could save £11,500 by sub contracting, and obtain the advantage of releasing some working and fixed capital as well as management time. Against this it might lose control of delivery and quality. Also future price quotations may not be so competitive.

20.2

Contributions are: –	X	Y	Z
	£	£	£
Sales Price	560	340	220
less:	250	140	80
Contribution per unit	310	200	140
lbs of Zebo per unit	20	10	5
∴Contribution per lb of Zebo	£15.50	£20.00	£28.00

∴. Chose Z then Y then X.
Total Contributions would be based in 1000 lbs of Zebo.
producing: –

$$200 \text{ of } Z = £28,000$$
$$100 \text{ of } Y = £20,000$$
$$50 \text{ of } X = £15,500$$

Note: It might be advisable in terms of longer tem planning of markets to sell all three products even though reducing current levels of profit – particularly if the material shortage is only likely to be short lived.

20.3 If the project is a one-off – with no continuing commitment to a price then both items would be charged at the realisable value: –

	£
Material 105	1,000
Machine	3,000
	4,000

If the information were to be the basis for a contract price into the future, then the appropriate values would be based on replacement cost.

	£
Material 105	10,000
Machine	50,000
	60,000

22.1 Gross Profit as % of Sales 19-1 50% 19-2 40% 19-3 60%.
Net Profit as % Sales 19-1 25% 19-2 18.4% 19-3 32.7%.

At Gross Profit comment on wide fluctuations in Stock in Trade levels and Purchases. Also mention possibility of price changes, theft or mistake.

At Net Profit note changes in selling expense levels: –

	19-1 %	19-2 %	19-3 %
Administration	10	10	10
Selling	15	11.6	17.3

22.3 19 × 1 Sales 500,000, Opening Stock in Trade 80,000, Purchases 290,000 less Closing Stock 120,000. Cost of Goods sold 250,000. Gross Profit 250,000. 19 × 2. Sales 600,000 Opening Stock in Trade 120,000 Purchases 360,000, Sub Total 480,000 less Goods destroyed 5000. Closing Stock 130,000. Cost of Goods Sold 345,000 Gross Profit 255,000.

22.5 Using 19-1 as base year 19-2 and 19-3 can be explained as percentages. This shows changes over five years. It may also be useful to split the figures as a percentage of revenue.

	19-1 %	19-2 %	19-3 %	19-1 %	19-2 %	19-3 %
Fees from hire of facilities	100	104	110	83	79	76
Fees from hire of equipment	100	150	217	10	14	18
Receipts from vending machines	100	112	115	7	7	6
	100	109	121	100	100	100
Salaries & Wages	100	110	127	133	134	140
Heating & Lighting	100	115	130	33	35	36
Repairs & Maintenance						
Buildings	100	80	60	8	6	4
Equipment	100	110	50	2	2	1
Goods for vending	100	75	97	5	3	4
Telephone etc.	100	117	136	12	12	13
Advertising	100	33	17	5	2	1
	100	107	121	198	194	199

Comment on high levels of increase in Salaries and Wages, Heating & Lighting and Telephone etc. over the three years. Also note the very high proportion of costs associated with salaries and wages and also heat and light. These two areas of cost appear crucial.

23.2 (a) On the assumption that Creditors and Debtors are paid at approximately the same time, it is an indication of the company's ability to meet its current liabilities from liquid current assets.

(b) The profit return on all longer term sources of capital to the business plus bank overdrafts. The profit is before charging any return on the sources of capital.

(c) It enables an assessment to be made of the actual period of credit allowed to customers by comparison with the official period and comparative firms.

(d) By showing what stake the shareholders have in the Total Assets, suppliers of other sources of capital can assess the amount of cover for their debts in the event of failure.

(e) This indicates how many times the profits could have covered this dividend and is therefore some guide to the likely stability of dividends. It also indicates how much profit is retained in the business.

23.4 1. A, C, E.
2. A, C, E.
3. E.
4. D, F (assuming current assets exceed current liabilities)
5. No Effect.

23.6

$$a = \frac{.1}{1.5} = 6.7\%$$

$$b = \frac{15.000}{100.000} = £.15 \text{ per share}$$

$$c = \frac{1.5}{.15} = 10.0$$

23.8 Selection of five from: –

Current Ratio 1.89: 1; Acid Test Ratio .78:1 (Note Only Bank and Debtor Balances included) Gross Profit/Sales 33⅓% Net Profit/Sales (no tax assumed) 13.3%. Net Operating Profit/Capital Employed $\frac{20 + \text{Debenture Interest } 3}{200} = 11.5\%$

Net Profit/Owners Equity $\frac{20}{140} = 14.3\%$ Stock Turnover $\frac{100}{30} = 3.3$ times.

Sales/Fixed Assets $\frac{150}{120} = 1.3$ times. Days Sales in Debtors = 122.

Net Worth/Total Assets $\frac{140}{290} = 48.3\%$ Fixed Assets/Net Worth $\frac{120}{140} =$

85.7%. Coverage of Fixed Charges $\frac{20+3}{3} = 7.7$ times.

23.10 Current Ratios 1) 2.4:1 2) 2.4:1, Acid Test Ration 1) 1.2:1 2) 1.2:1 Gross Profit/Sales 1) 21.3 2) 20.3 Net Profit/Sales 1) 5% 2) 4.5% Operating Profit/Capital Employed:

1) $\frac{30,000}{200,000} = 15\%$ 2) $\frac{38,000}{294,000} = 12.9\%$ Net Profit/Owners Equity:

1) $\frac{30,000}{200,000} = 15\%$ 2) $\frac{34,000}{234,000} = 14.5\%$ Stock Turn (using year end

figures 1) $\frac{472}{120} = 3.9$ times 2) $\frac{596}{188} = 3.2$ times. Sales/Fixed Assets 1) $\frac{600}{60}$

$= 10$ times 2) $\frac{748}{80} = 93$ times. Collection Period for Debtors 1) = 60.8 days

2) = 80 days Net Worth/Total Assets 1) $\frac{200}{300} = .67$ 2) $\frac{234}{446} = .52$ Cover-

age of fixed charges. 1) n/a 2) $\frac{38,000}{4,000} = 9.5$

23.12 (*a*) 1:1
(*b*) 5.2 times
(*c*) 9.2%
(*d*) 34.1 days
(*e*) 3.31 times

24.4 A central key ratio is explained in terms of subsidiary ratios branching from it. Each subsidiary is similarly dealt with until a pyramid develops with the base showing very detailed ratios and the top the final overall summary ratio.

The presentation allows the overall picture to be easily visualised, and key ratios to be quickly spotted.

24.7 *Liquidity*

The substantial increase in the previous four years on Current ratio shows a reduction in 19-1 to 2.5 which is in part accounted for by reduction in Acid Test ratio from 1.22 to 1. The change probably reflects management policy to reverse a trend towards inefficient use of liquid resources.

Profitability

The steady decline in the ratio of Net Profit/Owners Equity indicates a general reduction in the company's profitability rather than any temporary decline. The adequacy of this level of return must be judged against other comparable companies.

Use of Assets

The collection period for debtors has lengthened during the four years but reduced a little in the current period. The trend is in sympathy with the liquidity ratio and probably reflects management's difficulties with declining profitability, i.e. attracting customers.

Stock Turnover has reduced in every period. This is an unsatisfactory trend when taken in conjunction with all the other indicators.

Capital Structure

Times Interest changes covered. This ratio has not changed must and indicates that the company is not in immediate difficulties so far as covering interest payments is concerned. With declining profits this is at least some encouragement.

Summary

All the main indicators are showing adverse trends, i.e. Liquidity, Profitability and Use of Assets. From the evidence we have this tends to support a feeling that management has not been effective. Fortunately the company is not too highly geared and may survive to do better.

24.9

		19-2
(1)	Gross Profit % Sales	8.8%
	Net Profit % Sales	0.9%
	Current Ratio	3.2:1
	Acid Test Ratio	1.5:1
	Debtors − Collection Period in Days	16.8 Days
	Stock Turnover	13.9 Days
	Net Worth as % of Total Assets	64.9%
	Number of Times Fixed Charges Earned	8.0 times
	Operating Profit/Capital Employed	6.9%
	Earnings per Ordinary Share	£.20
	Price Earnings Ratio	7.5 times
	Dividend Yield	3.3%

(2) Comments: −

Gross Profit − tending to follow industry pattern but only third in rank.

Net Profit − following Gross Profit trend, second in rank, but overall the return seems low.

Current and Acid Test Ratios − nothing exceptional on interfirm basis although the level appears high for general standards.

Debtors — only one company is substantially better but may be setting a desirable standard.

Stock Turnover — some improvement is possible as evidenced by A and C.

Net Worth as % Total Assets — Both A and B appear to be more highly geared than P, which may indicate that future borrowing maybe a good source of raising funds.

Number of Times Fixed Charges Covered — Only one company has a better cover which reinforces the previous point.

Operating Profit/Capital Employed — P is showing up well in 19.2 at this level, compared to the other companies, but this is not a satisfactory return when borrowing on 8% Debentures.

Earnings per Ordinary Share — Despite earning the highest return on capital employed the ordinary shareholders are not benefiting, possibly because A is paying higher interest charges than A or C.

Price Earnings Ratio — P seems to be very much undervalued in comparison with A or C. There must be special external factors.

Dividend Yield — P seems to be average.

25.3 Sources of Funds: Profit for the year 4,400 + Depreciation of Plant in year 500 =   £4,900

Applications of Funds: Addition to Building 300 + Plant 1,000 + Drawings 3,000 =   £4,300

Net Increase in Working Capital   600

Items Increasing Working Capital. Reduction in Creditors 720 Reduction in Bank Balance 1,280 + 1,700 =   £3,700

Items Reducing Working Capital Loan 2,000 + Reduction in Stock 60 + Reduction in Debtors 1,040 =   £3,100

Net Increase in Working Capital   600

25.5 Sources of Cash

Cash Contribution from Profits + Depreciation	4,900
New Loan	2,000
Reduction in Stock	60
Reduction in Debtors	1,040
	8,000

Applications of Cash

Building	300	
Plant	1,000	
Drawings	3,000	
Reduction of Creditors	720	
		5,020

Increase in Cash (1,700 + 1,280)   2,980

26.1 (a)

$$5,300 \times .17 \times \frac{62}{365} = £153.05$$

(b)

$$9,000 \times .19 \times \frac{70}{365} = £327.95$$

The Bank will pay £9,000 − 327.95 = £8,672.05.

26.3 The amount borrowed is: –

£1,000 × ¼ =	250.0
750 × ¼ =	187.5
500 × ¼ =	125.0
250 × ¼ =	62.5
Equivalent loan for 1 year	625.0

$$r = \frac{200}{625 \times 1} = .32 \text{ or } 32\%.$$

26.4 £4,000 will accumulate to $4,000 (1+.1)^{10} = £10,375$.
Interest is ∴ £10,375 − 4,000 = £6,375.
(Using the tables 4,000 × 2.594 = £10,376 − note slight rounding errors).

27.1 The present value of an annuity of £5,000 p.a. for seven years at 12% = 5,000 × 4.564 = £22,820

or

$$\frac{1 - \dfrac{1}{(1+.12)^7}}{.12} \times 5,000 = £22,820$$

The offer of £20,000 would therefore appear less attractive than retaining the rental income.

27.3

$$R = \frac{Ar}{(1+r)^n - 1} = \frac{100,000(0.10)}{(1+0.10)^5 - 1}$$
$$= £16,380 \text{ per annum.}$$

27.4

$$R = \frac{100,000(0.15)}{(1+0.15)^5 - 1} = £14,832 \text{ per annum.}$$

28.1

	Year 19-1	Year 19-2
Purchase of machine	50,000	–
Sale of old machine	–	(8,000)
Installation Cost	10,000	–
Commissioning Cost	15,000	8,000
Rent of premises to date of completion	5,000 (9 months)	3,750
Training Labour		2,000
Working Capital	10,000	
Net Cash Outlay	90,000	5,750

28.2 The net cash outlays in 19-1 and 19-2 will reduce the companys tax bill by 50%, and the cash benefit actually obtained in the next year (i.e. after 9 months). Thus the year 19-1 saving of £45,000 will be received in year 19-2 and the £2,875 from year 19-2 will be received in 19-3 as follows: –

	19-1	19-2	19-3
Net Cash Outlay	90,000	5,750	
Cash Inflow: –			
Tax saving on outlay		(45,000)	(2,875)
Net Cash flows	90,000	(39,250)	(2,875)

figures in brackets = net inflows.

28.3

	Net Cash Flows	Present Value Factor for 15%	N.P.V. £
Year 19-1	90,000	.870	78,300
19-2	(39,250)	.756	(29,673)
19-3	(2,875)	.658	(1,892)

Net Present Value at start of project   £46,735

29.1 Exactly 3 years when the cumulative cash flow will be – nil –.

29.2

Year	Net Cash Flow	Present Value Factor for 10%	N.P.V. £
1	9,000	.909	8,181
2	(6,000)	.826	(4,956)
3	(3,000)	.751	(2,253)
4	(2,000)	.683	(1,366)

Net Present Value of Cash (inflow)   (394)

29.3

Year	Net Cash Flow	Present Value Factor for 12%	N.P.V. 12%	Present Value Factor for 14%	N.P.V. 14%
1	9,000	.893	8,037	.877	7,893
2	(6,000)	.797	(4,782)	.769	(4,614)
3	(3,000)	.712	(2,136)	.675	(2,025)
4	(2,000)	.636	(1,272)	.592	(1,184)
			(153)		70

12% Discount Rate gives N.P.V.   (153)
14% Discount Rate gives N.P.V.   70
                                        223

The IRR is $\dfrac{70}{223} \times 2\%$ below 14% = 14 − .63 = 13.37%.

30.1

	Internal Rate of Return	*N.P.V. using 12%*
Project A	16%	(£2,433)
Project B	14%	(£3,270)

Using IRR the choice would be Project A but using N.P.V. with 12% interest would suggest Project B. The crucial factor is therefore the rate of interest that funds would be invested at when generated by the project, if approximating to 12% then the N.P.V. is more realistic but if closer to the I.R.R. rates then they would give better solution.

30.3

Year	Net Cash Flow £	Factor for 12%	Present Value £
0	8,000	1.000	8,000
1	(4,000)	.893	(3,572)
2	(2,000)	.797	(1,594)
3	(6,000)	.712	(4,272)
			(1,438)

(1) The N.P.V. at 12% interest is £1,438.

(2) The Present Value of an annuity of £1 for three years at 12% interest = £2.402.

∴ Present Value £1,438 = 2.402 × The annual sum

∴ The Annual sum = $\dfrac{1438}{2.402}$ = £598.7

30.4 The Present Value of an annuity of £1 for six years at 12% interest = £4.111

Present Value £2624 = 4.111 × The annual sum

∴ Annual sum = $\dfrac{2,624}{4.111}$ = £638.3 which is a better annual return than for machine in 30.3.

31.1 £13,190 × P.V. factor an annuity of £1 = £50,000

P.V. factor for an annuity of £1 = $\dfrac{50,000}{13,190}$ = 3.79

Referring to the tables along the 5 period row gives 10% interest for 3.79.

31.4

	£
Cost of Asset 80,000 (1 − 0.4) =	48,000
Cost of Leasing 26,338 (1 − 0.4) =	15,803
P.V. factor for four years =	$\dfrac{48,000}{15,803}$ = 3.04

From P.V. of annuity tables this represents 12% interest over 4 years.

31.5 Factor for P.V. of an annuity of £1 for 10 years at 14% = 5.216

5,000 × 5.216 = £26,080 Capital Value of Lease.

32.1 As per the Chapter – scaling down estimates of gains, benefits or revenues and scaling up estimates of cost. The cut off rate of return may also be increased above the cost of capital. To improve judgement a number of profiles may be taken – Best, Most Likely and Worst so that a range of outcomes can be seen, which may be further extended by sensitivity analysis – where varying assumptions about individual components will indicate how important they are for success. The estimates of items such as sales may be helped by using subjective probability to produce an expected outcome from a range of estimates.

32.2

Units	Probability	Expected unit sales
100,000	.05	5,000
200,000	.20	40,000
250,000	.30	75,000
300,000	.40	120,000
350,000	.05	17,500
	1.00	Total 257,500

33.1

$$\text{Break even for Plant A} = \frac{\text{F.C.}}{\text{Contribution per £ Sales}} = \frac{30,000}{£0.50} = \frac{£60,000}{\text{Sales}}$$

$$\text{Plant B} = \frac{20,000}{£0.40} = \frac{£50,000}{\text{Sales}}$$

Profitability of Plant A

	£	£	£	£	£	£	£
Sales	40,000	50,000	60,000	70,000	80,000	90,000	100,000
Variable Cost	20,000	25,000	30,000	35,000	40,000	45,000	50,000
Contribution	20,000	25,000	30,000	35,000	40,000	45,000	50,000
Fixed Cost	30,000	30,000	30,000	30,000	30,000	30,000	30,000
Net Profit (loss)	(10,000)	(5,000)	0	5,000	10,000	15,000	20,000

Profitability of Plant B

	£	£	£	£	£	£	£
Sales	40,000	50,000	60,000	70,000	80,000	90,000	100,000
Variable Cost	24,000	30,000	36,000	42,000	48,000	54,000	60,000
Contribution	16,000	20,000	24,000	28,000	32,000	36,000	40,000
Fixed Cost	20,000	20,000	20,000	20,000	20,000	20,000	20,000
Net Profit (Loss)	(4,000)	0	4,000	8,000	12,000	16,000	20,000

Plant A has a higher break even point and only produces higher profits than Plant B when sales in excess of £100,000 p.a. are achieved. The relative riskiness depends on how strong the market demand is for the product. Unless there is a very high level of demand in excess of £100,000 Plant A is inherently more risky than plant B.

33.2

	£	£	£	£	£	£	£
Sales	40,000	50,000	60,000	70,000	80,000	90,000	100,000
(a) Net Profit (Loss)	(10,000)	(5,000)	0	5,000	10,000	15,000	20,000
Return on Shares of £100,000	(10%)	(5%)	0	5%	10%	15%	20%
(b) Contribution	20,000	25,000	30,000	35,000	40,000	45,000	50,000

Interest   £4,000
Fixed Cost £30,000

	34,000	34,000	34,000	34,000	34,000	34,000	34,000
Net Profit (Loss)	(14,000)	(9,000)	(4,000)	1,000	6,000	11,000	16,000
Return on Shares of £60,000	(23.3)%	(15)%	(6.7)%	1.7%	10%	18.3%	26.7%

The introduction of borrowed capital increases the break even point from sales of £60,000 to sales of £68,000 ($\frac{£34,000}{£0.50}$). On Sales of £80,000 the rate of return 10% is the same under both funding situations and equal to the loan rate. On Sales above £80,000 the return to Ordinary Shareholders is higher with the loan capital since they take profits in excess of £10,000.

34.1 The company receives £100,000 − £2,959 = £97,041 immediately (£100,000 × .12 × $\frac{90}{365}$ = £2,959)

The real rate of interest is: −

$$\frac{2,959}{97,041 \times \frac{90}{365}} = 12.37\%$$

34.3 $\dfrac{\text{Interest}}{\text{Market Price}} = \dfrac{5}{40} = 12.5\%.$

34.4 $12.5\% \times (1 - .52) = 6\%.$

35.1 $P = \dfrac{1}{(1 + .12)} + \dfrac{2}{(1 + .12)^2} + \dfrac{5}{(1 + .12)^2} = £6.47$

35.3 $P = \dfrac{D}{K - 9} = \dfrac{.60}{.1 - .05} = £12.00$

35.4 $\dfrac{.60}{.1 - 0} = £6.00$

35.6 £0.13 × 9.2 = £1.20.

36.1

			£	% weight
Equity	500 + 280	=	780	66.1
Preference		=	250	21.2
Debt	100 + 50	=	150	12.7
			1180	100.0

36.2

			£	% weight
Equity	500,000 × 2.50		1,250,000	82.2
Preference			125,000	8.2
Debt		95,000		
		50,000	145,000	9.6
			1,520,000	100.0

36.3

	Rate of Return	Book Weighting	Book WACC %	Market Weighting	Market WACC %
Equity	.12	66.1	7.93	82.2	9.86
Preference	.15	21.2	3.18	8.2	1.23
Debt	.14	12.7	1.78	9.6	1.34
		100.0	12.89	100.0	12.43

37.1 Good management, Patents, Trade Marks and special know how. Trading reputation, good or unique trading situation etc.

37.2 $50\% \times £80,000 = £40,000$.

37.4 £60,000 × 3.791 = £227,460

Appendix

Table 1

Compound Amount of 1

Period	1%	2%	3%	4%	5%	6%	7%	8%	9%	10%
1	1.010	1.020	1.030	1.040	1.050	1.060	1.070	1.080	1.090	1.100
2	1.020	1.040	1.061	1.082	1.102	1.124	1.145	1.166	1.188	1.210
3	1.030	1.061	1.093	1.125	1.158	1.191	1.225	1.260	1.295	1.331
4	1.041	1.082	1.126	1.170	1.216	1.262	1.311	1.360	1.412	1.464
5	1.051	1.104	1.159	1.217	1.276	1.338	1.403	1.469	1.539	1.611
6	1.062	1.126	1.194	1.265	1.340	1.419	1.501	1.587	1.677	1.772
7	1.072	1.149	1.230	1.316	1.407	1.504	1.606	1.714	1.828	1.949
8	1.083	1.172	1.267	1.369	1.477	1.594	1.718	1.851	1.993	2.144
9	1.094	1.195	1.305	1.423	1.551	1.689	1.838	1.999	2.172	2.358
10	1.105	1.219	1.344	1.480	1.629	1.791	1.967	2.159	2.367	2.594
11	1.116	1.243	1.384	1.539	1.710	1.898	2.105	2.332	2.580	2.853
12	1.127	1.268	1.426	1.601	1.796	2.012	2.252	2.518	2.813	3.138
13	1.138	1.294	1.469	1.665	1.886	2.133	2.410	2.720	3.066	3.452
14	1.149	1.319	1.513	1.732	1.980	2.261	2.579	2.937	3.342	3.797
15	1.161	1.346	1.558	1.801	2.079	2.397	2.759	3.172	3.642	4.177

Period	12%	14%	15%	16%	18%	20%	24%	28%	32%
1	1.120	1.140	1.150	1.160	1.180	1.200	1.240	1.280	1.320
2	1.254	1.300	1.322	1.346	1.392	1.440	1.538	1.638	1.742
3	1.405	1.482	1.521	1.561	1.643	1.728	1.907	2.097	2.300
4	1.574	1.689	1.749	1.811	1.939	2.074	2.364	2.684	3.036
5	1.762	1.925	2.011	2.100	2.288	2.488	2.932	3.436	4.007
6	1.974	2.195	2.313	2.436	2.700	2.986	3.635	4.398	5.290
7	2.211	2.502	2.660	2.826	3.185	3.583	4.508	5.629	6.983
8	2.476	2.853	3.059	3.278	3.759	4.300	5.590	7.206	9.217
9	2.773	3.252	3.518	3.803	4.435	5.160	6.931	9.223	12.166
10	3.106	3.707	4.046	4.411	5.234	6.192	8.594	11.806	16.060
11	3.479	4.226	4.652	5.117	6.176	7.430	10.657	15.112	21.199
12	3.896	4.818	5.350	5.936	7.288	8.916	13.215	19.343	27.983
13	4.363	5.492	6.153	6.886	8.599	10.699	16.386	24.759	36.937
14	4.887	6.261	7.076	7.988	10.147	12.839	20.319	31.691	48.757
15	5.474	7.138	8.137	9.266	11.974	15.407	25.196	40.565	64.359

Period	36%	40%	50%	60%	70%	80%	90%
1	1.360	1.400	1.500	1.600	1.700	1.800	1.900
2	1.850	1.960	2.250	2.560	2.890	3.240	3.610
3	2.515	2.744	3.375	4.096	4.913	5.832	6.859
4	3.421	3.842	5.062	6.544	8.352	10.498	13.032
5	4.653	5.378	7.594	10.486	14.199	18.896	24.761
6	6.328	7.530	11.391	16.777	24.138	34.012	47.046
7	8.605	10.541	17.086	26.844	41.034	61.222	89.387
8	11.703	14.758	25.629	42.950	69.758	110.200	169.836
9	15.917	20.661	38.443	68.720	118.588	198.359	322.688
10	21.647	28.925	57.665	109.951	201.599	357.047	613.107
11	29.439	40.496	86.498	175.922	342.719	642.684	1164.902
12	40.037	56.694	129.746	281.475	582.622	1156.831	2213.314
13	54.451	79.372	194.619	450.360	990.457	2082.295	4205.297
14	74.053	111.120	291.929	720.576	1683.777	3748.131	7990.065
15	100.712	155.568	437.894	1152.921	2862.421	6746.636	15181.122

Table 2

Present Value of 1

Period	1%	2%	3%	4%	5%	6%	7%	8%	9%	10%	12%	14%	15%
1	0.990	0.980	0.971	0.961	0.952	0.943	0.935	0.926	0.917	0.909	0.893	0.877	0.870
2	0.980	0.961	0.943	0.925	0.907	0.890	0.873	0.857	0.842	0.826	0.797	0.769	0.756
3	0.971	0.942	0.915	0.889	0.864	0.840	0.816	0.794	0.772	0.751	0.712	0.675	0.658
4	0.961	0.924	0.889	0.855	0.823	0.792	0.763	0.735	0.708	0.683	0.636	0.592	0.572
5	0.951	0.906	0.863	0.822	0.784	0.747	0.713	0.681	0.650	0.621	0.567	0.519	0.497
6	0.942	0.888	0.838	0.790	0.746	0.705	0.666	0.630	0.596	0.564	0.507	0.456	0.432
7	0.933	0.871	0.813	0.760	0.711	0.665	0.623	0.583	0.547	0.513	0.452	0.400	0.376
08	0.923	0.853	0.789	0.731	0.677	0.627	0.582	0.540	0.502	0.467	0.404	0.351	0.327
9	0.914	0.837	0.766	0.703	0.645	0.592	0.544	0.500	0.460	0.424	0.361	0.308	0.284
10	0.905	0.820	0.744	0.676	0.614	0.558	0.508	0.463	0.422	0.386	0.322	0.270	0.247
11	0.896	0.804	0.722	0.650	0.585	0.527	0.475	0.429	0.388	0.350	0.287	0.237	0.215
12	0.887	0.788	0.701	0.625	0.557	0.497	0.444	0.397	0.356	0.319	0.257	0.208	0.187
13	0.879	0.773	0.681	0.601	0.530	0.469	0.415	0.368	0.326	0.290	0.229	0.182	0.163
14	0.870	0.758	0.661	0.577	0.505	0.442	0.388	0.340	0.299	0.263	0.205	0.160	0.141
15	0.861	0.743	0.642	0.555	0.481	0.417	0.362	0.315	0.275	0.239	0.183	0.140	0.123
16	0.853	0.728	0.623	0.534	0.458	0.394	0.339	0.292	0.252	0.218	0.163	0.123	0.107
17	0.844	0.714	0.605	0.513	0.436	0.371	0.317	0.270	0.231	0.198	0.146	0.108	0.093
18	0.836	0.700	0.587	0.494	0.416	0.350	0.296	0.250	0.212	0.180	0.130	0.095	0.081
19	0.828	0.686	0.570	0.475	0.396	0.331	0.276	0.232	0.194	0.164	0.116	0.083	0.070
20	0.820	0.673	0.554	0.456	0.377	0.319	0.258	0.215	0.178	0.149	0.104	0.073	0.061
25	0.780	0.610	0.478	0.375	0.295	0.233	0.184	0.146	0.116	0.092	0.059	0.038	0.030
30	0.742	0.552	0.412	0.308	0.231	0.174	0.131	0.099	0.075	0.057	0.033	0.020	0.015

Period	16%	18%	20%	24%	28%	32%	36%	40%	50%	60%	70%	80%	90%
1	0.862	0.847	0.833	0.806	0.781	0.758	0.735	0.714	0.667	0.625	0.588	0.556	0.526
2	0.743	0.718	0.694	0.650	0.610	0.574	0.541	0.510	0.444	0.391	0.346	0.309	0.277
3	0.641	0.609	0.579	0.524	0.477	0.435	0.398	0.364	0.296	0.244	0.204	0.171	0.146
4	0.552	0.516	0.482	0.423	0.373	0.329	0.292	0.260	0.198	0.153	0.120	0.095	0.077
5	0.476	0.437	0.402	0.341	0.291	0.250	0.215	0.186	0.132	0.095	0.070	0.053	0.040
6	0.410	0.370	0.335	0.275	0.227	0.189	0.158	0.133	0.088	0.060	0.041	0.029	0.021
7	0.354	0.314	0.279	0.222	0.178	0.143	0.116	0.095	0.059	0.037	0.024	0.016	0.011
8	0.305	0.266	0.233	0.179	0.139	0.108	0.085	0.068	0.039	0.023	0.014	0.009	0.006
9	0.263	0.226	0.194	0.144	0.108	0.082	0.063	0.048	0.026	0.015	0.008	0.005	0.003
10	0.227	0.191	0.162	0.116	0.085	0.062	0.046	0.035	0.017	0.009	0.005	0.003	0.002
11	0.195	0.162	0.135	0.094	0.066	0.047	0.034	0.025	0.012	0.006	0.003	0.002	0.001
12	0.168	0.137	0.112	0.076	0.052	0.036	0.025	0.018	0.008	0.004	0.002	0.001	0.001
13	0.145	0.116	0.093	0.061	0.040	0.027	0.018	0.013	0.005	0.002	0.001	0.001	0.000
14	0.125	0.099	0.078	0.049	0.032	0.021	0.014	0.009	0.003	0.001	0.001	0.000	0.000
15	0.108	0.084	0.065	0.040	0.025	0.016	0.010	0.006	0.002	0.001	0.000	0.000	0.000
16	0.093	0.071	0.054	0.032	0.019	0.012	0.007	0.005	0.002	0.001	0.000	0.000	
17	0.080	0.060	0.045	0.026	0.015	0.009	0.005	0.003	0.001	0.000	0.000		
18	0.069	0.051	0.038	0.021	0.012	0.007	0.004	0.002	0.001	0.000	0.000		
19	0.060	0.043	0.031	0.017	0.009	0.005	0.003	0.002	0.000	0.000			
20	0.051	0.037	0.026	0.014	0.007	0.004	0.002	0.001	0.000	0.000			
25	0.024	0.016	0.010	0.005	0.002	0.001	0.000	0.000					
30	0.012	0.007	0.004	0.002	0.001	0.000	0.000						

Table 3

Amount of Annuity of 1 per period

Period	1%	2%	3%	4%	5%	6%	7%	8%
1	1.000	1.000	1.000	1.000	1.000	1.000	1.000	1.000
2	2.010	2.020	2.030	2.040	2.050	2.060	2.070	2.080
3	3.030	3.060	3.091	3.122	3.152	3.184	3.215	3.246
4	4.060	4.122	4.184	4.246	4.310	4.375	4.440	4.506
5	5.101	5.204	5.309	5.416	5.526	5.637	5.751	5.867
6	6.152	6.308	6.468	6.633	6.802	6.975	7.153	7.336
7	7.214	7.434	7.662	7.898	8.142	8.394	8.654	8.923
8	8.286	8.583	8.892	9.214	9.549	9.897	10.260	10.637
9	9.369	9.755	10.159	10.583	11.027	11.491	11.978	12.488
10	10.462	10.950	11.464	12.006	12.578	13.181	13.816	14.487
11	11.567	12.169	12.808	13.486	14.207	14.972	15.784	16.645
12	12.683	13.412	14.192	15.026	15.917	16.870	17.888	18.977
13	13.809	14.680	15.618	16.627	17.713	18.882	20.141	21.495
14	14.947	15.974	17.086	18.292	19.599	21.051	22.550	24.215
15	16.097	17.293	18.599	20.024	21.579	23.276	25.129	27.152
16	17.258	18.639	20.157	21.825	23.657	25.673	27.888	30.324
17	18.430	20.012	21.762	23.698	25.840	28.213	30.840	33.750
18	19.615	21.412	23.414	25.645	28.132	30.906	33.999	37.450
19	20.811	22.841	25.117	27.671	30.539	33.760	37.379	41.446
20	22.019	24.297	26.870	29.778	33.066	36.786	40.995	45.762
25	28.243	32.030	36.459	41.646	47.727	54.865	63.249	73.106
30	34.785	40.568	47.575	56.085	66.439	79.058	94.461	113.283

Period	9%	10%	12%	14%	16%	18%	20%	24%
1	1.000	1.000	1.000	1.000	1.000	1.000	1.000	1.000
2	2.090	2.100	2.120	2.140	2.160	2.180	2.200	2.240
3	3.278	3.310	3.374	3.440	3.506	3.572	3.640	3.778
4	4.573	4.641	4.779	4.921	5.066	5.215	5.368	5.684
5	5.985	6.105	6.353	6.610	6.877	7.154	7.442	8.048
6	7.523	7.716	8.115	8.536	8.977	9.442	9.930	10.980
7	9.200	9.487	10.089	10.730	11.414	12.142	12.916	14.615
8	11.028	11.436	12.300	13.233	14.240	15.327	16.499	19.123
9	13.021	13.579	14.776	16.085	17.518	19.086	20.799	24.712
10	15.193	15.937	17.549	19.337	21.321	23.521	25.959	31.643
11	17.560	18.531	20.655	23.044	25.738	28.755	32.150	40.238
12	20.141	21.384	24.133	27.271	30.350	34.931	39.580	50.895
13	22.953	24.523	28.029	32.089	36.766	42.219	48.497	64.110
14	26.019	27.975	32.393	37.581	43.672	50.818	59.196	80.496
15	29.361	31.722	37.280	43.842	51.659	60.965	72.035	100.815

Period	28%	32%	36%	40%	50%	60%	70%	80%
1	1.000	1.000	1.000	1.000	1.000	1.000	1.000	1.000
2	2.280	2.320	2.360	2.400	2.500	2.600	2.700	2.800
3	3.918	4.062	4.210	4.360	4.750	5.160	5.590	6.040
4	6.016	6.326	6.725	7.104	8.125	9.256	10.503	11.872
5	8.700	9.398	10.146	10.846	13.188	15.810	18.855	22.370
6	12.136	13.406	14.799	16.324	20.781	26.295	33.054	41.265
7	16.534	18.696	21.126	23.853	32.172	43.073	57.191	75.278
8	22.163	25.678	29.732	34.395	49.258	69.916	98.225	136.500
9	29.369	34.895	41.435	49.153	74.887	112.866	167.983	246.699
10	38.592	47.062	57.352	69.814	113.330	181.585	286.570	445.058
11	50.399	63.122	78.998	98.739	170.995	291.536	488.170	802.105
12	65.510	84.320	108.437	139.235	257.493	467.458	830.888	1444.788
13	84.853	112.303	148.475	195.929	387.239	748.933	1413.510	2601.619
14	109.612	149.240	202.926	275.300	581.859	1199.293	2403.968	4683.914
15	141.303	197.997	276.979	386.420	873.788	1919.869	4087.745	8432.045

Table 4

Present Value of Annuity of 1 per period

Period	1%	2%	3%	4%	5%	6%	7%	8%	9%	10%
1	0.990	0.980	0.971	0.962	0.952	0.943	0.935	0.926	0.917	0.909
2	1.970	1.942	1.913	1.886	1.859	1.833	1.808	1.783	1.759	1.736
3	2.941	2.884	2.829	2.775	2.723	2.673	2.624	2.577	2.531	2.487
4	3.902	3.808	3.717	3.630	3.546	3.465	3.387	3.312	3.240	3.170
5	4.853	4.713	4.580	4.452	4.329	4.212	4.100	3.993	3.890	3.791
6	5.795	5.601	5.417	5.424	5.076	4.917	4.766	4.623	4.486	4.355
7	6.728	6.472	6.230	6.002	5.786	5.582	5.389	5.206	5.033	4.868
8	7.652	7.325	7.020	6.733	6.463	6.210	6.971	5.747	5.535	5.335
9	8.566	8.162	7.786	7.435	7.108	6.802	6.515	6.247	5.985	5.759
10	9.471	8.983	8.530	8.111	7.722	7.360	7.024	6.710	6.418	6.145
11	10.368	9.787	9.253	8.760	8.306	7.887	7.499	7.139	6.805	6.495
12	11.255	10.575	9.954	9.385	8.863	8.384	7.943	7.536	7.161	6.814
13	12.134	11.348	10.635	9.986	9.394	8.853	8.358	7.904	7.487	7.103
14	13.004	12.106	11.296	10.563	8.899	9.295	8.745	8.244	7.786	7.367
15	13.865	12.849	11.938	11.118	10.380	9.712	9.108	8.559	8.060	7.606
16	14.718	13.578	12.561	11.652	10.838	10.106	9.447	8.851	8.312	7.824
17	15.562	14.292	13.166	12.166	11.274	10.477	9.763	9.122	8.544	8.022
18	16.398	14.992	13.754	12.659	11.690	10.828	10.059	9.372	8.756	8.201
19	17.226	15.678	14.324	13.134	12.085	11.158	10.336	9.604	8.950	8.365
20	18.046	16.351	14.877	13.590	12.462	11.470	10.594	9.818	9.128	8.514
25	22.023	19.523	17.413	15.622	14.094	12.783	11.654	10.675	9.823	9.077
30	25.808	22.397	19.600	17.292	15.373	13.765	12.409	11.258	10.274	9.427

Period	12%	14%	16%	18%	20%	24%	28%	32%	36%
1	0.893	0.877	0.862	0.847	0.833	0.806	0.781	0.758	0.735
2	1.690	1.647	1.605	1.566	1.528	1.457	1.392	1.332	1.276
3	2.402	2.322	2.246	2.174	2.106	1.981	1.868	1.766	1.674
4	3.037	2.914	2.798	2.690	2.589	2.404	2.241	2.096	1.966
5	3.605	3.433	3.274	3.127	2.991	2.745	2.532	2.345	2.181
6	4.111	3.889	3.685	3.498	3.326	3.020	2.759	2.534	2.339
7	4.564	4.288	4.089	3.812	3.605	3.242	2.937	2.678	2.455
8	4.968	4.639	4.344	4.078	3.837	3.421	3.076	2.786	2.540
9	5.328	4.946	4.607	4.303	4.031	3.566	3.184	2.868	2.603
10	5.650	5.216	4.833	4.494	4.193	3.682	3.269	2.930	2.650
11	5.988	5.453	5.029	4.656	4.327	3.776	3.335	2.978	2.683
12	6.194	5.660	5.197	4.793	4.439	3.851	3.387	3.013	2.708
13	6.424	5.842	5.342	4.910	4.533	3.912	3.427	3.040	2.727
14	6.628	6.002	5.468	5.008	4.611	3.962	3.459	3.061	2.740
15	6.811	6.142	5.575	5.092	4.675	4.001	3.483	3.076	2.750
16	6.974	6.265	5.669	5.162	4.730	4.033	3.503	3.088	2.758
17	7.120	5.373	5.749	4.222	4.775	4.059	3.518	3.097	2.763
18	7.250	6.467	5.818	5.273	4.812	4.080	3.529	3.104	2.767
19	7.366	6.550	5.877	5.316	4.844	4.097	3.539	3.109	2.770
20	7.469	6.623	5.929	5.353	4.870	4.110	3.546	3.113	2.772
25	7.843	6.873	6.907	5.467	4.948	4.147	3.564	3.122	2.776
30	8.055	7.003	6.177	5.517	4.979	4.160	3.569	3.124	2.778

Index